Good Father, Bad Father

How Following the Right Spiritual Father Can Lead You to Eternal Life

Eliseo Santos

Emerging Truth Productions

Wurtsboro, NY

Copyright © 2015 by Eliseo Santos

All rights reserved.

Emerging Truth Productions – Eliseo Santos
P.O. Box 785
Phillipsport, New York 12769
www.emergingtruth.net
Email: Emergingtruth@yahoo.com

Publisher's Note:

After you finish reading the book, please spread the word about this book and share the things you learned with your close friends and family members.

You can follow us on Facebook at https://www.facebook.com/emergingtruth

You can reach the author at https://www.facebook.com/ems1005

Thank You and God Bless.

Book Layout © 2014 BookDesignTemplates.com

Good Father, Bad Father: How Following The Right Spiritual Father Will Lead You To Eternal Life, Eliseo Santos. – 2nd Print Edition
ISBN 978-1516866113

To My Teachers- First and Foremost God and His Holy Word, then my Family and then the many teachers who have had a positive impact on my life.

Contents

Preface 1
Chapter 1: Who is the Good Father? 9
Chapter 2: The Reality of the Law of God 17
Chapter 3: The Road Map of History 23
Chapter 4: Daniel in Babylon 33
Chapter 5: Christ's Date of Birth 47
Chapter 6: The Apocalypse of Revelation 61
Chapter 7: The Seven Churches, Seals, and Trumpets 65
Chapter 8: The Church of Ephesus and the 1st Seal 69
Chapter 9: The Formation of the Bible 75
Chapter 10: The Church of Smyrna and the 2nd Seal 79
Chapter 11: The Church of Pergamos and the 3rd Seal 93
Chapter 12: The Church of Thyatira and the 4th Seal 115
Chapter 13: Christ, The Holy High Priest and Sole Mediator of Humanity 137
Chapter 14: The Church of Sardis and the 5th Seal 143
Chapter 15: Martin Luther and the Dawn of the Protestant Reformation 147
Chapter 16: The Jesuits and the Counter- Reformation 165
Chapter 17: The Inquisition 173
Chapter 18: The Church of Philadelphia and the 6th Seal 181

Chapter 19: Signs of the End Times 185
Chapter 20: The End of the 1260-Day Prophecy 195
Chapter 21: Suppression of the Jesuit Order 205
Chapter 22: Revelation 11 and the French Revolution 221
Chapter 23: Protestantism and the 2nd Beast of Revelation . 231
Chapter 24: Subversive Secret Societies in America 245
Chapter 25: Revelation 17 and 666 259
Chapter 26: End of 2300-Day Prophecy and the Investigative Judgment 271
Chapter 27: The Mark of the Beast 279
Chapter 28: The Three Angels Messages 285
Chapter 29: The Church of Laodecia and the 7th Seal 291
Chapter 30: The Seven Last Plagues 295
Chapter 31: Resurrection to Eternal Life or To Receive God's Judgment 305
Chapter 32: New Heaven and New Earth 313
Notes 319
Appendix 1 - Old Testament Prophecies of Jesus Christ and Their New Testament Fulfillment 322
Appendix 2 - Differences Between Teachings Found in the Bible and Teachings Taught By The Little Horn 323
Index 326

Preface

The purpose of this book is to explain to you the history that is not taught in schools, nor found in many historical textbooks. It is the history only found with the help of the Holy Spirit and Bible prophecy within the pages of the Bible. The Bible was written primarily for the many men and women living today who are far removed from the glorious miracles of God and His Son Jesus Christ. The Bible was written to be understood. It was written to ultimately glorify the Holy Spirit, which has led and directed the authors of all the books of the Old and New Testament.

The Bible is as relevant today as it was two thousand years ago. Back then, when Christ 1st visited the planet, the Jewish religious leaders were not focused on the fulfillment of Bible prophecy, they ultimately caused the Jewish nation to reject their God and Creator Jesus Christ. Likewise today, many religious leaders do not focus on the fulfillment of Bible Prophecy. Thus, the people God has given the religious leaders to lead to heaven are not ready for the 2nd Coming of Christ. Many people today are distracted with the entertainment of this world, which ultimately takes away the precious time you and I have left before the many remaining prophecies of the Bible are fulfilled before our very eyes. These prophecies will lead the way to the fulfillment of the greatest prophecy ever written, the most important words ever written with ink and paper, the 2nd coming of

Christ and the end of the world as we know it. At Christ's 2nd Coming, many who died in the hope of Jesus Christ will be resurrected into their eternal glory. There will also be a group of people who will live through the most difficult times of trouble and tribulation this world has seen, and at the 2nd Coming of Christ they will be transformed and go to heaven without dying. Those who believed and followed the words of Christ to receive their eternal bodies of perfection will witness the 2nd Coming of Christ in the sky with his fleet of angels. In the words of Apostle Paul,

> *"Behold, I show you a mystery; We shall not all sleep, but we shall be changed, In a moment, in the twinkling of an eye, at the last trump; for the trumpet shall sound and the dead shall be raised incorruptible, and we shall be changed. For this corruptible must put on incorruption, and this mortal must put on immortality. [...] O death, where is thy sting? O grave, where is thy victory? [...] But thanks be to God, which gives us the victory through our Lord Jesus Christ." 1 Corinthians 15:51-53,55, 57*

Wouldn't you also like to have the victory over death? Then, out of love for humanity, God has given us the Bible to be our manual for the way in which we should live our lives in these final End Times. If you desire to live forever alongside the Good Father God and His Son Jesus Christ, then reading, studying, and believing the Words of the Bible will help you develop your relationship with God. Beyond in the pages of this book you will not find any future date for the 2nd Coming of Jesus Christ and the End of the world. Christ says clearly that "Of that day and hour, knoweth no man, no, not the angels of heaven, but my Father only," (Matthew 24:36). Instead, the Bible explains itself and thus, it gives the reader signs of clear and discernible events that will occur, which will be the signals of the 2nd Coming of Christ. All Bible prophecies have foretold the history of the world from the time they were written to modern times. The Bible also foretells of the near future of the 2nd Coming of Christ. It is with this certainty that I can say that we are living in the final years on this planet before the 2nd Coming of Christ.

In knowing this truth, I feel it is my responsibility before God to actually warn and wake up as many people as possible to the reality of the spiritual warfare that has existed for a long-time between the Good Father God and the Bad Father Satan. This conflict is evident in the deaths of many Christians throughout the world, and the deaths of many innocent people and children. This conflict will end once and for all on the day Jesus Christ makes His 2nd Coming, where every eye will see Him and His glory in the sky. In the words of the Apostle John, "Behold, he cometh with clouds; and every eye shall see him, and they also which pierced him: and all kindreds of the earth shall wail because of him. Even so, Amen," (Revelation 1:7).

In saying these things, you must also recognize that the blessed hope for all humans in this world is reaching for eternal life. Only Jesus Christ can give access to those who remain faithful to His honest promises. Those who will live forever with Him in Heaven and in the New Earth believe in His life, death, resurrection, and His words found in the Old and New Testament. Yes, you reading this book can attain eternal life. John 3:16,17 states, "For God so loved the world, that he gave his only begotten Son, that whosoever believeth in him should not perish, but have everlasting life. For God sent not his Son into the world to condemn the world; but that the world through him might be saved." This being said, we must also not lose sight of God. God is not only merciful and patient with the sins of humanity, but God also must carry out His justice to put an end to evil. God's system of justice is the fairest because it is the only one in which you can attain eternal life.

In these End Times, Satan will not openly seek the destruction of mankind, but will do so in secret. Satan seeks to surprise the world, especially Christians who primarily follow their religious leaders without taking the time and effort to understand the Bible. God has made His Words of Eternal wisdom available to Christians out of His abundant mercy for human souls. Satan's ultimate deception includes his arrival as an anti-Christ, who will be a man who looks like Christ and acts like Christ in performing healing miracles, but he will teach things that are not written in the Bible. The Apostle John writes in Revelation 12:12, "Therefore rejoice, ye heavens, and ye that dwell in them. Woe to the inhabiters of the earth and of the sea! For the devil is come down unto you, having great wrath, because he knoweth that he hath but a short time." This verse is even more relevant today as the 2nd Coming of Christ quickly approaches. Satan in these End Times will work through distraction and deception. These principles of evil are seen in the words of the Apostle Paul in 1 Thessalonians 5:3,4 "For when they shall say, peace and safety, then sudden destruction cometh upon them, as travail upon a woman with child; and they shall not escape. But ye, brethren, are not in darkness, that that should overtake you as a thief." Paul here describes a scenario where peace and safety will be used to distract people from realizing the sudden destruction that will come upon the world.

Therefore, Satan will work through all different types of ways to get as many people to forfeit their eternal life and to believe in lies, which ultimately leads to Satan's mark of the beast. Later on you will find out what the mark of the beast really means using the Bible to

Good Father, Bad Father

interpret itself. Satan and fallen demonic angels will also try to deceive many with the appearance of many familiar ghosts and spirits, all which stem from the erroneous belief in the immortality of the soul. By believing in this lie you allow for Satan and his demons to impersonate dead relatives, friends, and even dead historical figures. If you don't believe in the immortality of the soul, Satan and his demons will not waste their time on trying to trick someone who knows the truth concerning the state of the dead, (Ecclesiastes 9:5).

If you are a Christian, you have to be also be on guard for Satan has developed many ways to trick Christians with false theories such as the Secret Rapture, (Rev. 7:14); the theory that the Ten Commandments are no longer valid after the resurrection (1 John 2:3-4, Romans 3:31); the theory that speaking in indiscernible noises and languages is acceptable, when it is not (1 Corinthians 14:9-22). One of the last deceptions Satan has planned is to fool the world to believe in alien visitors from other worlds in preparation for the 2nd Coming of God,

> *"And I saw three unclean spirits like frogs come out of the mouth of the dragon, and out of the mouth of the beast, and out of the mouth of the false prophet. For they are the spirits of devils, working miracles, which go forth unto the kings of the earth and of the whole world, to gather them to the battle of the great day of God Almighty. – Rev.16:13-14"*

These demonic spirits posing as aliens will come to reunite the world and its armies in battle against Jesus Christ and His 2nd Coming. However, this last attempt by Satan to use God's creation against Him in war and battle will prove to be no contest, (Rev. 19:19-20).

One of Satan's lies in the modern times, that has hindered the spiritual growth of many, is the theory of evolution. The Bible clearly states in Psalm 19:1, "The heavens declare the glory of God, and the firmament shows his handy work. " Thus, if you take a look at the sky you will notice that the Sun and the moon appear to be the same size and this is evident in a solar eclipse. What scientists won't tell you or admit to is that it's impossible for the phenomena of the solar eclipse to exist as a result of chance. The Sun is 400 times larger than the moon in terms of equatorial radius, however the sun's average distance away from the earth is also 400 times greater than the moon's average distance away from the earth. As a result of these things it causes the Sun and moon to appear the same size when viewing the celestial bodies from the earth. This could have only been done with the intelligent design of God the creator.

Keep in mind, the solar eclipse is visible on the only planet in the solar system with life. This signifies that God, who wants to make His presence known to mankind, designed the solar eclipse to be one of the many signs of His existence. Only God could have measured and viewed the sun and the moon and placed them in their precise location in space so that these signs would forever be evident on earth. In Psalms 33:6, "By the Word of the Lord were the heavens made." Genesis 1:14 states, "Let there be lights in the firmament of the heaven to divide the day from the night; and let them be for signs, and for seasons, and for days, and years." The theory of Evolution does not account for this and the many other simple facts that baffle humans and scientists alike at the greatness of the Almighty Creator.

The firmament or atmosphere shows God's handiwork daily. It is composed with several complex layers of the atmosphere that work together in purifying all water on the planet, protecting human life from harmful UV Rays, keeping the temperatures on earth warm enough for life to exist, and continue on earth. It is by considering and believing in God, the Good Father, especially as a Creator, in which can help further develop your faith in God and thus, further strengthen your relationship with God.

With these things in mind, I hope that you get the most out of the information found in this book. May God lead you, the reader, with the Holy Spirit to actually learn the many lessons there are to learn from God's words found in the Bible.

Chapter 1: Who is the Good Father?

Out of the many people and histories that are covered in the Bible, the most important person is the person from which all light and truth comes from, the Good Father God. It's important to gain a basic biblical understanding of the existence of God to then be able to completely understand the reality of the world today. Even though you and I are finite beings seeking to comprehend the infinite greatness of God, we can only gain the necessary help from the Word of God and the Holy Spirit. It is the Bible through the direction of the Holy Spirit, which opens the understanding of the eternal realities of life in heaven.

In the 1st Letter of John, John briefly and concisely explains the various properties of God the Father and His Son, and how through Christ and His righteousness we can gain eternal life. The Apostle John was one of the twelve Apostles who saw Jesus die on the Cross and later saw Him alive after Christ's resurrection. He describes God as being composed of three intelligent beings the Good Father, the Son, and the Holy Ghost. John states in 1 John 5:7, "For there are three that bear record in heaven, the Father, the Word, and the Holy Ghost: and these three are one." Therefore, God exists via the Holy unified entity of God the Father, the Son Jesus Christ, and the Holy Ghost. What does this mean? The three are one in power, justice, love, mercy, and truth. According to the Gospel of John 1:14, "The

Word" is a symbol of Christ, "And the Word was made flesh, and dwelt among us, (and we beheld his glory, the glory as of the only begotten of the Father,) full of grace and truth." Therefore, Jesus Christ was eternal, living alongside God the Father before He became human and dwelt among humanity for 33 ½ years.

While Jesus was with John and the other Apostles, there were many instances when the greatness of Christ was displayed in His love and compassion for humanity evident in His teachings and miracles. The compassion and love displayed by Jesus Christ was congruent to the compassion and love God displayed in the Old Testament, in His patience staying with Israel during good and bad times. John goes on to describe God as a God of pure love, in 1 John 4:15, 16, "Whosoever shall confess that Jesus is the Son of God, God dwelleth in him, and he in God. And we have known and believed the love that God hath to us. God is love; and he that dwelleth in love dwelleth in God, and God in him." Therefore, a key component of the Love of God is the belief and faith that Jesus is the Son of God. It was this belief and faith that caused many to see miracles occur in their lives through the aid of Jesus Christ, who was and will always be the Son of God.

Another important component of the Love of God is as John states in 1 John 5:3, "For this is the love of God, that we keep his commandments and his commandments are not grievous." In the Gospel of John 15:10, Jesus Christ on the night of the last supper, told the disciples, "As the Father have loved me, so have I loved you: continue ye in my love. If ye keep my commandments, ye shall abide in my love: even As I have kept my Father's Commandments, and abide in his love." According to the previous verses, it is by following the Ten Commandments that God gave to Moses at Mt. Sinai and that

Good Father, Bad Father

Jesus Christ kept on earth, which causes us to enter into the love of God. If you love God, you do as He says and you recognize that God and Jesus Christ never change. In the Book of Hebrews 13:8, Paul states "Jesus Christ the same yesterday, to day, and forever." In the Old Testament, Proverbs 30:4 states, "Who hath ascended up into heaven, or descended? Who hath gathered the wind in his fists? Who hath bound the waters in a garment? Who hath established all the ends of the earth? What is his name, and what is his son's name, if thou canst tell?" Here it shows that the act of creation of the earth involved God the Father and God the son, whose name we know to be Jesus Christ.

Although finite beings have but a limited understanding of the eternal greatness and love of God, from what is written in the Holy Scriptures, you are made aware of the importance in believing in Jesus Christ as the Son of God, and with this faith, keeping the Commandments of God. The Lord Jesus Christ tells us plainly the significant part of salvation is in believing in Him as the Son of God. To fully believe this is to embrace the love of God, which is the love of His commandments. In the Gospel of John 3:16,17

"That whosoever believeth in him should not perish, but have eternal life. For God so loved the world, that he gave his only begotten Son, that whosoever believeth in him should not perish, but hath eternal life. For God sent not his Son into the world to condemn the world; but that the world through him might be saved."

Therefore, it is through the belief in Jesus Christ as the Son of God, who died and resurrected, for our sins that we might be saved.

Eliseo Santos

The human language fails to accurately describe how grandiose is the Good Father and His Son, and the Holy Spirit. But let us turn to the Words of God, inspired by the Holy Spirit to comprehend the greatness of God. First, it is important to understand that Jesus, the Creator, existed before He became human. Jesus plainly states to the Jewish religious leaders, while He was on earth in John 8:58, "Verily, Verily, I say unto you, Before Abraham was, I am ...." Because Jesus was with God in heaven, before the Creation of the world, then His eternal greatness is tied with the eternal greatness of the Good Father. When Jesus was asked by The Apostle Philip, to show them the Father, Christ responded, "Have I been so long time with you, and yet hast thou not known me, Philip? He that hath seen me hath seen the Father; and how sayest thou then, Show us the Father?" In the Book of Daniel Ch. 7:9-10, describes the scene of the Good Father in heaven. Daniel describes the Good Father as

> *I beheld till the thrones were cast down, and the Ancient of Days did sit, whose garment was white as snow, and the hair of his head like the pure wool: his throne was like the fiery flame, and his wheels as burning fire. A fiery stream issued and came forth from before him: thousand thousands ministered unto Him, and ten thousand times ten thousand stood before him: the judgment was set, and the books were opened."– Daniel 7: 9-10*

Daniel explains the throne of God and the wheels of God, as a fire, which is describing the intense glory of God, but also the blazing speed at which the heavenly messengers travel from earth to heaven updating God on the events occurring on the earth. Due to the fact that Jesus Christ was and still is God, he now takes up the role of High Priest in the Most Holy place in the Temple Sanctuary of God. The

Good Father, Bad Father

reality of Jesus as a High Priest in the Heavenly Temple of God, is presented in The Book of Hebrews 2:17,18, 3:1 where Paul states,

"Wherefore in all things it behooved him to be made like unto his brethren, that he might be a merciful high priest in things pertaining to God, to make reconciliation for the sins of the people. For in that he himself hath suffered being tempted, he is able to succor them that are tempted. Wherefore, holy brethren, partakers of the heavenly calling, consider the Apostle and High Priest of our profession, Christ Jesus."

After dying on the cross and becoming the sacrificial lamb that takes away the sins of the world (John 1:36), Jesus Christ also became the High Priest that intercedes before God on behalf of humanity, in the Heavenly Temple of God. Thus, what makes Jesus Christ so special is not only that He was God and became man, but he also became the sacrificial lamb, and the resurrected High Priest. Christ now, from heaven, hears prayers and forgives the sins of those who pray to Him. Christ now hears the prayers of those who are poor in spirit, and of those who mourn, and those who are meek, (Matthew 5:3-5). Christ also hears the prayers of those who hunger and thirst, not only after food and water, but also after righteousness, (Matthew 5:6). Christ hears the prayers of the merciful, the pure in heart, and those who make peace, (Matthew 5:7-9). Christ, not only hears the prayers of those who are persecuted and hated for Christ's sake, but also hears the prayers of those with a broken spirit, and a humble heart, (Matthew 5:10,11; Psalm 51:17; Isaiah 57:15). Like God the Father, Jesus Christ entered in the Most Holy Place. Christ is described in a like manner as his Father, in the Book of Daniel 7: in 13, 14 when it states,

Eliseo Santos

> *I saw the night visions, and behold, one like the Son of man, came with the clouds of heaven, and came to the Ancient of Days, and they brought him near before him. And there was given to him dominion, and glory, and a kingdom, that all people, nations, and languages, should serve him: his dominion is an everlasting dominion, which shall not pass away, and his kingdom that which shall not be destroyed. – Daniel 7:13-14*

Thus, Daniel is describing Jesus' arrival at the Most Holy Place after 2300 years prophecy is completed[1]. This momentous occasion began the End Times of the Planet, which occurred in 1844. Jesus Christ, after His death and resurrection regained dominion of the planet, by becoming the first human to overcome death living without the blemish of sin, and thus establishing once and for all the way to eternal life.

In Daniel 8:11-14 explains that there was and still exists a power that sought to place itself in opposition to Jesus and His temple ministry. Daniel 8: 11-14,

> *Yea, he magnified himself even to the prince of the host, and by him the daily sacrifice was taken away, and the place of his sanctuary was cast down. And a host was given to him, against the daily transgression, and it cast down the truth to the ground, and it practiced and prospered. Then I heard one saint speaking, and another saint said unto that certain saint which spake, How long shall be the vision concerning the daily sacrifice, and the transgression of desolation, to give both the sanctuary and the host to be trodden under foot? And he said unto me, Unto two thousand and three hundred days, then shall the sanctuary be cleansed.*

---

[1] See Chapter 26 for details

Good Father, Bad Father

Therefore, there has throughout human history arisen an evil power that pretends to be like a god on earth, forgiving sins, and even having the audacity to institute a priesthood, when priests are no longer needed for daily sacrifice after the death and resurrection of Jesus Christ. Paul states in Hebrews 7:27 how Jesus Christ's High-Priesthood is more efficient and perfected version of the human Jewish High-Priesthood, "Who needeth not daily, as those high priests, to offer up sacrifice, first for his own sins, and then for the people's: for this he did once, when he offered himself." Continue reading in order to find out who is the power, that opposes the authority of Jesus Christ and His system of Salvation in the Heavenly sanctuary. The Heavenly sanctuary was the Temple of God from which the earthly Tabernacle and Temple of Jerusalem were modeled after (Hebrews 8:1-5). The evil powers that oppose Christ will soon be named later on in the book.

God and Jesus Christ will ultimately win this current spiritual war between Good and Evil. In Revelation 19: 11-16, describes the Messiah, Jesus Christ, who was sadly rejected the 1st time around by the Jewish religious leaders who had gained control over the minds of the general Jewish population. Hopefully many more Jewish people this time around will expect the 2nd return of Christ, who will now come with the great power and great glory that their ancestors believed the Messiah would return the 1st time Christ came to earth. Now Christ will come to earth with the host of heavenly angels ready to put an end to evil once and for all. John states,

And I saw heaven opened, and behold a white horse, and he that sat upon him was called Faithful and True, and in righteousness he doth judge and make war. His eyes were as a flame of fire, and on his head were many crowns; and he had a

name written, that no man know, but he himself. And he was clothed with a vesture dipped in blood: and his name is called The Word of God. And the armies which were in heaven followed him upon white horses, clothed in fine linen, white and clean. And out of his mouth goeth a sharp sword, that with it he should smite the nations: and shall rule them with a rod of iron: and he treadeth the winepress of the fierceness and wrath of Almighty God. And he hath on his vesture and on his thigh a name written, KING OF KINGS, AND LORD OF LORDS. – (Revelation 19: 11-16).

Therefore, Christ's foretells He will lead the angelic forces of good into battle to put an end to Satan's usurped authority and his evil human accomplices by throwing them in the lake of fire. Find out who else will join Satan in the shower of God's wrath...

Chapter 2: The Reality of the Law of God

To further understand Satan's role in reality, it is best to view each individual's life as a dramatic courtroom drama. Satan is the corrupt prosecuting attorney, who brings the accusation of sins before the Judge, who is God. Satan seeks God to impose the death penalty on all sinners. Satan and his fallen angels setup and frame every individual to sin. Then Satan, being the prosecuting attorney, seeks the death penalty on all the individuals he frames to make a mockery of the law of God. Satan corrupts the environment for sin, and plants the evidence for people to sin. The Bad Father even manipulates the crime scene of sin to remove any evidence of himself and his fallen angels. He controls the flow of information you receive to have you believe that you and you alone are fully responsible for your actions.

In other words, your actions can only be considered free when you choose an action that is not controlled by Satan. To continue choosing Satan's choices will only cause an unconscious slavery and you will believe you have freewill. But your freewill is only limited by the amounts of choices you have control over. Compared with the overwhelming amount of choices Satan and his fallen angels control and influence daily, the only choice in which you have complete control is to follow God according to the Words of His Bible. In order to say no to Satan and his matrix of choices, you will require your own free will and will power. Satan distracts humanity with so many choices that are not worthwhile, especially considering that by rejecting Satan and his artificial world you can attain eternal life. Satan's manipulation of reality occurs while people believe that they are freely choosing what is best for them to do, while not realizing that Satan and his agents have great control and influence over the availability and popularity of mainstream choices.

A simple example of Satan's manipulation of reality was in the Garden of Eden. Satan in the form of a serpent, first questions the reality created by God. Satan reverses the bad choice and markets it as a good choice. When Eve took of the fruit from the tree knowledge of good and evil, then she based reality on her own limited experience, instead of the reality and the infinite experience of God. She instead succumbed to the lie of Satan. In other words, Eve based her decision on what momentarily pleased her eyes rather than on God's infinite wisdom. God's wisdom was reflected in His words to Adam and Eve when He said " You can eat of all the other trees of the Garden but not from the tree of knowledge of Good and Evil," (Genesis 2:16-17; 3:2-3). She goes to Adam and subverts his freewill under the popular will or peer pressure that is based on the limited experience of Eve eating a fruit because it looked good. When Eve takes the fruit from the tree of Knowledge of Good and Evil, she takes note that nothing has happened to her by taking of the fruit and that she is not dead. Nothing has happened until, Eve as a wife, convinces her husband to do something he does not want to do. Adam eats of the fruit from the Tree of Knowledge of Good and Evil and only then do their robes of light disappear and then they realize they are naked.

This example is a microcosm of what occurs when evil is advertised as good. It begins with only a small portion of the

Good Father, Bad Father

population doing this evil. It is not until this evil is done by at least more than half of the population, then you start seeing the consequences of these actions in society. Thus, the lesson here is that evil always exists and is always on the move. However the effects of evil are not discerned immediately in the short-term because evil always advances using the lie of goodness. Thus, in the long-term the truth will be made clear and evident, after the bright light of truth dissipates the short-term lie and leaves behind evidence of its lie. As water mixed with wine when left out in the sun leaves behind a stain and odor of its presence, likewise when truth is mixed with lies and it is observed for a long-period of time it will leave behind evidence of its lies. Thus, in light of these examples, in the grand courtroom drama in which each individual is brought in daily due to Satan's framing, setups, and traps for every individual to sin, then it is imperative for every human being to be aware of Satan and his agents.

After setting up his human prey, Satan then seeks the death penalty. The only way for anyone to live and experience eternal life would be for your defending attorney to be also the Judge of the courtroom. In order to equalize the balances of justice that Satan was using against humanity, Jesus paid the ultimate sacrifice so that the balances of justices will forever fall on His favor and that of His children. This was made possible when Jesus Christ, being part of the trinity of God, along with the Good Father, and the Holy Spirit, came to earth and lived a sinless life and died a cruel death. He then resurrected so that He can now become a legitimate representative in this grand human courtroom for all sinners. Because Jesus became human, he can now be a legitimate representative of the earth before God. Christ's death and resurrection also prevents Satan from laying any claim to this planet and its people. Thus, Christ's death and resurrection is great news and a victory, because God and Jesus Christ knows Satan would never seek to die for anyone or anything. Because God is all-knowing and all-mighty then, Jesus can put down His infinite life and take it back up again, especially if it is for saving the Creation in which He Himself loves with a divine compassion that human words fail to describe.

When you go to Jesus Christ with your sins, and confess to Him all of the wrong doing you have done in your life, similar to how a defendant goes to their defense attorney and confesses in private whether they actually did or did not do the crime they are accused of by Satan. If you lie or do not fully confess your sins, how can your defense attorney Jesus Christ, defend your case before the Good Father? By doing so you give unnecessary power to the Bad father whose power and strength is the ability to lie and to manipulate the truth of reality to accomplish his goals. Once your sins are confessed, your defense attorney Jesus Christ will give you spiritual legal advice. Jesus Christ first wants you to believe and have your eyes set on Him. In doing so, you will be justified in the eyes of the Good Father through the Son's mediation. John 3:16 states, "For God so loved the world, that he gave his only begotten Son, that whosoever believeth in him should not perish, but have everlasting life." Then He asks of you to develop a love and faith in Jesus Christ as the Son of God and have faith in His 2nd Coming. As Paul states in 1 Thessalonians 5:7-9, "For they that sleep sleep in the night; and they that be drunken are drunken in the night. But let us, who are of the day, be sober, putting on the breastplate of faith and love; and for an helmet, the hope of salvation. For God, hath not appointed us to wrath, but to obtain salvation by our Lord Jesus Christ." Third, Jesus Christ wants you to repent of your sins and stop sinning. In Matthew 4:16-17, it states

"The people which sat in darkness saw great light; and to them which sat in the region and shadow of death light is sprung up. From that time Jesus began to preach, and say 'Repent, for the Kingdom of Heaven is at hand.'" If you are able to do these three things daily then, you will be able to have your sins pardoned, forgiven, and forgotten by the Good Father, and then you will be on your way to eternal life.

Chapter 3: The Road Map of History

To prove His authenticity and teachings, God developed a way to differentiate the Judeo-Christian beliefs found in the Bible from other religious texts. The way in which God did this was through the incorporation of many prophecies in the Bible. God has verified to many people throughout the centuries that He is not only a being of divine intelligence by foretelling future events thousands of years before they occur, but God is also a loving Good Father who gave humanity these prophecies for their spiritual well-being. It is with the fulfillment of Bible prophecies throughout the centuries up until the present that a Christian can with certainty and confidence proclaim the Word and the love of God, in a world of widespread apathy and skepticism.

If you ask any person who does research, they would agree with the idea of history being important. Not only is history in general important to the world, but it is also important in understanding the present time period in relation to the Book of Daniel and Revelation. The Bible is a view of history directed by the Holy Spirit. Once you understand the history taught by the Bible it then becomes the greatest friend to an individual and also to mankind. An individual will with greater accuracy predict what will happen in the future, if he observes the trends and patterns of the past and recognizes the prophecies covered in the books of the Bible. By the very nature of Biblical prophecies foretelling future events, history by default is used as the primary source of information for explaining the prophecies in the Bible.

When reviewing the Bible passages that contain a prophetic message, it's first important to know when the prophetic passage was written to know the historical context. Once you identify when the prophetic passage was written, then you must study the historical events that occurred afterward up until the present. By doing this, then you will be able to determine which historical events and patterns correlate with the prophetic message. For example, the events of the Book of Daniel took place during the height and the fall of the Babylonian empire from 605-539 B.C. Therefore, all the prophecies found in the Book of Daniel refer to events that occurred from the historical reign of the Babylonian empire and onward in history.

Another key rule of interpretation when trying to figure out the meaning of a prophetic passage is the significance of the symbols that are being used given the context. Most of the prophets of the Bible wrote their prophetic passages in symbols that are meant to be revealed at a certain time and place. For many of the prophets of the Old and New Testaments, there are prophetic passages that have fulfillments before and after the time of Christ on earth. The Bible guides you, the reader, in figuring out the meaning of the symbols used, and how they relate to the Bible passages in the book. In other words, the Bible "interprets" itself as to the meanings of the symbols used in a particular passage. The Apostle Peter writes about biblical interpretation when he says

We have also a more sure word of prophecy; whereunto ye do well that ye take heed, as unto a light that shineth in a dark place, until the day dawn, and the day star arise in your hearts: Knowing this first, that no prophecy of the scripture is of any private interpretation. For the prophecy came not in old time by the will of man: but holy men of God spake as they were moved by the Holy Ghost, (2 Peter 1:19-21 KJV).

Therefore, it is with great certainty in which an individual can understand the meanings of symbols used in the prophetic passages of the Bible. It is by comparing related prophetic passages and seeing the concordance of the symbols used in these passages. Often times related prophetic passages were written more than 500 years apart from each other, and yet they use the same prophetic symbols in similar ways. For example, one of the important symbols of Bible prophecy is the word of "waters." Unlike the symbol of "water," used in some prophetic passages and parables in either a literal sense or a symbolic sense given the context, the meaning of "waters" is plainly stated in the Book of Revelation 17:15 (KJV), "The Waters which thou sawest, where the whore sitteth, are peoples, and multitudes, and nations, and tongues." The angel who spoke to John is explaining an earlier scene that was shown to John in Revelation 17:1 where the symbol of "waters" was used. The actual prophetic passage states, "And there came one of the seven angels which had the seven vials, and talked with me, saying unto me, Come hither; I will shew unto thee the judgment of the great whore that sitteth upon many waters," (Revelation 17:1 KJV). Continue reading to learn more of the great harlot or whore that is seated upon many waters, or in other words, the whore that has a worldwide following, support, and influence.

Before you can understand the great significance of this symbolic whore, it is important to understand and be well grounded in ancient world history and its relation to the Book of Daniel and modern history.

As an example of the importance of ancient world history in understanding the world and its traditions, the popular spring holiday of Easter, has its origins in pagan traditions and customs, most of which are not taught in ancient world history. The holiday was instituted by the Roman Catholic Church to celebrate the resurrection of Jesus Christ. However, the name Easter has its origins from the Teutonic goddess Eostra (sometimes Eostre), who was the goddess of the spring. In an attempt to increase the amount of loyal Roman Catholics in the Teutonic region of Europe, the early leaders of the Roman Catholic Church decided to create the spring celebration now known as Easter. The newly created festival of Easter coincided with the pagan feast of Eostra[2]. The feast of Eostra was not only to celebrate spring, but also to celebrate more hours of sunlight and warmth that the sun would provide during the warmer months. Keep in the mind; none of the modern conveniences of indoor heating and air conditioning were available during this time. Thus, spring and the warmer weather was a much welcomed change when compared to the frigid temperatures of winter. The American People's Encyclopedia describes how the Roman Catholic Church used popular pagan sun beliefs to create the Easter holiday. It states, "The Church endeavored to give Christian significance to such of the pagan rites as could not be rooted out. Joy at the rising of the sun and the spring awakening of

---

[2] Pg. 18, Easter, American People's Encyclopedia, Vol. 07, Grolier Inc., New York, 1967,
Library of Congress Catalog Card Number 67-10584

Good Father, Bad Father

nature became joy at the rising of the Sun of Righteousness or the resurrection of Christ from the grave."[3] In other words, the early Roman Catholic Church of the Dark Ages intermingled the popular Teutonic Spring solar fertility festival with the commemoration of the resurrection of the Son of God on the Sunday after Passover. There are other historians who point to Easter's pagan origins originating from "Ishtar" which was the Babylonian chief goddess whose titles included the queen of heaven, great mother, and goddess of fertility.[4] Like in many ancient cultures, the spring festival was held during the same time of year as Easter. Festivals held during the Spring season were at a time when many pagans celebrated the longer daylight hours and the warmer temperatures, which were signs of the increased fertility and foliage of the earth.

The Roman Catholic Church's mixture of the pagan spring festivals actually took away from God's appointed Spring Festival, which was the Passover or the Feast of Unleavened bread, and the feast of the first fruits. The context of the death and resurrection of Christ gives an added significance to the Passover feast. The Passover Feast which began when the People of Israel exited the sandy slums of slavery in Egypt to the Land flowing with milk, honey, and freedom, which was found in Canaan. God told Moses of a new feast of Passover, which involved selecting a spotless lamb without blemishes or deformities. And during the night of Passover this perfect lamb would be killed and the blood of this perfect lamb was to cover to the doorposts of the homes of the people of Israel. It was through the blood of this lamb that every household of Israel would be

---

[3] Pg.18, Easter, Ibid.
[4] ("Ishtar." Microsoft® Student 2009 [DVD]. Redmond, WA: Microsoft Corporation, 2008.)

Eliseo Santos

saved. Through the blood of the lamb, the people of Israel would not be harmed by the passing of the Angel of Death during the 10th plague that would kill the firstborn of all of Egypt.

This one-time event typified the future sacrifice of Jesus Christ, who was the spotless or sinless Lamb of God. The sacrifice of the blood of the Infinite God, who was made into human flesh, would cover the sins of finite humanity. It is through the one-time sacrifice of an infinite God and His later resurrection that allows for the mediation of finite humanity. Because God became the lamb and the high-priest, then He will forever be the person in which any individual can turn to and seek forgiveness for their sins. Those who pray for forgiveness and repentance do so only under His name, Jesus Christ.

During the Passover before His death, Jesus Christ said to His Apostles "do this in remembrance of me" when referring to the breaking of the bread and drinking of the wine, which in Jewish tradition is pure unfermented grape juice. According to the historical background of the Passover and the context of the time and place of His Last Passover meal, Jesus Christ was referring to the Feast of unleavened bread, not the communion of the Roman Catholic Mass. In the Roman Catholic Mass, an unnecessary mystery surrounds the wine and communion wafer. That mystery is the claim of the Roman Catholic priest is able to convert the communion wafer and wine into the actual body and blood of Christ, which is, in essence, another sacrifice of Jesus before the communicants. The transubstantiation often times occur in the Monstrance where the communion wafer is kept usually in a golden graven image or idol of the sun. The Bible states the sacrifice of food to idols or graven images is an abomination, (Revelation 2:14,20 KJV). In the Old Testament, God experienced a similar problem with the people of Israel, who were in

Good Father, Bad Father

the midst of idolatry or spiritual fornication with food was sacrificed to the queen of heaven. For example, in Jeremiah 44:19 reads, "And when we burned incense to the queen of heaven, and poured out drink-offerings unto her, did we make her cakes to worship her, and pour out drink-offerings unto her, without our men?" The prophet Jeremiah was here writing shortly before the Babylonian invasion in 586 B.C. At this time, the widespread pagan beliefs were practiced amongst the women and eventually the men of Israel. In Alexander Hislop's *The Two Babylons*, he describes what these cakes really were and where they come from and how they still persist today in Roman Catholicism

> *The round disk, so frequent in the sacred emblems of Egypt, symbolized the sun. [...] These are the letters on the wafer that are worth reading. These letters are I.H.S. What mean these mystical letters? To a Christian these letters are represented as signifying, "Iesus Hominum Salvator," "Jesus the Savior of Men." But let a Roman worshipper of Isis (for in the age of the emperors there were innumerable worshippers of Isis in Rome) cast his eyes upon them, and how will he read them? He will read them, of course, according to his own well-known system of idolatry: "Isis, Horus, Seb" that is, "The Mother, the Child, and the Father of the gods," – in other words, "The Egyptian Trinity. [...] The initials pay the semblance of a tribute to Christianity while Paganism in reality has all the substance of the homage bestowed upon it."* [5]

The above citation should underscore why history is important and why knowing history gives an individual understanding of the origins of many pagan traditions and customs. Many pagan traditions and customs crept into the Early Christian church, converting the essence

---

[5] Alexander Hislop, Two Babylons, Pg. 134, 136, 1853

and substance of Biblical Christianity into idolatrous paganism. Today, these pagan beliefs that have seeped into mainstream Christianity are far away from the simple, pure, unfermented, and unleavened teachings in which Christ advocated on earth. Jesus Christ laid down His human life to uphold and defend these Biblical teachings, and resurrected, and was glorified by His same teachings. Like in the times of Jeremiah, if there is not a return to the Words, Laws, and principles of God, then catastrophe and disasters await. In Jeremiah 44:22, 23, Jeremiah gives a warning and as well as an explanation for why God allows horrible things to happen,

> *So the Lord could no longer bear, because the evil of your doings, and because of the abominations which ye have committed, therefore is your land a desolation, and an astonishment, and a curse, without an inhabitant, as at this day. Because ye have burned incense, because ye have sinned against the Lord, and have not obeyed the voice of the Lord, nor walked in His law, nor in His statutes, nor in His testimonies; therefore this evil is happened unto you, as at this day, (Jer.44:22,23, KJV)*

While the Good Father God can be extremely patient, there is a limit to how much evil he will allow from the Bad Father to do amongst humanity. Due to using our free will, God can allow bad things to happen to people so that they can come back and seek God. Humanity is in control of whether they choose to be Children of the Good Father and Children of the Bad Father. Thus, they can either take responsibility and work for the Good Father and carry out His will in the world, which begins and ends with Christ and his principles and teachings. It's only the belief in Christ and His Biblical teachings and principles of God that leads to eternal life.

Good Father, Bad Father

Alternatively, by rejecting the Good Father and His principles in the Bible, you will be accountable before God for using your free will to take part in the evil that is done in the world, which leads to death for you, and all the children of the Bad Father. Satan will also eventually die for his responsibility in causing the sins of mankind. The Children of the Good Father are those who in realizing their wrong doings, seek forgiveness and seek to become obedient to God and His commandments, and seek to do His will on earth. The Children of the Bad Father are those who don't see anything wrong in their actions, and thus, they don't seek to change, but they seek to do their own will. Often times, an individual's will is a function of the popular will that is manipulated by Satan. The Good Father seeks to spend time with His Children, while the Bad Father ultimately seeks to kill his children, and thus distracts them as much as possible before they face death. Following Satan, and the will of the majority will usually end in chaos, destruction, and death. Thus, this is why God wants humanity to listen to Him and separate ourselves from Satan and the popular will and listen to the will of God, found in the Bible and the Ten Commandments.

In understanding the history of the Kingdoms found in the Book of Daniel then it will help you further understand the Bible, its prophecies, its symbols, and ultimately the world you live in today. It will also help you further understand the history of the battle between the Good Father and the Bad Father.

Chapter 4: Daniel in Babylon

The Book of Daniel is one of the most important books in the Bible for several important reasons. The first of which is it outlines the four kingdoms, which will control the earth from the height and the downfall of the Babylonian empire until the 2nd coming of Jesus Christ. The prophecies of Daniel were given to humanity as a guide for future generations to know the historical roadmap of events that will lead to the climactic event of the 2nd return of Christ. Without this basic historical understanding of the Bible and its symbols, then it leads to confusion when trying to interpret the symbols of the Bible and usually leads to errors in interpretation. To prevent and minimize human errors in the interpretation of the Bible, it is best to look for other places in the Bible where the same subject matter is stated, and look for other areas in the Bible where the symbols in question are used.

If you are not familiar with the context of The Book of Daniel, then let me explain the background history. Daniel and many Israelites were taken captive by the Babylonian King Nebuchadnezzar into slavery. King Nebuchadnezzar and his Babylonian army destroyed Jerusalem and also destroyed the 1st temple of God that was built by Solomon. Many Israelites were taken into captivity in Babylon, which was also the name of the main capital city. There was no city in ancient human history that could come close to how magnificent and majestic was the city of Babylon. The city was shaped into a perfect square. Each side of the city was approximately 15 miles (24 km) for a total perimeter of 60 miles (96 Km) and an area of 225 square miles (576 sq. km)[6] . The well-known historian Herodotus describes the "powerful and renowned city" of Babylon being situated in "a wide plain [Plain of Shinar], a vast city in the form of a square with sides nearly 14 miles long and a circuit [perimeter] of some fifty-six miles and in addition to its enormous size it surpasses in splendor any city of the known world." [7]

When the Israelites were taken captive into Babylon, Daniel and several other Israelites became servants of King Nebuchadnezzar. As servants, they studied in the Babylonian schools and learned the Babylonian language to be translators and interpreters for King Nebuchadnezzar. Daniel Ch. 2 begins by explaining how King Nebuchadnezzar had strange reoccurring dreams. These dreams were so strange and out of the ordinary that Nebuchadnezzar called his counsel of magicians, sorcerers, and other so-called psychics and mystics. Due to the bizarre nature of this dream, Nebuchadnezzar mandated that his counsel of dream interpreters, psychics, and other intuitive counselors tell the king what happened in his dream and give him an interpretation of the dream. To prove the psychic or predictive abilities of his mystical counselors, King Nebuchadnezzar decided instead of telling them the contents of his dream, it was best for these so called psychics to prove themselves by telling him the events that transpired in his own dream. The group of psychics, magicians and

---

[6] pg.4, The Illustrated Guide to Bible Prophecy, Orion Publishing, 2005
[7] pg. 79, The Histories, Penguin Classic, Translated by , Aubrey De Selincourt, 2003

Good Father, Bad Father

sorcerers admitted that it was impossible for them to tell Nebuchadnezzar the contents of his own dream. The King became so enraged that he issued a death sentence to all "the wise men" of the Babylonian Court. Enter Daniel, who was made aware of King Nebuchadnezzar's decree to kill all "the Wiseman" including him and other Israelites through Arioch, who was Captain of the King's Guard. Upon hearing this Daniel immediately went to the King and asked Nebuchadnezzar to delay his decree for a short time until he can tell the King the contents of his significant dream. (Daniel 2:1-16)

Daniel and his three Israelite friends, Hananiah, Mishael, and Azariah came together and prayed to God to reveal to them the grave mystery of Nebuchadnezzar's dream and its interpretation. God that same night revealed to Daniel Nebuchadnezzar's dream and its proper interpretation. The next day Daniel was able to prove the King of Babylon the legitimacy of his abilities as a prophet of God, by telling the King what occurred during his dream and its interpretation. (Daniel 2:17-26) The dream was as follows:

Thou, O king, sawest, and behold a great image. This great image, whose brightness was excellent, stood before thee; and the form thereof was terrible. This image's head was of fine gold, his breast and his arms of silver, his belly and his thighs of brass, His legs of iron, his feet part of iron and part of clay. Thou sawest till that a stone was cut out without hands, which smote the image upon his feet that were of iron and clay, and brake them to pieces. Then was the iron, the clay, the brass, the silver, and the gold, broken to pieces together, and became like the chaff of the summer threshing floors; and the wind carried them away, that no place was found for them: and the stone that smote the image became a great mountain and filled the whole earth. (Daniel 2:31-35 KJV)

Eliseo Santos

When Daniel gave the interpretation of King Nebuchadnezzar's dream, he says that the head of gold represented the King of Babylon, whose kingdom rose to prominence from 608-538 B.C. He states: "Thou, O king, art a king of kings: for the God of heaven hath given thee a kingdom, power, and strength, and glory. And wheresoever the children of men dwell, the beasts of the field and the fowls of the heaven hath he given into thine hand, and hath made thee ruler over them all. Thou art this head of gold," (Daniel 2:37-38). The other parts of the statue (silver chest and arms, brass thighs, iron legs, and clay and iron feet) symbolize the following world kingdoms that will follow the Babylonian empire.

To understand the meaning of the other symbols of silver, bronze, iron, iron and clay of the prophecy of Daniel chapter 2, it's best to read the 2nd major prophecy in Daniel Chapter 7. It is here in which the reader is given more details concerning the corresponding kingdoms 1st shown in Daniel chapter 2. The vision of Daniel chapter 7 begins with Daniel seeing four beasts come out of the sea. The 1st beast was a lion with eagle's wings; the 2nd was a bear with three ribs in its mouth, and the bear was in a position where one side was higher than the other. (Daniel 7:1-5) The 3rd beast was a leopard with four heads and wings (Daniel 7:6); and the fourth beast is unlike the other beasts as Daniel states:

> *After this I saw in the night visions, and behold a fourth beast, dreadful and terrible, and strong exceedingly; and it had great iron teeth: it devoured and brake in pieces, and stamped the residue with the feet of it: and it was diverse from all the beasts that were before it; and it had ten horns. I considered the horns, and, behold, there came up among them another little horn, before whom there were three of the first horns plucked up by the roots: and, behold, in this horn were eyes*

Good Father, Bad Father

like the eyes of man, and a mouth speaking great things.–
(Daniel 7:7-8 KJV)

Daniel further describes this Little Horn will speak blasphemies against God, will wear out the Saints of God, and also would think to change the times and the law of God (Ten Commandments). This Little Horn would be a given a "time, times, and a dividing time," where it will exercise its power over many (Daniel 7:25). The 1st beast of Daniel 7 relates to the head of gold from Daniel 2, and that was the Kingdom of Babylon. The 2nd beast of Daniel 7 relates to the chest and arms of silver, which was the Medo-Persian empire. The 2nd beast of Daniel 7 conquered and brought down the Babylonian empire in 539 B.C.[8]. The 3rd leopard beast of Daniel 7 relates to the thighs of bronze and this was the empire of ancient Greece. The 4th beast of Daniel 7 relates to the iron legs of Daniel chapter 2 and that was the ancient Roman Empire. Finally, the Little Horn power of Daniel 7 that arises from the 4th beast corresponds to the feet of iron and clay of Daniel 2.

To identify the Little Horn power of Daniel 7 and its relation to the feet of iron and clay of Daniel 2, you must understand the symbols being used in these two passages. The symbol of iron and clay from Daniel 2 is in accordance with the language of Daniel 7. From the 4th beast or 4th Kingdom would arise a powerful and influential Kingdom, the Little Horn. Thus, this Little Horn would consider itself to be of Roman origin as well as it would presume itself to being a god on earth. Therefore, the feet of iron and clay in Daniel 2 alludes to the unique mixture of great political and religious power that will

---

[8] Babylon, Funk& Wagnalls New Encyclopedia Volume 3, New York, 1971, Library of Congress#72-170933

rise from the fall of the Roman Empire. When you read in Daniel 7:25 (KJV), you will see that this Little Horn would also speak blasphemy against God. Daniel states, "And he shall speak great words against the most High, and shall wear out the saints of the most High; and think to change times and the laws." To speak blasphemy against God is defined as either for any man to proclaim himself as a god (John 10:33). Also, blasphemy is considered for any man to either proclaim to have the power to forgive sins (Luke 5:18-26) or proclaim to do God's service by killing anyone else in the name of God (John 16:2-4). Any man or human institution to proclaim any or all definitions of blasphemy is for them to take the place of Christ on earth. For Christ is the only man who can proclaim Himself as God, forgive sins, and judge other human beings and carry out judgment in the form of punishment. The meaning of the symbols of iron and clay from Daniel 2 is evident when you read verse 34 and 35. There you read "a stone was cut out by no human hand" and "the stone that struck the image became a great mountain and filled the whole earth." This stone correlate with verse 27 of Daniel 7 when it states "And the kingdom and the dominion and the greatness of the kingdoms under the whole heaven shall be given to the people of the saints of the Most High." Therefore "the stone that is cut by no human hand" refers to the Kingdom of God that will be instituted by God after the 2nd coming of Christ. When Christ returns, he will end the Little Horn power and the world as we know it today. Thus, the symbol of iron and clay of Daniel 2 refers to not only a mixture of political and religious clout, but a power that seeks to become like God. In the same way clay hardens to become similar to stone, this false religious system seeks to become like God and write their own laws in stone. God who wrote His law (The Ten Commandments) with the power of His finger on

Good Father, Bad Father

two slabs of rock to signify that His laws stand forever. The false man-made religion attempts to place itself as a god to create a worldwide Kingdom through human manipulation similar to that of a pottery maker using his hands to mold the clay into his own form or liking. Therefore, this is why God describes His Kingdom in Daniel 2:34-35 as a "stone cut out without hands" because it is a religious kingdom that existed long before Adam and Eve were alive. Thus, it is a religious kingdom instituted by God and His Ten Commandments rather than man. After this the "stone cut out without hands" destroys the statue and image by destroying the Iron and clay kingdom, it will then destroy the whole statute and to such an extent that there will be left no sign of them for eternity. This is seen in Daniel 2:35 when it states that "the iron, the clay, the brass, the silver, and the gold, broken to pieces together, and became like the chaff of the summer threshing floors; and the wind carried them away, that no place was found for them." The reason why no place was found for them is because "the stone cut out without hands" became "a great mountain, and filled the whole earth." (Daniel 2:35). Thus, the prophetic symbols are trying to say that after the 2nd Coming of Christ, God will judge all the people that have existed throughout history. After God's punishment is complete, they will no longer exist and be forgotten. God's Kingdom will become a great mountain. This great mountain is an allusion to another biblical symbol of Mount Zion (Psalm 51, Hebrews 12, Revelation 14) or a mountain of the salvation of God's people.

In other words, it will be God's people who will be part of the new eternal kingdom of God on earth. After the judgment and punishment of the Bad Father and all of his children throughout the centuries, then God's people will live forever on a recreated planet earth. God will restore His intended vision for human life on earth that he made long ago in the Garden of Eden. Evidence of this interpretation is further shown in Daniel 7:21-22, 26-27 (KJV):

> *I beheld, and the same horn [Little Horn] made war with the saints, and prevailed against them; Until the Ancient of days came, and judgment was given to the saints of the most High; and the time came that the saints possessed the Kingdom. [...] But the judgment shall sit, and they shall take away dominion, to consume and to destroy it unto the end. And the kingdom and dominion, and the greatness of the kingdom under the whole heaven, shall be given to the people of the saints of the most High, whose kingdom is an everlasting kingdom, and all dominion shall serve and obey him.*

You may be asking, so who will be part of God's kingdom? The Kingdom of God will be formed from people from every walk of life imaginable on the face of the earth. They all share the common bond of recognizing the truth about God, and reality. They will also strive to live a life based on the truth. Their sins will be forgiven and forgotten on the condition they admit and confess their sins in prayer to God, and repent of these sins or eventually stop doing them. For many people this spiritually painful process, to stop sinning, is similar to the spiritual pain felt by many drug addicts who at times suffer anguishing withdrawal symptoms from whatever drug they once delighted. This spiritual suffering is also suffered by many who are shunned by the world and their friends, families, and acquaintances on account for believing and following the words of God. The saints of God have at one time or another experienced this type of spiritual suffering, which is the type of sacrifice that is pleasing to God, as it states in Psalms 51:16,17 KJV "For thou desirest not sacrifice; else would I give it: thou delightest not in burnt offering. The sacrifices of

God are a broken spirit: a broken and a contrite heart, O God, thou wilt not despise." Another source of this spiritual suffering of the Saints is that they have been persecuted throughout history by the Little Horn power. Many people throughout the centuries have been hated, persecuted, spied, killed, burned, beheaded, and tortured for their crime being in the eyes of the Little Horn power, the faith in the truth of Christ and His words in the Bible. Christ says

> *"Blessed are ye, when men shall hate you, and when they shall separate you from their company, and shall reproach you, and cast out your name as evil, for the Son of man's sake. Rejoice ye in that day and leap for joy: for, behold, your reward is great in heaven; for in the like manner did their fathers unto the prophets," (Luke 6:22-23).*

All of this information is relevant because this Little Horn power still exists today. It will once again have the political and religious clout on a global scale to persecute the people of God on the face of the earth using every piece of modern technology at its fingertips. The Little Horn power has embedded itself upon the structure of the Roman Empire as stated in Daniel:

> *The fourth beast shall be the fourth kingdom upon earth, which shall be diverse from all kingdoms, and shall devour the whole earth, and shall tread it down, and break it in pieces. And the ten horns out of this kingdom are ten kings that shall arise; and another shall rise after them; and he shall be diverse from the first, and he shall subdue three kings. – (Daniel 7:23)*

It is important to pay attention to the description of the 10 horns because Daniel says that the ten horns are ten kings and thus, the little horn is also a king. In order to further understand the symbols of the horns being equal to kings, you must read Daniel Ch. 8.

In Daniel Chapter 8, Daniel sees a ram at the side of the river Ulai and this ram is killed by a goat that charges at the ram with its large, and prolific horn. Then this large prominent horn becomes broken and then it is uprooted by four horns, that each grows towards the four cardinal directions. Then Daniel once again describes the Little Horn saying,

> *Out of one of them came forth a little horn, which grew exceedingly great toward the south, toward the east, and toward the glorious land. It grew great, even to the host of heaven; and some of the host of the stars it cast down to the ground, and trampled upon them. It magnified itself, even up to the Prince of the host, and the continual burnt offering was taken away from him, and the place of his sanctuary was overthrown. And the host was given over to it together with the continual burnt through transgression; and truth was cast down to the ground, and the horn acted and prospered. – Daniel 8:9-12 (RSV)*

The angel explains to Daniel the Ram that he saw was the Kingdom of the Medes & Persians. The angel further explains to Daniel that the goat he saw with the prominent horn was the Kingdom of Ancient Greece led by their first king, who was Alexander the Great, (Daniel 8:20). The four horns that grew from the fall of the prominent horn represented the four generals that divided up the empire of ancient Greece after fall of the Alexander the Great. These four generals were Cassander, Lysimachus, Seleucus, and Ptolemy. Keep in mind Daniel had this prophecy at least 200 years before it was fulfilled in detail.

Good Father, Bad Father

In Daniel Ch. 5, you see the events that occurred when the Medo-Persian Empire conquered Babylon, in 539 B.C. Daniel Ch. 5 which describes the events that occurred during the night Babylon fell to Medo-Persia. After Daniel revealed, the head of Gold was Babylon, and the subsequent parts of the statue were the kingdoms that would conquer the previous kingdom. On the night Babylon was conquered, Daniel was called to the feast of Belshazzar, the grandson of Nebuchadnezzar. That night during this celebration, Belshazzar took out of storage the gold and silver vessels (cups) that were used in the services in the temple of God built by Solomon, (Daniel 5:1-4). Then during this feast as Belshazzar and the nobles of Babylon were drinking copious amounts of wine, there suddenly appeared a mysterious man's hand that began to write a phrase on the wall. (Daniel 5:5-6) This greatly terrified King Belshazzar and the guests so much that Belshazzar called for his "wise men." In other words, the astrologers, and enchanters of the Babylonian courts were contacted by Belshazzar to see if they could read the writing on the wall. Belshazzar felt as if the writing on the wall was a terrible omen. Belshazzar felt so afraid that he was compelled to offer purple clothing synonymous with Babylonian royalty, and the third post in the Kingdom and a chain of gold, (Daniel 5:7-9). The Babylonian Queen and other nobles told the king not to worry and call the Prophet Daniel, who had revealed to his grandfather the interpretation of his significant dream detailed in Daniel 2. King Belshazzar calls in Daniel and explains to him his situation. Belshazzar even offers him the purple clothing, gold chain, and the third position in the Kingdom, which he respectfully declines, (Daniel 5:10-24). Daniel then reveals the significance of the writing on the wall reads ME'NE, ME'NE, TEK'EL, UPHAR'SIN which translates into the following "ME'NE,

God has numbered the days of your Kingdom and bought it to the end, TEK'EL You have been weighed in the balances and found wanting: PE'RES, Your kingdom is divided and given to the Medes and Persians," (Daniel 5:25-28). Belshazzar believed the writing on the wall was a terrible omen, and indeed it was. When Daniel gave him the grim news that very night, the Bible goes on to say Belshazzar was killed when the Medes and Persians under Darius The Mede or Cyrus, conquered Babylon when he was 62 years old, (Daniel 5:28-30).

Later on in Ch.8, Daniel sees an angel who explains to him that the Medes & Persians will follow the Kingdom of Babylon. Daniel had a vision of the ram with two horns and a goat with a large prominent horn. The explanation for this dream was given by the Angel Gabriel in verse 20, "As for the ram, which you just saw with the two horns, these are the kings of Media and Persia," (Daniel 8:20). This verifies that Medo-Persia is the bear with three ribs in its mouth from Dan. Ch.7 and the ram with two horns from Daniel Ch.8 are one and the same. The three ribs in the mouth of the bear of Dan. 7 represent the three kingdoms conquered by Medo-Persians to expand their kingdom westward, northward, and southward as suggested in Daniel 8. Thus, the three ribs represent its three major conquests over Egypt, Babylon, and Lydia.

After the Medo-Persians, the Bible foretold the arrival of the Kingdom of Ancient Greece. The vision of Daniel Ch.7 highlights the characteristics of the Kingdom of Greece, which the Prophet Daniel was shown in the description of the leopard with four wings and four heads. The leopard with wings denotes the speed and ferocity with which the army of Greece was able to wipe the Medo-Persian army off the map in 331 B.C. The Leopard's four heads represent the subsequent four generals who would each become a king of a different sector of the Kingdom in 301 B.C. Keep in mind, Daniel had the prophetic vision of Daniel Ch.7 in first year of Belshazzar in 555 B.C. and the prophetic vision of Daniel Ch.8 in 553 B.C. approximately 225 years before Alexander conquered the Medo-Persian kingdom. Daniel received his prophetic visions, close to 250 years before the Kingdom of Greece was split into four divisions. The Bible in Daniel Ch. 7 focuses more on the rapid speed and the unique future four heads of Ancient Greece with its description of the four-headed leopard beast with wings. Daniel Ch.8 focuses on the first King of Greece and the subsequent four divisions of the Greek empire. The Prophet Daniel was accurate with his description of Alexander the Great as "the prominent horn" or the "first king of Greece." After the prominent horn broke with Alexander's unexpected death, in its place grew 4 horns or 4 kings.

As a result of the Bible foretelling the arrival of the Kingdom of Medo-Persia and Greece, then it leads us to understand that the Iron legs from Daniel 2 and the 4th terrible beast of Daniel 7, refer to the Ancient Roman Empire. The validity of the Prophecy of Daniel 2, 7, 8 is verified by several people throughout history. In the 3rd century A.D., Hippolytus an early leader of the Christian church saw at first hand the fulfillment of Daniel living during the times of the oppressive and the perilous Roman Empire. In Daniel 8:24, God states concerning the 4th beast and the little horn that grows from it, "His power shall be great, and he shall cause fearful destruction, and shall succeed in what he does, and destroy mighty men, and the people of the saints." Did the Rome cause "fearful destruction and the death of saints"? Let's ask Hippolytus, who states in his Treatise on Christ and Antichrist,

> *Rejoice, blessed Daniel! There has not been in error! All these things have come to pass. After this again thou hast told us of the beast dreadful and terrible. It has iron teeth and claws of brass; it devoured and brake in pieces and stamped the residue with the feet of it. Already the Iron rules; already it subdues and breaks all in pieces; already it brings all the unwilling into subjection; already we see these things ourselves. Now we glorify God, being instructed by thee.*[9]

If the 4th beast of Daniel Ch. 7 is the ancient Roman Empire and then what is the little horn that surges from the Roman Empire and uproots three horns in its place? Daniel Ch. 7 verse 8, (KJV) states "I considered the horns, and behold, there came up among them another little horn, before whom there were three of the first horns plucked by the roots: and, behold, in this horn were eyes like the eyes of man, and a mouth speaking great things." The arrival of the little horn was fulfilled by the Roman Catholic Papacy. In 538 AD, the Pope after destroying three horns, which were the three different Kingdoms of the many Germanic tribes that appeared after the fall of the Roman Empire in 476 AD. The three uprooted kingdoms were the Vandals, Heruli, and Ostrogoths. Later on in the book, you learn in greater detail how this occurred.

Before discussing in detail the history of Christianity and the formation of Roman Catholicism, it is important to review the many biblical prophecies concerning Jesus Christ of Nazareth, and all the historical evidence concerning His life, miracles, death, and resurrection.

---

[9] Our Day In The Light Of Prophecy, London, 1917, Review and Herald Publishing -Pg.126

Chapter 5: Christ's Date of Birth

An important revision to the life of Jesus Christ of Nazareth was his birth date. Many erroneously believe Christ was born on Christmas day. The origins of Christmas will reveal the truth concerning the holiday itself, and whether or not Jesus was actually born on Christmas day. Christmas is actually a mixture of different pagan traditions, which venerated the sun. The year-end solar cult festivals during this time of year were widespread in the world at that time. The American People's Encyclopedia states concerning the origins of Christmas,

> *It is not surprising, therefore, that a great variety of ancient seasonal customs and beliefs from a number of different sources-Roman, Celtic, Teutonic, Western Asian, and Christian- have clustered round this composite observance: solar, solstitial[concerning the solstice], calendrical, and ecclesiastical, derived from Graeco-Roman, Nordic, Germanic, and Slavonic sources. These customs often have only remotely related to the Christian Feast of the Nativity [Christmas] as such, though the occurrence of the commemoration in the greater part of Europe in the darkest and coldest part of the year has given prominence to fires and lights and to outward signs and symbols of renewal in nature and the sun[10].*

---

[10] pg. 62, Christmas, The American Peoples, Volume 5 Grolier Incorporated, New York, Copyright 1967, Library of Congress Catalog Card Number: 67-0584,

The winter solstice marked the shortest day and the longest night of the year, where many pagans believed the sun was temporarily dead before it resurrected on Dec. 25th. This resurrection of the Sun was marked by longer daytime hours, which progressed to the summer solstice. The Bad father of lies, Satan took advantage of these solar phenomena in order to trick the masses into believing the "resurrection of the sun god" from death on the Winter Solstice.

A pagan tradition that was celebrated during the Winter Solstice was the Yuletide that was celebrated in Teutonic and Celtic Europe. The Yuletide was marked by fire rituals and ceremonies involving the use of vegetation. Some common examples of these rituals and ceremonies were in the burning of the Yule log, and the use of Evergreen trees, ivy, mistletoe, and holly as decorations.[11] Many of the customs of the Yuletide still exist today including the gift exchanges, carols, wassailing, feasting, and rejoicing. The only festivity to not survive to the modern-day was mortuary customs that have their origin in the Cult of the dead that was held in November. As a side note, the actual tradition of the use of Christmas trees has its origin in Babylon. The Prophet Jeremiah when speaking to Israel concerning God's thoughts:

> *Thus saith the LORD, Learn not the way of the heathen, and be not dismayed at the signs of heaven; for the heathen are dismayed at them. For the customs of the people are vain: for one cutteth a tree out of the forest, the work of the hands of the workman, with the axe. They deck it with silver and with gold; they fasten it with nails and with hammers, that it move not. – Jeremiah 10: 2-4 KJV.*

---

[11] pg. 63, Christmas, Ibid.

Good Father, Bad Father

Here God considers the practice of decorating a tree with gold and silver, which are the colors associated with the sun and moon, as a pagan practice in which he forbids his people, Israel from practicing. If Christians consider God and Jesus Christ to be the same, then they should not take part in the modern-day Christmas festivities. The modern-day Christmas tree is the practice in which God strongly condemns Christians to practice. Another key point in this passage is when God mentions "be not dismayed at the signs of heavens," which is in reference to the prevailing belief at the time of the apparent death of the sun at the winter solstice and subsequent rise of the sun on December 25th. God advises his people Israel to not be dismayed, like the majority people during the Winter solstice at the apparent death of the sun. God considers these things to be vain, superstitious, and, false which is of no benefit to His People.

The second pagan tradition to influence Christmas has its origins in Medo-Persia. From Persia rose the religion of Mithras, which gained widespread popularity throughout the Roman Empire. The Mithraic religion celebrated an important festival on December 25th, which was called in Latin *Natalis Solis Invicti* [Birth of the Unconquerable Sun]. In the Early period of the Christian Church, Mithras was the popular Roman state religion that rivaled the popularity of Christianity in the 2nd – 3rd centuries. However in the 4th century, the early church compromised Jesus Christ's truth, ethics, and morality by agreeing to join the compromise of Constantine and to accept his Sunday law. It was in this vein, the earliest record of Christmas was found recorded in the Philocalian calendar of Rome in the year 336 AD. The Christmas holiday was at this time referred to the "Feast of the Nativity", which coincided the Mithraic *Natalis Solis Invicti* on December 25th. Some scholars suggest that in order to get more people to join the new state religion of Roman Catholicism, which was created via Constantine's Edict of the Venerable Sun in 321 AD, Christmas was created as a means of not just competing with the popularity with the Mithraic *Natalis Solis Invicti*, but it was also a way for many to accept Jesus Christ at only face value via the Feast of Nativity.

Unlike other religious figures, Jesus Christ is central to understanding the Old and New Testament, and central to Biblical Christianity. First, the name Jesus Christ is the English form of the Greek translation (*Iesus Christos*) of the Hebrew *Yoshua Mashiakh*, which is the shortened version of the Hebrew name *Yehoshuah Mashiakh*. The name *Yehoshuah* means Yahweh is deliverance. The Hebrew word *Mashiakh* translates into Messiah, which means anointed one. The Greek word *Christos* was a translation of the Hebrew *Mashiakh* and was popularly used by the early followers of Jesus Christ.[12] The concept of a Messiah is tied to the Ancient Hebrew culture detailed in the Old Testament, where the king of Israel was anointed with oil. This is shown in the 2nd Book of the Prophet Samuel, 5:17, "But when the Philistines heard that they had anointed David king over Israel, all the Philistines came up to seek David." Therefore, to call Jesus the Messiah or the *Christos* means to acknowledge Him as the King of not only Israel, but of the world. He was the Son of God who created the world and also turned himself into a physical human descendant of King David and Abraham and thus, Jesus Christ is the Messiah in the sense of being King of the universe. When Christ was crucified on the cross, Pontius Pilate wrote a title to identify Jesus Christ of Nazareth. He wrote this title in the

---

[12] Jesus Christ." Microsoft® Student 2009 [DVD]. Redmond, WA: Microsoft Corporation, 2008.

Good Father, Bad Father

three primary languages of the region at the time Latin, Greek, and Hebrew, (John 19:19-20) He placed this title written in three languages on the cross, "Jesus of Nazareth, the King of the Jews," in Latin, this title translated to *Iesus Nazarenus, Rex Iudaeorum*.

Another important point that is lost in the translation is the fact that there were many people called "Jesus" or *Yoshua* at the time of Christ. Likewise, there were many who were named Simon, and many named Judas, and also many were named Mary. In order to distinguish people on records or in a conversation, their place of birth or where they were raised, then became a second identifier of a person's name. If this did not work, or if they were many in a particular area called by a certain name, then another name was given to them, similar to what in modern times is referred to as a nickname. In Matthew 4:18, you see that the Apostle Peter had the name of Simon, but Peter became his nickname. In Matthew 26:6, you read there was a man called "Simon The Leper" and in Matthew 27:32 there is a "Simon of Cyrene" who helped Jesus Christ carry His cross. There was also John the Baptist, and John the son of Zebedee, who became John the Apostle, (Matthew 4:21).The Jesus Christ that is known today was also known as "Jesus of Galilee" (Matthew 26:69) and "Jesus of Nazareth" (Matthew 26:71). Keep in mind, the city of Nazareth was in the district of Galilee, (Luke 2:4). The followers of the real Jesus Christ of Nazareth recognized in His teachings and miracles how God was not only uniquely divine, but also the King of the World and the Universe. They recognized that He is the creator along with God the Father and the Holy Spirit, due to not only His many marvelous miracles but also due to Christ impeccable character, determination, and service, which many people should learn today.

Eliseo Santos

This fundamental revision of the birth date of Jesus Christ has created confusion, and unbelief in God and God's word found in the Bible. Many people who search for the truth come across these facts and use it to dismiss the existence of God, while not understanding the context of these facts prove that throughout history Satan has tried to deceive humanity through things that which appeal to our human senses. Satan knowing the Sun's appeal to mankind sought to deify the unconscious stellar creation of God. Satan has long sought to have mankind to worship him either through free will, coercion or deception. Jesus Christ came to earth to educate and tell the truth about reality, salvation, and the proper way to worship God and take care of your human brothers and sisters. Unlike the other gods and goddesses of ancient Rome, Greece, Medo-Persia, Babylon, and Egypt, the real Jesus Christ was the very definition of humbleness, fearlessness, and patience. The real Jesus Christ lived His life obeying the commandments and the will of the Good Father in heaven. Due to Christ's reverence and devotion to the Good Father, it gave His followers a leader and model to follow. The American Peoples Encyclopedia reiterates the idea of Christ's teachings being unique and genuine, "Certain of his teachings were distinctive. He invariably presented God as a Father, whose power, love, and authority, and forgiveness were extended to men. He used the title Father in addressing God, and taught His disciples to pray, 'Our Father,'"[13] . Therefore, with Christ's exemplary life many have a hope of achieving the goal of eternal life.

---

[13] Pg. 509, Jesus Christ, APE, Vol.10, Grolier Incorporated, New York, 1967, Library of Congress Catalog Card Number:67-10584

Good Father, Bad Father

The previous quote highlights what Christ said in the Book of Revelation 1:8 (KJV) "I am the Alpha and Omega, the beginning and the ending, saith the Lord, which is, and which was, and which is to come, the Almighty." Christ is everything to Christianity. All the themes of the Bible point to Him and Him alone. His life and existence combines both the Old and New Testament to give hope to individuals in achieving what He has accomplished; namely teaching the truth of reality, alleviating physical, mental, spiritual suffering, and taking part in the resurrection of the Body and Spirit to eternal life. Christ is both the beginning foundation and the end goal. If an individual is compared to a tree, Christ is both the rock upon which the tree grows firm roots in the firm soil, and at the same time He is the light of truth in which the branches of all strong trees grow towards. Christ is the vehicle, the GPS, and the road, which leads to eternal life. Christ is the teacher, the student, and the principal. Since Christ takes on many different responsibilities for the salvation of humanity, then therefore all you need to do is just rely on Him, and His teachings that are found in both the Old and New Testament. It is due to the nature of Christ and His many different roles in the process of salvation that gives certainty to achieving eternal life.

So if Christ was not born on December 25th like most of humanity believes today, when was He born? To answer this question, let's take a look at the Word of God to find important clues to find out the approximate birth date of Jesus Christ. The first important clue is found in Luke Ch.2 Verse 8, where it states the shepherds were out at night with their flock. This key clue rules out the birth of Jesus being in late December because inferring from the verse it was warm enough for the Shepherds and their flock to be outside at night. The second important clue is found in Luke 1:5 where it states, "In the days of Herod, king of Judea, there was a priest named Zachariah of the division of Abijah." This verse gives you two important pieces of information: King Herod was still alive and also Zachariah, John the Baptist's father, was a member of the 8th out of 24 priestly division of Abijah. Why is this significant? Because now you are aware of when Zachariah was in the Temple and now know when John the Baptist conceived. Therefore, you can know the approximate date of the birth of Jesus Christ, by knowing when His cousin John the Baptist was conceived and born. In 1 Chronicles Ch. 24: Verses10, 19 "the eighth to Abijah… These had as their appointed duty in their service to come into the house of the Lord, according to the procedure established for them by Aaron their father, as the Lord God of Israel had commanded him." The Jewish calendar begins in the spring during the month of Nisan, and therefore the 1st division of Jehoiarib served in the Jewish temple for 7 days. In following week, 2nd division of Jedaiah served in the Jewish Temple. The 3rd week would be the feast of the unleavened bread, (Passover) and all the priests of the 24 priestly divisions were present in the Temple to serve. Then the schedule resumed in the 4th week with the 3rd division of priests and this continued throughout the year. In the 10th week of the Jewish year, the priests of the 8th division Abijah served in the Jewish Temple after the feasts of Passover and the Pentecost required all the priests to serve in the temple. According to Luke Ch. 1: Verses 23-24, when Zachariah's time of service was completed, he returned home and his wife Elizabeth became pregnant and for five months remained at home. Zechariah completed his Temple service on the 3rd Sabbath of the 3rd Month of the Jewish year, or (June-July). Afterwards, he returned home and Elizabeth conceived his son, John. Therefore, John the Baptist was conceived on the 3rd Sabbath of the 3rd month of the

Good Father, Bad Father

Jewish calendar. It is important to know when John the Baptist was conceived because Jesus Christ was conceived in the Womb of Mary through the Holy Spirit in the 6th month of the Elizabeth's pregnancy, (Luke Ch. 1:Verses 26-45). The 6th month of Elizabeth's pregnancy was the 9th month of the Jewish year Kislev (Nov. -Dec.). This would mean that in the 12th -1st month (Mar. -Apr.) of the Jewish calendar would be the approximate date of the birth of John the Baptist. Therefore, Jesus Christ would be born on the 6th -7th month of the Jewish year which translated to (Sept. - Oct.) of the Year of 4 B.C.

In order to understand the why the year 4 B.C. is the year of Christ's birth it is important to review some important history that occurred in area of Judea in the Middle East during a time when Rome started to gain a presence in the region. When Christ was born, Herod was in the position of Procurator of Judea. It was in this position Herod the Great would rule Judea from 37 B.C. to 4 B.C. as King of Judea. It was during the last year of his reign and his life when Jesus Christ was born in 4 B.C. After the death of Herod the Great, Judea and Palestine was split amongst his three sons of which, Herod Archelaus served as ethnarch of Judea from 4 B.C. to 6 A.D. It was Herod the Great who would seek to kill Jesus after he was visited by the wise men from the East who made Him aware of the birth of the Messiah, the King of Israel. Herod the Great who feared the birth of Jesus would pose a challenge to his rule and authority and therefore, he gave one of the most diabolic orders ever given by a ruler and that was the death of all male babies under two years old in the region of Bethlehem (Matthew 2:16). After the visit from the wise men, an angel came and told Joseph and Mary to immediately leave for Egypt. When Herod died the angel came via a dream to inform Joseph and Mary that they can return to Israel. Upon returning to

Israel, Joseph became aware of Herod's son Archelaus became the ethnarch of Judea (Matthew 2:19-22). Due to this, Joseph and Mary settled in Galilee, in the city of Nazareth.

A key piece of evidence that Jesus was born in 4 B.C. is found in Luke 3:1 which states, "Now in the fifteenth year of the reign of Tiberius Caesar, Pontius Pilate being governor of Judea, and Herod the Tetrarch of Galilee, and his brother Philip tetrarch of Ituraea [present-day Lebanon]." This bit of information is important because it then gives historical confirmation of the following historical fact. The fact was that Jesus Christ of Nazareth was baptized by John the Baptist (John 1:15-34), and this milestone occurred when he was 30 years old, (Luke 3:23).[14] The ministry of Christ lasted for three and a half years (Luke 13:7), thus at the time of Christ's death and resurrection he was 33 and ½ half of years old.[15] The reason why this is certain is first because Christ was born in autumn (Late September- Early October) and He died in the spring (in late March- Mid April). Many scholars state that Tiberius Caesar came into power in 14 A.D. after the death of Augustus Caesar in the same year.[16] However, Tiberius came to power two years before Augustus died in 12 A.D. according to 2nd century Roman Consul Dion Cassius.[17] In Book 56, Ch.26 of the Cassius work, Dion Cassius gives the account that

---

[14] pg. 508, Jesus Christ, American Peoples Encyclopedia-Vol.10.-1967-Grolier Incorporated
[15] Pg. 508, Ibid. - Wojcik, Daniel. "Millennium." Microsoft® Student 2009 [DVD]. Redmond, WA: Microsoft Corporation, 2008
[16] Tiberias Caesar,Pg.18-810 APE- Vol.18-1958-Spencer Press Inc.
[17] "Dio Cassius." Microsoft® Student 2009 [DVD]. Redmond, WA: Microsoft Corporation, 2008

Good Father, Bad Father

Augustus Caesar recognized Tiberius as emperor of Rome in 12 A.D., two years before the death of Augustus Caesar.[18] Dr.Philip Schaff, who wrote in the "History of the Christian Church," gave further evidence of 12 A.D. being the starting year of Tiberius' reign by stating the existence of coins from Antioch in Syria from the date A.U. 765 [A.D. 12], with the head of Tiberius and the inscription, Kaisar, Sebastos(Augustus).[19] Thus, Tiberius Caesar was recognized as emperor, while Augustus was still alive in 12 A.D. Therefore, if Jesus was 30 in the 15th year of the reign of Tiberius Caesar, then Jesus turned 30 years old in the Fall of 27 A.D. Thus, if Christ's ministry lasted 3 and ½ years after he was 30 years old, then this leads us to His death and resurrection occurring in the spring of 31 A.D.[20]

There are two principles of timekeeping that guide individuals to navigate the apparent confusion of keeping time under different calendars. The first is someone's age and birth year, and the other is the anniversary of a certain event or the celebration of annual, or weekly holiday. All of these principles are used in the Gospels to help readers to figure out when Jesus Christ was born, died and resurrected through including the information concerning the 15th year of Tiberius was 30th year of Christ's life on earth, and the beginning of his 3 and ½ year ministry.

It is also important to review the significance of the Jewish Holidays and festivals in accordance with the life of Christ. Christ was born on the 15th day of the 7th Jewish month of Tishri, which

---

[18] Our Day in The Light of Prophecy, pg. 230, By W.A.Spicer, Review and Harold Publishing Assn., 1917 London

[19] pg. 120, footnote, Vol.1 as quoted in ODLP,pg. 230

[20] See note 1 in the Notes Section at the End of the Book

coincided with the feast of tabernacles. The feast of tabernacles was a harvest festival held after Yom Kippur, which is on the 10th day of Tishri. All the people of Israel would build temporary tents, and booths to commemorate the time Israel left outside of Egypt. At the time of Christ, all Jewish people from the Middle East would come to Jerusalem during their visit to the Temple in Jerusalem, and thus Jerusalem became overcrowded with visitors. The Feast of Tabernacles, the Feast of Unleavened Bread, and the Passover, were all the yearly Jewish festivals in which every man of Israel was supposed to appear before God in the Temple of God, (Deuteronomy 16:16-17). Christ's birth on the feast of tabernacles has the additional meaning, because it is a commemoration of not only Israel's exit from Egypt, but also it is a commemoration of the humble birth of Jesus Christ, the Son of God. Jesus Christ was with the eternal God before He decided it was time to go to earth and begin the plan of salvation of the human race from sin, suffering, and death, all of which cause by Satan's interference in human life. Christ stood from His throne, which is located to the right of the Good Father, and came to earth in the humblest of dwellings instead of remaining in the awe-inspiring Kingdom of heaven. The Feast of Tabernacles reminds the Jewish People of the temporary dwellings in which their ancestors made while traveling out of Egypt to the promised land of Canaan, (Leviticus 23:41-44). For Christ, in the Feast of Tabernacles Christ surrendered his pure divinity to become mixed and live with his creation, the human race. Humanity at the time was not conscious of how they desperately they need His help of the truth of salvation and eternal life. The Feast of Tabernacles is marked with a Holy day or Sabbath on the first day and another Holy day or Sabbath on the 8th day, outside of the weekly 7th Day Sabbath (Leviticus 23:39). In the case of Christ's birth, it also coincided with the High Holy Day Sabbath, which was of part of the 1st day of feast of Tabernacles and also it fell on the weekly 7th Day Sabbath. On the eighth Day, when Christ was named Yehoshuah and circumcised, it was also considered a Holy Day weekly Sabbath, which coincided the Holy Day Sabbath of the 8th Day of the Feast of Tabernacles, (Luke 2:21-24). During the times of Moses, the Feast of Tabernacles, the people of Israel and elsewhere were reminded of the law of God, and the law of God was also celebrated. It states in the Book of Deuteronomy 31:11-13,

When all of the people of Israel come to appear before the Lord thy God in the place in which he shall choose; and thou shalt read this law before all of Israel in their hearing. Gather the people together, men and women, and children, and thy stranger that is within thy gates, that they may hear, and that they may learn, fear the Lord your God, and observe to do all the words of this law: And that their children, which have not known anything, may hear, and learn to fear the Lord your God, as long as ye live in the land whither ye go over Jordan to possess it.

The quote above highlights the mission of Christ on earth, and His commission to the Apostles in Matthew 28:19-20, "All the power is given unto me in heaven and in earth. Go ye therefore, and teach all the nations, baptizing them in the name of the Father, and of the Son, and the Holy Ghost. Teaching them to observe all the things whatsoever I commanded you: and, lo, I am with you always, even unto the end of the world." The alignment of Christ's birth with the Feast of Tabernacles was also symbolic of Christ's mission to come and teach the people of Israel and the world the proper way to worship God, and the proper way to keep the law. As mentioned previously, Christ did not come to abolish the Ten Commandments.

Instead, He came to live them and fulfill them, in order to lead the Children of God by example to their eternal life and to their Good heavenly Father.

Take note of the other Jewish festivals in which were significant to the life of Jesus Christ and to the establishment of Christianity. After being born of the 1st day of the Feast of Tabernacles held on 10/4/ 4 B.C., Jesus would die on another major Jewish festival, Passover. On this day, the 14th day of the first Jewish month of Nissan of the year 31 A.D., Jesus became the Passover Lamb that takes away the sins of the world. The Passover celebrate Israel's exit from the physical slavery of Egypt. In Christ, the Passover lamb is symbolic of Jesus Christ becoming the only method of salvation made available to human beings from God, in order to save people from the slavery of the mind and soul that is caused by lies, sin, death, and the evil of the Bad Father.

Chapter 6: The Apocalypse of Revelation

In 96 AD, John, the original Apostle and witness to the crucifixion of Jesus Christ, wrote arguably the most important book of not only the Bible, but ever written with ink and paper. This book has guided millions of Christian Bible Believers throughout history. Those who through the grace of God have been able to learn, and accept the conspicuous conclusions of this book have faced the fiercest opposition in the face of the earth that man has ever known. This book reveals to the world who is the bad father, and more importantly, reveals how the bad father works in this world through his accomplices throughout history. The Bad Father of lies and his human henchmen wish to accomplish Satan's goal, which he has wanted since the Garden of Eden. Satan's main goal is a new world order, where he will impersonate Christ, to steal for himself the rightful glory, and worship away from God. This book also identifies the traits of The Good Father's church and people since the time of Christ. It also identifies the Church and people of the Bad Father. This book also does something no other book does, but it foretells of the destruction of humanity, which will lead to the 2nd coming of the only Lord and Savior Jesus Christ.

It also describes in vivid details the "new heaven and new earth" that will be created for man to reclaim their divine destiny to live forever side by side their creator. Imagine a world without fear, terror, anxiety, depression, and pain. Think about a world where death and evil no longer exist, where people no longer need to worry about how they look, their health, and their well-being. A world where everything of value, your eternal life, your very own beautiful mansion are given to you without price. At the cost of the infinite life of Christ, you will gain free unlimited access to things so advanced, that humanity still has not heard of or seen them. A world where man, woman, and child can receive the body, mind, and spirit made in God's perfect image reflected in Adam and Eve before sin. A world where man, woman, and child are a walking testament of God's love. It is God's love that can transform the weak to the strong; liars to truth tellers; and the ignorant to wise. God's love can also transform the homeless to mansion owners; miserable to elated; mediocrity to excellence; selfish to selfless; filthy to clean; and doubters to believers. This special book is none other than the Book of Revelation, the Book where John reveals the history from the times of Christ to the events that will soon captivate the world that are taking shape today.

The Bible begins with the Book of Genesis a book that describes the alienation of mankind from the tree of life (Gen. 3:22). Through Satan's evil influence, the destiny of mankind changed from deserving eternal life to deserving death (Gen. 2:17). After being removed from God's Garden of Eden, humanity has now changed to needing to work and plan to create food (Gen. 3:19). God had envisioned mankind having a holy dominion over the planet. In other words, a dominion where everyone rules themselves through the law of God and their free will. Once the great lies and sins entered the world, humanity lost dominion of the earth (Gen. 3:24). These were humbling events for humanity. Along with the realization of their nakedness and separation from the pleasant presence of God, Adam and Eve realize the great error in their ways for not obeying the loving Words of the Good Father. Adam and Eve repented from listening to the words of error of the Bad Father.

The Book of Revelation is the book in which everything that was destroyed by the Bad Father is restored to its rightful place. In the Book of Revelation, you read about the restoration of the tree of life (Rev.2: 7), and mankind's victory over death and evil (Rev.2:11). You also read of God's preparation of the eternal Garden and the New Jerusalem for His people (Rev.2:17). Man's dominion and also God's kingdom are restored to its rightful place (Rev.2:26). Instead of being naked or clothed in human clothes, people will be again clothed in white heavenly robes (Rev.3:5). God, the Good Father, will feed, clothe, and shelter His Children forever. There will no longer be any separation from God because He will live with us forever and ever. Imagine what a great blessing it will be to have the Creator as your neighbor.

Chapter 7: The Seven Churches, Seals, and Trumpets

In the beginning of Revelation, John writes the messages to the Seven Churches. These are specific messages of hope to strengthen God's people who keep the Commandments of God, and the faith of Jesus Christ. For each of the Seven Churches there is a specific town that was part of the early Christian Postal route located in Asia Minor in Modern-day Turkey.[21] Each of the Seven Churches has a commendation or special word of praise from God and also advice or counsel, and a rebuke by Christ to improve upon their weakness. These Seven Churches are each a prophetic message for the future of God's true people who continue to follow the Ten Commandments of God and keep the faith of Jesus Christ (Revelation 14:12). In total the Seven Churches not only provide a historical frame of reference in the Book of Revelation, but they also serve to demonstrate the characteristics of the strengths and weaknesses of God's people.

The Seven Churches correlate with the Seven Seals of Revelation 6. The Seven Seals are symbolic of the seven seals that were placed on scrolls in ancient times. Usually, a scroll with seven seals

---

[21] The Letter to Seven Churches of Asia" By W.M. Ramsay, Ch.15, pg.112, http://www.ccel.org/ccel/ramsay/letters.pdf

Eliseo Santos

contained classified information that can only be opened or revealed by the person who met the criteria to receive the scroll. Therefore, the scroll with the seven seals in Revelation could only be opened by Jesus Christ, who died, resurrected and ascended to Heaven.

In Revelation 4 and Revelation 5, there are two different scenes described in heaven. The first scene in Revelation 4 describes the scene of the throne of God. There are the 24 elders and four different types of Seraphim described as beasts or kings with six wings giving worship to the Creator of the Universe. Then in Revelation 5, describes the scene of the Lamb receiving the scroll or book with seven seals from the Right hand of the Creator. John writes in Revelation 5:2-12,

> *And I saw a strong angel proclaiming with a loud voice, 'Who are thou worthy to open the book, and loose, the seals thereof,?' And no man in heaven , nor in earth, neither under the earth, was able to open the book, neither to look thereon. And I wept much, because no man was found worthy to open and to read the book, neither to look there on. And one of the elders saith unto me, Weep not: behold, the Lion of the tribe of Juda, the Root of David, hath prevailed to open the book, and to loose the seven seals thereof. And I beheld, and, lo, in the midst of the throne and of the four beasts, and in the midst of the elders, stood a Lamb as it had been slain, having seven horns and seven eyes, which are the seven Spirits of God sent forth into all the earth. And he came and took the book out of the right hand of him that sat upon the throne. And when he had taken the book, the four beasts and four and twenty elders fell down before the Lamb, having every one of them harps, and golden vials full of odours, which are the prayers of saints. And they sung a new song, saying, Thou art worthy to take the book, and to open the seals thereof: for thou wast slain, and hast redeemed us to God by thy blood out of every kindred, and tongue, and people, and nation, And hast made us unto our God kings and priests: and we shall reign on the*

Good Father, Bad Father

earth. And I beheld, and I heard the voice of many angels round about the throne and the beasts and the elders: and the number of them was ten thousand times ten thousand, and thousands of thousands; Saying with a loud voice, Worthy is the Lamb that was slain to receive power, and riches, and wisdom, and strength, and honour, and glory, and blessing.

John describes the scene when Jesus returned to heaven after the ascension into heaven in 31 A.D. The lamb that was slain represents Jesus Christ who is the only one worthy of opening the Seven Seals because He is one with God, the Creator of the universe and the only one to overcome sin and death. When John describes the Lamb with 7 horns and 7 eyes, it describes Jesus having the perfect kingdom or being all-mighty and omniscience. The beasts mentioned by John are different from the beasts of the Daniel 7 they actually represent an elite rank of angels that have six wings. Lucifer was part of this elite rank of angels, but after his fall Gabriel took his place.

The Book of Daniel and Revelation share similar parallel chapters. Therefore, similar to how the prophecy of Daniel Ch.2 relates to the prophecy of Daniel Ch.7, and how Daniel Ch. 7 relates to Daniel Ch.8, there is a similar set-up in Revelation. The Seven Churches of Revelation Ch2, and 3 correlate with the Seven Seals of Ch. 6. The Seven Seals correlate with the seven trumpets of Revelation 8 and 9, 11. Thus, the Seven Churches are God's people from the Times of Christ until His 2nd coming. The Seven Seals help the reader understand and amplify the meaning of the Seven Churches. The seven seals help the reader understand the Seven Trumpets, which describe the war between the people of God and the other communities of the world from the Times of Christ and His 2nd Coming.

Another important part of these scenes is the worship that is freely given to God for His awesomeness and greatness. The 24 elders of the Throne of God freely toss their crowns before the Throne of God similar to the elation of graduation that causes students to toss their mortarboards in the air. The scene of the Throne of God is similar to a Hockey game, when someone performs a hat trick and the audience in unison tosses their hats on the ice to celebrate the greatness of the feat. Thus, the scenes described in Revelation Ch. 4 and Ch.5, express the indescribable feeling of elation, joy, and also the recognition of the immense greatness of the All-mighty Creator God. This is described in Revelation Ch. 4, where John writes of the scene of the 24 elders of Heaven. They continue to say, in an expression of their limitless gratitude, "Thou art worthy, O Lord, to receive glory, and honour and power: for thou hast created all things, and for thy pleasure they are and were created,"(Revelation 4:10-11). Thus the sole purpose of worship, concerning God was that the 24 elders recognize without God they themselves don't exist. It was from the limitless love and mercy of God, that brought our planet and our ancestor's Adam and Eve and us into existence and into redemption. To not recognize God as the creator eventually leads humanity to self-destruction characterized by greed, death, and selfishness.

Chapter 8: The Church of Ephesus and the 1st Seal

The first of the Seven Churches is the Church of Ephesus. This Church represents the Early Christian Church following the ascension of Jesus Christ into heaven from 31 AD. The Church of Ephesus translates to Desirable in Greek. Ephesus was the early church that had desirable qualities of being faithful, pure, and diligent church. It was a church where every member woke up every day thinking about ways to distribute the love and truth of the Good News of eternal life through Jesus Christ. The Church of Ephesus correlates with the 1st of the Seven Seals. Similar to how in Daniel 2, the head of Gold, correlated with 1st beast to come out of the sea, which was the lion beast with wings or Babylon in Daniel 7. Jesus Christ describes this church, by stating:"

> *I know your works, your toll, and your patient endurance, and how you cannot bear evil men, but have tested those who call themselves apostles but are not, and found them to be false; I know you are enduring patiently and bearing up for my name's sake, and you have not grown weary. But I have this against you that you have abandoned the love you had at first. Remember therefore from when thou art fallen, repent, and do the first works; or else I will come unto thee quickly, and will remove thy candlestick out of his place, except thou repent. But this thou hast, that thou hatest the deeds of the Nicolaitans,*

> *which I also hate. He that hath an ear, let him hear what the Spirit saith unto the churches; To him that overcometh will I give to eat of the tree of life, which is in the midst of the paradise of God. – (Rev. 2:2-7,KJV)*
>
> *And I saw, behold a white horse: and he that sat on him had a bow; and a crown was given unto him: and he went forth conquering, and to conquer. – (Rev. 6:2, KJV)*

John describes the words of Jesus as he describes the qualities of the early church. The early Christian Church of the Apostles from 31 A.D.-100 A.D. was the clean and pure church in teachings and work ethic. The church would spread the message of Christ from Jerusalem to Rome, and throughout Asia Minor, the Middle East, and Africa. The white horse represents the desirable humble qualities of this Church and how it was patient; and actively involved in spreading the word and truth about Christ in Latin, Greek, Hebrew, and Aramaic. The bow of the horseman represents how it was able to send the message very far away from its initial starting point of Jerusalem. The crown represents how the early Church of Ephesus was successful in winning souls for Christ, and this alludes to the crowns in which all saved Christians will receive once they enter heaven. Imagine, this early church did all of this without any modern technology that people have available today. It relied upon the Holy Spirit to spread the message of Christ and it succeeded.

The early Christians from 31 – 100 AD, faced opposition and infiltration like many of the future churches. The early Christians hated those who impersonated Apostles, but were not, and also hated those who taught false teachings concerning God and Jesus Christ that were not found in the Bible. The early church of Ephesus also handled the problem of fraudulent Christians who claimed to have been

Good Father, Bad Father

followers of Jesus Christ, but in reality they were spies or wolves in sheep's clothing. The problem of fraudulent Christianity continued due impart through the development of Gnosticism.[22] Through Gnosticism biblically-foreign ideas of God were introduced into the Christian community at that time under the guise of secret knowledge, in continuation of the ancient mystery cults mixed with Christianity. Jesus alludes to this when He says in the message to the Church of Ephesus, "thou hatest the deeds of the Nicolatians, which I also hate. Other Christian historians say that there are two possible definitions for the word "Nicolatians". The first possible definition is the definition of Nicolatians is derived from two Greek words Nikos and Laos. Nikos means "to subdue or gain control over" and Laos translates into people in ancient Greek.[23] Thus, when both words are combined, then it paints a clearer picture of what Christ was trying to say: He hates how some will infiltrate the early Christian Church for the sole purpose of gaining control over the people.

Similar to how Satan's greed for power was an abhorrence to Christ and God, so is Christ disgusted with those who join the Christian Church for the sole purpose of gaining power and authority over Christian believers. God hates false religious systems that distort the Word of God for their own selfish desires because it creates unnecessary confusion that is ultimately exploited for gain on the part of those who distort the Word of God. Another possible take on the meaning of the Nicolatians comes from the Greek word Nicolah,

---

[22] *Gnosis* means revealed knowledge in Greek (Perkins, Pheme. "Gnosticism." Microsoft® Student 2009 [DVD]. Redmond, WA: Microsoft Corporation, 2008
[23] http://www.lightsource.com/ministry/refuel-with-rick/articles/who-were-the-nicolaitans-and-what-was-their-doctrine-and-deeds--14510.html

which translates to "Let us eat." Thus, the doctrine of the Nicolatians could also refer to the eating of food sacrificed to idols, which later on Jesus expresses his displeasure in other messages, to the other churches of Revelation Ch.2 and 3.[24]

Despite the danger of false spiritual and unbiblical doctrines entering the early Christian Church, early Christian believers had to also be aware of persecution through espionage. The significance of Christian persecution throughout history is established by the historical facts of the persecution of the early Christian Church. Often times important history relating to the persecution of the Christian Church is distorted to support the state religion and the papal throne. In the book "Bloody Theater: Martyrs' Mirror of the Defenceless Christians, by Thielem J. Von Bracht, translated by L.Daniel Rupp," tells of individual martyrdom accounts starting from the Times of the Apostles to the age of Protestantism. Von Bracht accounts show the similarities in the crude and grotesque handling of innocent Christians by Imperial Rome, were not that far different from the Roman Church inquisitions during the Middle Ages, in terms of the process of questioning and torturing Christian believers to renounce their faiths.[25] Concerning Nero's persecution, he noted how there was an irrational hatred toward those who confessed to being followers of Christ, and this hatred is what motivated Nero to kill as many Christian saints.

One of the worst religious persecutions of history and the first widespread persecution of the Christian Church happened under Nero in 64 A.D. Nero used the crisis of the burning of Rome as an excuse

---

[24] http://www.gotquestions.org/Nicolaitans.html
[25] pg. 50, Bloody Theater: Martyrs' Mirror of the Defenceless Christians, by Thielem J. Von Bracht, translated by L.Daniel Rupp

Good Father, Bad Father

to attack Christians. When Nero burned the City of Rome, it did not impact the Christian and Jewish area of the city. Keep in mind, all Christians during this time still observed God's fourth commandment and thus they were considered by pagans to be Jews. Nero did not know the great influence of his persecution on future kings, Popes, and rulers throughout the world. Nero was the first ruler to take on the task of using his power to kill Christians for no other reason than being a faithful Christian. By doing this, Nero became the mold by which intolerant rulers, who are inflamed by the Bad Father of lies, would treat Christians. The process of "ab ordo chao" or order out of chaos is a process in which Satan and his children have been using for centuries to accomplish their goals. Nero staged the burning of the city of Rome in such a way to blame the event on Christians. This then turned the public opinion against Christians to develop a willing and compliant populace who will become spies, agents, and foot soldiers in the persecution of Christians.

Chapter 9: The Formation of the Bible

The use of the Old Testament was vital in the early years of the Church to convert many Jews to the upgraded Judaism, which is Christianity. The prophecies of Christ throughout the Old Testament were the key to seeing the authenticity of Christ in His words and actions. Old Testament Prophecies further establish Christ's divine nature and context for His actions'. The special truths of Bible prophecy created a unique picture for you to see the many strong, and intricate connections that exist between the Old and New Testament. It is in viewing the interrelatedness between the Old and New Testament in which you begin to appreciate the gospel and the New Testament of Jesus Christ. The American Peoples Encyclopedia, states

> *"The Hebrew Old Testament continued to be the Holy Scripture to Jesus and the first generation of Christians. Between 60 and 90 A.D. it was supplemented by the Gospels, Pauline Epistles, and other New Testament books, but in Orthodox Christian circles the Old and New Testament were considered equally sacred."*[26]

---

[26] pg.142, Old Testament, American Peoples Encyclopedia, Vol.14, Grolier

Eliseo Santos

As the early Christian church progressed to eventually become part of the Roman Catholic system, the Old Testament lost its significance within the church's life and teachings.[27] In the eyes of many early Roman Catholics, the Old Testament became only important theoretically. When the Roman Church was further removed from the glory of God on earth, then Roman Catholic theologians, priests, and popes, relied more and more on human wisdom instead of the divine wisdom from the Holy Bible. Then the word of God was further restricted by the Roman Catholic Highpriests of the organized religion by banning the common man from owning and reading the Holy Scriptures.[28] The Roman Catholic Church usurped the inherent personal ability of an individual to develop a personal relationship with their Good Father God. Eventually the Roman Catholic Church would face the consequences of hiding the Word of God from the people. Martin Luther and the other reformers of the Protestant Reformation would seek to restore the rightful place of the Holy Scriptures as the sole authority on all matters of faith and morals instead of the Pope. The Protestant reformers would gain support from many people who have not had access to the Word of God in the Bible. The invention of the Printing Press aided the spread and distribution of the Bible in the local language. The Old Testament would also reclaim its rightful place as the foundation of the Christian faith through the laws and prophecies that proclaim the character and greatness of God.[29]

Incorporated,NewYork,1967,Library of Congress Catalog Number:67-10584

[27] pg.142, Old Testament, Ibid.
[28] pg.142, Old Testament, Ibid.
[29] pg.142, Old Testament, Ibid.

Good Father, Bad Father

The formation of the New Testament was guided in several phases. At least nine of Paul's letters had been in distribution after 90 AD.[30] In the first phase of the New Testament, public Christian gatherings and private meetings were the center where the four gospels (Matthew, Mark, Luke, and John) were read. Copies were given to the people using the local language such as Greek, Latin, Hebrew and Aramaic, the language spoken by Jesus Christ.[31] The public readings of the Gospels became a common practice for Christians in Rome by at least 150 A.D.[32] There are some Christians today that doubt the authenticity of the letters of Paul. These claims are illegitimate due to fact that the letters of Paul were contemporary records and therefore they are "historical sources of the first order."[33] With the additional, books of the Acts of Apostles, Revelation, and several letters by the other Apostles Peter, and John, the New Testament increased to collection of 22 books by 200 AD. Beyond this point however there was no uniform agreement on the number books that should be included in the Holy Bible. For example, in the 3rd century, the churches of Alexandria increased the number of books in the New Testament to 30 or 31.[34] In the 4th century, 367 AD the Latin Church (Church of Rome) and the Greek Church had agreed upon the 27 books that are still found today in the New Testament. The Church of Syria only regarded 22 books in their New Testament and the Church of Ethiopia added 35 books to their New Testament.[35]

---

[30] Pg. 435, New Testament, A.P.E.Vol.13, Grolier Incorporated, New York, 1967-Library of Congress Catalog Card Number-67-10584
[31] Pg. 435, New Testament, Ibid.
[32] Pg. 435, New Testament, Ibid.
[33] pg.436-The Letters of Paul, New Testament, Ibid.
[34] Pg.435, New Testament, Ibid.

The early spread of Christianity was aided by the access and proliferation of the Holy Scriptures of the Old and New Testaments.

---

[35] Pg.435, New Testament, Ibid.

Chapter 10: The Church of Smyrna and the 2nd Seal

The second of the seven churches is the church of Smyrna which covers the early Christian period during 100-313 AD. The name Smyrna is derived from the word Myrrh, which is sweet smelling and was used in many cultures to make perfume and incense. In order, to get the sweet smell for Myrrh it had to be crushed. Interestingly enough, during this period the early Christian Church saw heavy persecution by the Romans. This church correlates with the second of the seven seals, which is the Red Horse that carries the sword of persecution. This is what Jesus says concerning the Church of Smyrna and the second seal, or the Red Horse:

I know thy works, and tribulation, and your poverty, (but thou art rich) and the blasphemy of them which say they are Jews, and are not, but are the synagogue of Satan. Do not fear what you are about to suffer. Behold, the devil is about to throw some of you into prison, that you may be tested and for ten days you will have tribulation. Be faithful unto death, and I will give you the crown of life. He that hath an ear, let him hear what the Spirit saith unto the Churches; He that overcometh shall not be hurt of the second death. – (Rev. 2:9-11, KJV)

And there went out another horse that was red: and power was given to him that sat thereon to take peace from the earth, and

Eliseo Santos

that they should kill one another: and there was given unto him a great sword. – (Rev.6:4)

Christ in these messages describes the time period from 100-313 A.D. During this period, the Christian persecution was rampant. Historians take note of the 10 official persecutions against Christianity by the Imperial Roman government.[36] All of these persecutions that occurred during this period were an accurate fulfillment of the 2nd seal of the Red horse, which carried the great sword of persecution. During this time period, many Christians were taken to the Roman Coliseum and other amphitheaters throughout the Roman Empire. There many Christians died violent deaths at either the hands of gladiators, wild beasts or animals (lions, tigers, leopards,). Also, many Christians were burned alive, in the same way in which Myrrh is used as incense

The general process for arraignment of Christians after they were captured was as follows. There was first a questioning of the individual concerning the accusations of being a Christian, no matter if they were already well-known to be one. If the accused agreed to the charge of being a Christian, then they were sentenced by the local governor or they were sentenced before the Augustus or Caesar in Rome. Before they were punished, they were given a chance to recant or deny their faith, which would require them to give an offering to a statue of a Pagan god, and worship before the statue. The overwhelming majority of Christians chose to face the punishment and stayed faithful until death, and in doing so would gain the Crown of Eternal life. The general process of interrogation and torturous treatment of Christians by the Roman Empire, continued under the

---

[36] See Note 2 at the End of the Book

Good Father, Bad Father

Roman Catholic Church and the inquisitions of the Middle Ages. Just as Daniel foretold in Daniel Ch. 8 how the Little Horn, Roman Catholic Church, will continue to have the same characteristics of the Roman Empire and seek to become like a god on earth by speaking presumptuous words against God, the Most High (Dan.8:23-25). The "ten days of tribulation" Christ referred to was the Diocletian Persecution that occurred during 302-312 AD (remember the prophetic day is a historical year from the Book of Daniel), (Pg.110-120, Diocletian, the precursor to Constantine, reorganized the Roman Empire into 101 provinces, divided into twelve larger regions that were each called a diocese.[37] The twelve dioceses were then grouped into four major regions as foretold in Daniel 8. The message for the Church of Smyrna foretold from John's time the persecution of this early Christian period. Jesus Christ accurately foretold the persecution that God's true people suffered during the time period. Jesus Christ mentions that God's true people who. It would be from the Christian and Roman structure that the future Roman Catholic Church or Little Horn will arise as the Prophecy of Daniel 8 foretold.

The Church of Smyrna was one of the greatest churches in the Christian era. It was a church characterized by the courage, valor, and tenaciousness. In the face of danger and persecution, they continued to preach the Word of God, fully knowing well that if they were caught they would be taken to prison. Eventually, many Christians were sentenced to the most barbaric, humiliating, excruciating forms of death known to mankind.[38] The brave ability to meet the cruelest death in peace, calm, and sometimes in prayer, is what actually caused

---

[37] "Diocletian." Microsoft® Student 2009 [DVD]. Redmond, WA: Microsoft Corporation, 2008.
[38] See note three at the End of the book

so many Romans and non-Christians who witnessed these public executions to join and seek God. During Nero's persecution, Tacitus commented that many of the common people who witnessed these cruel deaths understood the fact the Christians did not die because they were criminals or did something wrong.[39] Christians did not die for the common good of the people. Many Christians during the time of Nero, and other Roman Emperors died to satisfy the unreserved cruelty and the unmitigated blood thirst of the Roman Emperors and their Bad Father Satan. Christians had the faith and courage to meet the death of persecution because Jesus was able to do the same for humanity. Many Christian followers were martyrs who died to give glory to God and validate His Holy Words. When seeing the death of a Christian for his faith, the common man understood that an individual's conviction about the reality of the Good Father God, Jesus Christ, and the Holy Spirit is what caused them to look forward to eternal life. As Christ died and resurrected, so would all those who follow in the footsteps of Christ. Christians were prepared to meet death for the sake of refusing to change or submit to the state-approved false conceptions of God. Through their valor and bravery, Christians showed how the truth is more valuable than a life forced to accept a false reality matrix. Tertullian's well-known passage concerning the Blood of Christian Martyrs served as the fertilizer for the growth of the Early Church explains the underlying cause of the growth of the church despite facing persecution:

> *If we are mown down by you, we increase and grow; the blood of the Christians is the seed of the church. For who is there*

---

[39] pg.51, The Bloody Theatre, Thielem Von Bracht,, Translated by L. Daniel Rupp, 1837,Published By David Miller, 1837

Good Father, Bad Father

among you that, when he sees such things [bloodshed of innocent Christians], is not constrained to inquire what there may be intrinsically in this matter? Who is he that, after having examined the matter, does not resolve, and having resolved, does not desire to suffer with them? This sect [referring to the Christians using the pagan expression], can never be destroyed or extirpated, which when it appears to be cut down, is then only built up. For everyone who witnesses such great patience and sufferings, seeing them beaten and torn, is induced to inquire into the cause of all this; and having come to the knowledge of the truth, he follows immediately.[40]

Jesus foretold that many early Christians would experience trouble by those "who call themselves Jews, but are a synagogue of Satan." Many early Christians experienced in similar way what Jesus Christ went through. Jesus was rejected by the Jewish religious leaders and High Priests, who turned the people of His origin against Him, and they delivered Him to the Romans for execution. Likewise, many early Christians were handed over to the Roman authorities for trial and execution. Jesus Christ refers to the Jewish population that descended from the Jewish people during the time of Christ. Many of the Jewish people who were under the guidance of the Jewish religious leaders, who refused to believe that Jesus Christ was the Son of God. They did so despite the many Old Testament prophecies that were fulfilled with the Life of Jesus Christ.[41] The rejection on the part of Jewish religious leaders and many Jewish People came even despite His many miracles, and His many words of wisdom and prophecies that are still true today. Matthew Ch. 23 describes in detail the corruption of the religious leaders during the time of Christ, and the many leaders of major organized religions. To learn why Jesus

---

[40] Pg.85, *The Bloody Theater*, By Thielem J. Von Bracht,
[41] See Appendix 1

Eliseo Santos

Christ referred to some Jews as "synagogue of Satan," it is best to read Matthew 23:33-39, where Jesus Christ states when speaking to the Pharisees and other religious leaders during his time,

> *Ye serpents, ye generation of vipers, how can ye escape the damnation of hell? Wherefore, behold, I send unto you prophets, and wise men, and scribes: and some of them ye shall kill and crucify; and some of them shall ye scourge in your synagogues, and persecute them from city to city: That upon you may come all the righteous bloodshed upon the earth, from the blood of righteous Abel unto the blood of Zacharias son of Barachias, whom ye slew between the temple and the altar. Verily, I say unto you, All these things shall come upon this generation. O Jerusalem, Jerusalem, thou that killest the prophets, and stonest them which are sent unto thee, how often would I have gathered thy children together, even as a hen gathered her chickens under her wings, and ye would not! Behold your house is left unto you desolate. For I say unto you, ye shall not see me henceforth, till ye shall say, "Blessed is he that cometh in the name of the Lord."*

This Synagogue of Satan is composed of the religious leaders within the Jewish community who were opposed the light of God and the truth of Jesus Christ. The Jewish religious leaders were prepared to lead the Jewish nation into the darkness of a ritualized tradition without God and His Son. Another example of the Messianic prophecies and the evidence that supports the existence of the Good Father and His Son Jesus Christ, is found in the Old Testament Zechariah Ch.9: verse 9 states, "Rejoice greatly, O daughter of Zion; shout, O daughter of Jerusalem: behold, thy King, cometh unto thee: he is just, and having salvation; lowly, and riding upon an ass, and upon, a colt the foal of an ass." Here the prophet Zechariah foretells how Jesus Christ entered into Jerusalem in the year 31 A.D. on the

Good Father, Bad Father

Sunday before His death and resurrection. The Messianic prophecy of Zechariah 9:9 was fulfilled in Matthew 21:4-7. Where it states

> *"All of this was done, that it might be fulfilled which was spoken by the prophet, saying 'Tell ye the daughter of Sion. Behold, thy King cometh unto thee, meek, and sitting upon an ass, a colt, the foal of an ass.' And the disciples went, and did as Jesus commanded them. And brought the ass, and the colt, and put on them their clothes, and they set him thereon."*

The fulfillment of this prophecy should have been evident to the biblical scholars of Israel at the time. However, instead of believing in the plain prophetic fulfillment of the Word of God, many Jewish religious leaders were not prepared to relinquish their power, influence, and goals and humble themselves before the Messiah King Jesus. Instead of listening to the truth of Jesus Christ and the inspired words of God found in the Old Testament Patriarchs, Prophets, and Kings, the Jewish nation listened and believed the words of their religious leaders. The warped conception and understanding of God led them to prefer rather their own selfish interests and goals instead of the reality of God and the eternal well-being of the Jewish nation. Instead of embracing the truth of the Good Father God, that Jesus Christ was the Son of God, the Jewish religious leaders believed the lie of the Bad Father, which was Jesus was just a man. They did so, even against all the indicators of Bible Prophecy that He was otherwise. The Jewish religious leaders knew Christ would be born in Bethlehem. They even told the wise men that came to visit Christ that He would be born there. The Jewish religious leaders, even knew that King Herod killed all male children under two years old and you can say they did not raise any objection to the horrible action. Based on these facts, Jewish religious leaders were later furious to find out 30 years later that Jesus Christ, the Babe born in Bethlehem was alive and was full of the Holy Spirit working miracles, preaching insightful teachings, and revealing the true nature of their corruption. Jesus even prophesied how the early Christian church, which was the remnant of the Jewish nation, would be chased, persecuted, tortured, and killed by their once Jewish brethren for proclaiming the truth of Christ. The Jewish religious leaders were even aware of the resurrection of Jesus Christ as a fulfillment of His own prophecy. In knowing this truth, they did not accept Jesus as the Son of God. The Jewish religious leaders bribed the eyewitnesses to lie, and they themselves lied to their congregations to maintain the power and control they had over the minds of the Jewish nation, (Matthew 28:12,13). Christ at the end of His rebuke of the Jewish religious leaders reminisces about all the times in which He and His Good Father have spoken to Israel. From heaven, Christ and God had intervened to free and protect Jerusalem from Egypt and the belligerent neighbors that surrounded Canaan. But despite all the divine miracles and interventions, the religious leaders of Israel led the people away. At times, the people under the surrounding influence of the Bad Father, who using the pagan neighbors led Israel to walk away from God to worship foreign gods. Despite all this, Jesus Christ adds that He is ready to accept His Jewish nation back, on the condition they accept Him as the Son of God. Many Jews have to accept Jesus Christ as their savior, redeemer, sacrificial lamb, and eternal High Priest, who is now intervening on behalf of all of humanity in the Temple of God in Heaven.

After the death and resurrection of Christ and the subsequent spread of the Gospel of Christ, the Jewish religious leaders still maintained control over the Jewish nation. The religious leaders

Good Father, Bad Father

spread malicious lies in trying to cover the truth of the Resurrection of Jesus of Nazareth. These lies taught by the rabbis, scribes, and Pharisees, and other religious leaders led the people to persecute the Apostles and the early Christian church out of Jerusalem, after stoning Stephen in 34 AD. In 70 AD, the Romans came and encircled the city of Jerusalem. The Roman Soldiers destroyed the Temple as Jesus foretold to His disciples in Matthew 24:1-2, "And Jesus went out, and departed from the temple; and his disciples came to him for to show him the buildings of the Temple. And Jesus said unto them, 'See ye not all these things? Verily I say unto you. There shall not be left here one stone upon another, that shall not be thrown down.'" This prophecy served as a confirmation that no longer was there to be any shedding of the blood of lambs, goats, and other animals for the sins of the people. Jesus Christ Himself became the infinite sacrifice for humanity. Even despite this fulfillment of the words of Jesus Christ, the anointed Son of God, the Jewish religious leaders still did not want to admit any wrongdoing. In not accepting Jesus Christ and His teachings, they lost sight of the Law and the teachings of the Good Father. Another key moment, and a sign of the complete rejection of Jesus Christ and His divinity as the Son of God was when the Jewish religious leaders motivated by greed for power and lust for prestige sought another Christ. After rejecting the many prophecies of the truth of Jesus Christ in the Old Testament, which were already established in the historical truth, they allowed themselves to be captivated by the lies of the Bad Father.

They took scripture and twisted to serve their own selfish goals, one of which was to overthrow their Roman oppressors. It seems that rabbis at this time blinded themselves to not only the prophecies of Christ, but also of Daniel, who foretold that the Roman power will not be overthrown by any other nation until the 2nd Coming of Christ. Thus, the Jewish religious leaders found in Simon Bar Kokhba, a false messiah and anti-Christ that became in the eyes of the Jewish religious leaders their Christ and Messiah according to their conceptions not based on biblical truth. Bar Kokhba was one of many historical false Christs who put themselves in the shoes of God. Bar Kokhba led Jerusalem into war against their Roman oppressors. This was the result of years of the burning animosity between the Romans and Jews. When it reached its limits a conflict started between Israel and the Romans that lasted from 132-135 A.D. The cause of this conflict was Hadrian's desire to Romanize Judea, and to allow Jews only to visit Jerusalem on one day per year and to ban circumcision. Keep in mind, Jesus Christ advocated spiritual circumcision rather than physical circumcision. Spiritual circumcision being the parts of the character and habits that are trimmed and refined to keep the Ten Commandments of God. Paul sums up the issue in 1 Corinthians 7:19, "Circumcision is nothing, and uncircumcision is nothing, but the keeping of the Commandments of God." Bar Kokhba led a rebellion against the Roman Empire, that sought to dethrone the Romans for the purpose of regaining sovereignty over Israel. One of the well-known Jewish religious leaders at that time, included Akiba Ben Joseph, who was an influential religious leader of the Jewish nation during 132 AD. The Jewish religious leaders and Akiba Ben Joseph sought to justify their rebellion as being part of God's plan for the People of Israel, by stating that Bar Kokhba was the Christ and Messiah of the Bible. The Encyclopedia Encarta states Bar Kokhba was accepted by Akiba Ben Joseph and other Jewish leaders as a messiah or false Christ. Akiba proclaimed Bar Kokhba was the Messiah, or leader, the Jews believed would be sent by God to restore Israel and reign

Good Father, Bad Father

righteously over humankind".[42] The belief and acceptance of the lie of Bar Kokhba as a Christ by the Jewish religious leaders is a complete rejection and denial of God, His Son, and the Holy Spirit. Many Prophets under the inspiration of the Holy Spirit, prophesied the truth concerning God and His Son Jesus Christ. The Prophet Daniel even prophesied the kingdoms of the earth, after the fall of Babylon, for the Jewish nation and people to not believe in the lies of their corrupt religious leaders. More specifically, Daniel foretold that from the Roman Empire would come the Little Horn power. According to Daniel 2 and 7, and 8, the Little Horn power will remain in power until the 2nd Coming of Christ, and so far he is correct with the existence of the Roman Catholic Church, which has been in existence since the times of Constantine in 321 A.D, that is approximately 1700 years. However, because the Jewish nation blindly followed their Rabbi's words and the words of other religious leaders, it led to the deaths of many innocent people and it caused the dispersion of the Jewish nation. This is an important case study of what happens when a groups of people blindly follow their religious leaders, without investigating the truth and also the truth about God and Jesus Christ that is found in the Old and New Testament.

Despite all the 10 persecutions, the Early Christian Church grew in far and wide throughout the known world. All Early Christian churches shared the characteristics of the Church of Jesus and the Apostles and that it was a Church that kept the 10 commandments, especially the 4th commandment and the 7th Day-Sabbath or Saturday. Meaning that every Saturday, all Early Christians gathered

---

[42] Glatzer, Nahum Norbert. "Simon Bar Kokhba." Microsoft® Student 2009 [DVD]. Redmond,WA: Microsoft Corporation, 2008.)

together for prayer, worship, sermons, and reading from the Holy Scriptures. It is a popular misconception for many modern Christians to believe that Early Christians celebrated their weekly day of devotion on Sunday instead of Saturday. The Early Christian Church was more faithful to God and His words and commandments than many Modern Christians today. Jesus said in Mark 2:27-28, "The Sabbath was made for man, and not man for the Sabbath. Therefore the Son of man is Lord also of the Sabbath." Therefore, the God of Creation, created the Sabbath not just for the Jewish nation, but also for all of mankind. The 7th Day Sabbath was a day to not only of rest from servile work, but also a day to spend with God in prayer and studying and reflecting on the eternal truths found in the Bible. God rested, blessed, and sanctified the 7th- Day Sabbath, for it is a symbol of His love for humanity evident in His creation of the earth. This is the position in which the Apostles had concerning the Sabbath because the Apostles were aware that the Sabbath was a non-negotiable day of worship. The 7th-Day Sabbath is non-negotiable because it was the 4th Commandment and the Commandments are part of the Law of God, and thus immutable. John says in the 2nd Letter of John verse 6, concerning the Love of God and the Commandments of God, "And this is love, that we walk after his commandments. This is the commandment, that, as ye have heard from the beginning, ye should walk in it." In other words, John here tells the early Christian Church t o continue to follow the Ten Commandments of God.

All the Early Christians no matter in which region they were located kept the 7th Day Sabbath. Josephus said, "There is not any city of the Grecians, nor any of the Barbarians, nor any nation whatsoever, whither out custom of resting on the Seventh day hath come!,"[43] The previous quote suggests that the custom of resting on the 7th Day Sabbath is a custom that has existed in many parts of the world long before the arrival of Christ and the Christians. Philo expressed this same fact on record saying the Seventh Day festival is a festival, not native to any city, but of the universe.[44] The evidence of the Sabbath being kept in many different regions outside of Israel, was the exponential growth of the early Christian Church in Asia Minor, the Middle East, Africa, the Mediterranean, and all throughout Europe. During the 2nd and 3rd centuries, the Christian Gospel was spreading in parts throughout Africa, in Carthage, Ethiopia, Egypt, and other parts and also spreading in parts of India and China.

The Historian Mingana, in his Early Spread of Christianity, states "As early as A.D. 225 there existed large bishoprics or conferences of the Church of the East (Sabbath-keeping) stretching from Palestine to India,".[45] Lloyd in The Creed of Half Japan recounts the controversy that occurred amongst Buddhist monks in 220 A.D. who were keeping the Biblical 7th Day Sabbath. He states, "The Kushan Dynasty of North India called a famous council of Buddhist priests at Vaisalia to bring uniformity among the Buddhist monks on the observance of their weekly Sabbath. Some Buddhist monks had been so impressed by the writings of the Old Testament that they had begun to keep holy the Sabbath.[46] Therefore, the early Christian church stayed to true to Christ's mission found in Matthew 28:18-20, "All power is given unto me in heaven and in earth. Go ye therefore, and teach all nations,

---

[43] pg.100, M'Clatchie, Notes and Queries on China and Japan (edited by Dennys, Vol.4 Nos 7,8,
[44] pg.99, Ibid.
[45] Mingana, Vol. 10, pg. 460, Early Spread of Christianity
[46] Lloyd, pg. 23 The Creed of Half Japan

baptizing them in the name of the Father, and of the Son, and of the Holy Ghost: Teaching them to observe all the things whatsoever I have commanded you: and, lo, I am with you always, even unto the end of the world." Despite all the persecution faced by the church of Ephesus and the church of Smyrna, they were able to spread the Gospel as far West as Ireland and the British Isles and as far-east as India and China. The belief in the Son of the Good Father was widely accepted because it is true; Christ did resurrect. Satan thought the best way to handle the problem would be to kill all the Christians, but all that did was increase the popularity and legitimacy of Christianity.

Chapter 11: The Church of Pergamos and the 3rd Seal

Persecution proved ineffective as a means of limiting the growth of Christianity. After more than two centuries of intermittent persecution, Christianity increased in size, strength, and span within society. The Bad Father of lies came up with the plan to corrupt the early Christian church from the inside out. This leads us to the third of the seven churches, which was the Church of Pergamos. The name Pergamos means Elevation and during the time period of 313-538 AD, the religious precepts and doctrines of man were elevated over the divine precepts of the Good Father that are found in the Bible. The Church of Pergamos correlates with the third seal symbolized by the black horse whose rider holds a pair of balances. The Church message of Pergamos, and the third seal states:

I know thy works, and where thou dwellest, even where Satan's seat is: and thou hold fast my name, and thou holdest fast my name, and hast not denied my faith, even in those days wherein Antipas was my faithful martyr, who was slain among you, where Satan dwelleth. But I have a few things against thee, because thou hast there them that hold the doctrine of Balaam, who taught Balak to cast a stumbling block before the children of Israel, to eat things sacrificed unto idols and practice immorality. So hast thou also them that hold the doctrine of the Nicolaitans, which thing I hate. Repent; or else I will come unto thee quickly, and will fight against them with the sword of

Eliseo Santos

my mouth. He that hath an ear, let him hear what the Spirit saith unto the Churches; To him that overcometh will I give to eat of the hidden manna, and I will give him a white stone, and in the stone a new name written, which no man knoweth saving he that receiveth it. – (Rev. 2:13-17; KJV)

And when he had opened the third seal, I heard the third beast say, Come and see. And I behold, and lo a black horse; and he that sat on him had a pair of balances in his hand. And I heard a voice in the midst of the four beasts say. 'A measure of wheat for a penny, and three measures of barley for a penny; and see thou hurt not the oil and the wine. – (Rev.6: 5-6; KJV)

The name of this church signifies elevation because during this time period, the early Christian church became corrupted. The mixture of pure Christianity based on the Word of God, became mixed with ancient pagan traditions. These human pagan traditions have their origins with ancient occult secret societies and pagan cults that rose to prominence during the kingdoms of Egypt, Babylon, Medo-Persia, Greece, and Rome. Therefore, the Black horse is a symbol of the spiritual corruption that entered into the early Christian church with noxious elements that included Gnosticism, ancient order secret societies that were especially prominent amongst the Roman aristocracy, and pagan sun worship. In other words, the early Christian churches of Ephesus and Smyrna proclaimed mostly the truth concerning God and His Son, Jesus Christ and the Holy Spirit. The corruption and contamination of the early Christian Church of Pergamos was evident when it began using its authority to accept non-Biblical doctrines. Because we all sin and capable of sinning, then we cannot trust human doctrines and have to put trust solely in the plain spoken truth of the Word of God. The corrupted early Church, then deemed these non-Biblical doctrines as an official part of the Christian experience, when in reality it went against the Biblical precepts of God and the Commandments of Jesus Christ. The teachings of the Church became at variance with Biblical teachings. Thus, the institutionalized Roman Catholic Church became a stumbling block for many within the Early Christian Church.

During this time the people of God were primarily located in Rome, which Jesus refers to as the seat of Satan. It was here where Constantine, who as emperor of Rome, shocked all Roman Citizens at the time when he declared his conversion to Christianity. In 312 AD, Constantine before his battle at the Milvian Bridge against Maxentius, was said to have seen a flaming cross appear in the sky, and the Latin words *In Hoc Signo Vinces*. 'In this sign you will conquer,'.[47] The miracle involving the sun is what caused Constantine to join Christianity. Constantine became the bridge by which the pure biblical doctrine became mixed with the pagan doctrines of sun worship.

The mixture between the pure Christian doctrines of the Bible with the ancient pagan rituals of Sun worship is what caused the stumbling block for the Early Church. Jesus refers to this Old Testament story in the Numbers 22-25, where Balak was a King of Moab, who believed he could curse the people of Israel. He then sent an envoy to the Prophet Balaam seeking his help in cursing the people of Israel. Instead of cursing Israel, God had Balaam bless Israel three times. But later in Numbers 31:8 and 16, God reveals that Balaam had

---

[47] Constantine I or Constantine the Great, pg, 409, American Peoples Encyclopedia, Grolier, NY1967

a role in the corruption of the people of Israel in through the use of the women of Moab, which also caused them to eat food sacrificed unto idols and bowed down to the gods of Moab, which included Baal-Peor. Thus, the leaders of the Christian church such as the Bishop of Rome and others at the time represented Balaam, who had a part in bringing a curse upon the Early Christian church by mixing in the pagan sun worship. This was done at the request of Constantine, who in the example above is an example of Balak. The compromise between by their religious leaders is shown by the example of the 3rd seal or the Black horse whose rider is carrying a balance. The corresponding voice of one of the four living creatures or seraphim or six-winged angels says, "a measure of wheat for a penny, and three measures of barley for a penny, and see thou hurt not the oil and wine." This signifies that during the era of the black horse, the people of God, represented by the wheat and barley, are sold out at a cheap price by their religious leaders. The religious leaders were unable to harm the oil and wine that was a symbol of the biblical truths and doctrines that were taught by the Holy Spirit in the Bible, which means they are preserved for the future people of God. The Constantine compromise between the Pagan religion of the Roman State with the pure and increasing popular Christianity, was the official creation of the Roman Catholic Church. The Bishop of Rome at that time, Sylvester and all future Bishops of Rome and popes became beneficiaries of Constantine's unification of paganism and Biblical Christianity.[48]

---

[48] "Saint Sylvester I." Microsoft® Student 2009 [DVD]. Redmond, WA: Microsoft Corporation, 2008.).

Good Father, Bad Father

Constantine enacted the legal framework for the Roman Catholic Church. Due to Constantine, Roman Church officials gained the legal authority of the Roman Church to possess land, property, and wealth.[49] Constantine and Pope sought to gain power and control to build a kingdom on earth. This is what Jesus refers to as the meaning of the doctrine of the Nicolatians, which is to power and control over others especially Christians. The Roman Church's official deviation from the Word began in 321 A.D when the Law of Constantine the Great opened the door for the Pope to begin his temporal power. [50]In other words, Constantine gave the Roman Catholic Church the power that only up until then could be employed by the Roman Caesar. As foretold by Daniel more than a millennium before hand in 539 B.C., the Roman pontiff started to transform into the Little Horn of Daniel 7. Like Daniel said the Little Horn would grow from the Ancient Roman Empire and sure enough Constantine's law gave the Roman Church the entitlement to the land of Rome. Now the Bishop of Rome became also the owner of all of the land and the wealth of the vicinity. The Pope became like a pharaoh with power and authority, not from the Good Father, but from the Bad Father. Later on, when describing the 1st beast of Revelation 13, this will be more fully understood.

After the Roman church's new ability to hold property, then Constantine went to Turkey to transform the City of Byzantine into Constantinople. It became the Eastern outpost of the Roman Catholic Church and the Roman Empire. In Daniel 2, Daniel's interpretation of

---

[49] pg. 293, Papal States, APE, vol.14, Grolier Incorporated, New York, 1967,Library ofCongress Catalog Card Number:67-10584

[50] pg. 84, National Sunday Law, Appendix 9, 2007 AT Publications

Eliseo Santos

Nebuchadnezzar's dream of the statue of different metals, accurately foretold the Kingdom of Iron that would be divided east and west, which was fulfilled in the Ancient Roman Empire.

Constantine's sign of the sun was the sign by which Satan used in all forms of paganism throughout the world. Satan used the symbol of the Sun to corrupt the Early Church of God, which became a vehicle by which he would use to conquer the world. The keeping of the Day of the Sun, instead of the 7th Sabbath day instituted by God, was the continuation of the ancient pagan rituals from Egypt and Babylon. When Jesus says "eating food sacrificed to idols," in other words eating the "Eucharist" or "host" he is also referring to the continuation of the ancient pagan rituals from Egypt and Babylon. It was during the Church of Pergamos, in which the traditions of the world became mixed with the pure Biblical doctrines. The advice found in 1 John 2:15-17, was not only relevant to Christian leaders of that day and age but also Christians in modern times. John wrote,

> *Love not the world, neither the things that are in the world. If any man love the world, the love of the Father is not in him. For all that is in the world, the lust of the flesh, and the lust of the eyes, and the pride of life, is not of the Father, but is of the world. And the world passeth away, and the lust thereof; but he that doeth the will of God abideth forever.*

Therefore, if you seek the Good Father, then you will do the things in which the Good Father asks which is to believe in His Son Jesus Christ and follow the Ten Commandments. You are justified through your faith by believing Jesus Christ is the Son of God, and the Law of God prepares you to live forever with God. In terms of the Church of Pergamos, the leaders of the early Christian Church who were in

Good Father, Bad Father

Rome became carried away with the power and prestige of the world. They elevated their self-interest over the interests of the Christian followers and brought them the stumbling block of Sunday worship. Constantine in 321AD made an edict or law establishing the first ever Sunday Law.[51] This law is what allowed for the new Christian counterfeit religion to gain popularity amongst the Roman people, and it caused confusion amongst God's early church. Constantine and the leaders of Rome at the time were not aware that the Ten Commandments of God is not just something practiced in this earth, but is practiced throughout all the Creation of God in every region of the universe for eternity. This is seen in the words of Isaiah 66:23, 24 where he writes a vision of the eternal keeping of the Law of God, and the punishment of those who transgress the Ten Commandments of God, "And it shall come to pass, that from one new moon to another and from one Sabbath, to another, shall all flesh come to worship before me, saith the Lord. And they shall go forth, and look upon the carcasses of the men, that have transgressed against me." Thus, the Seventh-Day Sabbath is very important to God and will continue to be from eternity to eternity.

The faithful Christians of the early Church now encountered a Roman Catholic Papal authority that now authorized a different day of weekly worship that was not instituted and endorsed by Christ. Remember Christ said in Matthew 5:17-18, "Think not that I come to destroy the law, or the prophets: I am not come to destroy, but to fulfill. For verily, I say unto you, till heaven and earth pass, one jot or one tittle shall in no wise pass from the law, till all be fulfilled."

---

[51] Edict of Constantine, Encyclopedia Britannica, ninth edition, article "Sunday" as quoted in
pg.84-National Sunday Law

Eliseo Santos

During the times of Constantine, the Early Church encountered one of the first threats to the pure biblical doctrine endorsed by Christ, and later the Apostles, and the early Church. Sunday became the new official day in which all needed to keep under the human authority of the corrupt religious leaders and not under the authority of God. Throughout the centuries up until now many Christians are still not aware of the significance of the 7th Day Sabbath (Saturday) that Christ and His Apostles advocated while on earth. In Mark 2:27, 28, Christ says Concerning the Sabbath, "The Sabbath was made for man, and not man for Sabbath: Therefore the Son of man is Lord of also of the Sabbath." Thus, the Lord's Day is not Sunday as many today believe, it is in fact the same Sabbath that God wrote with His finger on tablets of stone on Mount Sinai (Exodus 31:17,18). This in turn inundated the church with many new converts who in not understanding the Judeo roots and history of Christianity, lost sight of the true significance of Christ and His roles as Creator, Savior, and the only Mediator between God and humanity. Due to Christ being the highest representative of God and mankind, Jesus was the Lamb of God that takes away the sins of the world. Christ is now the High Priest who petitions before God on behalf of those who pray in His name and carry out His will on earth.

Like Daniel foretold long ago, the Little Horn would grow from Ancient Rome, (Dan. 7:7-8). The ancient traditions in pagan Rome made their way into the early Christian church led by Constantine's conversion to Christianity and subsequent Sunday law. Constantine's Sunday law would be the beginning of the cover-up of the truth of God's law, specifically the 4th Commandment of the 7th Day Sabbath. In order to verify if the Roman Catholic Papacy was the

Good Father, Bad Father

Little Horn, you will have to read the description of the Little Horn given in Daniel 7:23-25,

Thus he said, The fourth beast shall be the fourth kingdom upon the earth, which shall be diverse from all kingdoms, and shall devour the whole earth, and shall tread it down, and break it in pieces. And the ten horns out of this kingdom are ten kings that shall arise: and another shall rise after them; and he shall be diverse from this first, and shall subdue three kings. And he shall speak great words against the most High, and think to change times and laws: and they shall be given into his hand until a time and times and the dividing of time.

After the fall of the Roman Empire in 476 A.D., Europe became fragmented into different Germanic Kingdoms. These Ten Germanic Kingdoms were the ancestors of the Modern European nations that still hold the languages and occupy the general region occupied after the collapse of the Roman Empire. The Ten Germanic Kingdoms were:

The Heruli – Were eliminated in 493 A.D.

The Vandals – In 534 A.D. they were plucked out by Justinian's General Belisarius

The Ostrogoths – Were eliminated in 538 A.D. and plucked out by Justinian. They were removed from Rome, which allowed the Papacy to rule unopposed from the City of Rome.

The Suevi – Portugal.

The Burgundians – Switzerland

The Anglo-Saxons – Great Britain

The Visigoths – Spain

The Franks - France

The Alamanni – Germany

The Lombards – Romania

From 538 A.D. and onwards would begin 1260 years of Papal power during the Dark and Middle Ages. Daniel describes this time period as a "time, times, and half a time," (Daniel 7:25). A time is a year Daniel 4:32 "seven times" = "seven years") Thus, a time = 1 year; Times = Two years; and half a time = half a year. In total, it equals 3 ½ prophetic years, or 1260 prophetic days, or 42 Prophetic months.

The persecution suffered during the time of the Church of Pergamos was less widespread when compared to the Church of Smyrna. Despite the spread of Christianity during this time period not growing as fast the two previous churches, there was still some persecution. There was notable persecution in the country of Armenia, which in 387 AD, came under the influence of the two powerful forces in the Byzantine region: the Eastern Roman Empire and the Persian Sassanid Kings.[52] Zoroastrianism was the official Sassanid state-approved religion in the region and the Sassanids implemented forced conversions to reduce the amount of Armenian Christians.[53] This created unfavorable conditions for Christians in the region well into the next century. A revolt in Armenia in 451 A.D. forced Persia to rescind its anti-Christian policies. This historical example led the Bad Father of lies to develop a new technique to kill and reduce the number of Christians in the Middle-East region. The Middle East was the center of the pure Biblical Christianity for many centuries after the resurrection of Christ. The Bad Father realized that to reduce the amount of Christians in the Middle East he would require a new

---

[52] Ibid, pg.427, 428, Persia, The Sassanids, A.P.E, Vol. 14., Grolier Incorporated, New York, NY
[53] pg.427, 428, Persia, The Sassanids, Persia. Ibid.

Good Father, Bad Father

religion where physical warfare is cherished over the spiritual warfare of telling the truth. A religion that would claim its origin from the Judeo-Christian God and Patriarchs, but yet would deny Judeo-Christian principles such as the Ten Commandments, the Good Father, the Son Jesus Christ, and the Holy Spirit. Unlike the Judeo-Christian justification by faith, it would instead teach justification by works. A religion that claimed to be a religion of peace and yet violent warfare would be deeply embedded within its very being through honor killings, Jihads, and a thirst of bloodshed. A religion where the religious leaders have control over the minds of the many innocent people and provokes them to unnecessary violence, bloodshed, and destruction that brings generations of strife and misery. A religion that does not utilize the spiritual sword of the word of God, which describes Paul in Hebrews 4:12, "For the word of God is quick and powerful, and sharper than any two edged sword, piercing even to the dividing asunder of soul and spirit, and of the joints and marrow, and is a discerner of the thoughts and intents of the heart." This is the sword in which Jesus Christ uses in Revelation 2:12 to introduce the Church of Pergamos, and the sword in which He warns of the Church of Pergamos He will use against its false doctrines. The Bad Father's new religion in the Middle-East would eventually support the Bad Father's other false religious mixture of Pure Biblical doctrine with false pagan principles, known as the Roman Catholic Church. The Roman Catholic Church and the Muslims[54] during the Crusades entered in a campaign of forced conversions, where either you were killed for being a Bible-believing Christian or accepted the unholy doctrines of either religion. Like the

---

[54] See Note at the End of the book

Roman Empire became controlled by two separate powers one from Rome and the other from Constantinople, the Roman Catholic Church created many subdivisions of religious entities that work with the Roman Church to eliminate and oppose biblical Christianity and to strengthen to the authority of the Pope.

Another important factor concerning the Church of Pergamos is the formation of a church leader who will also have significant political authority. First, the title of "Pontifex Maximus," was a pre-Christian pagan title of the member of the pagan College of Priests who had jurisdiction over civil and religious affairs.[55] When the Roman monarchy dissolved, the number of the priests (pontiffs) eventually increased to fifteen under Lucius Cornelius Sulla (138- 78 B.C.)[56] Under Julius Caesar (100-44 B.C.) the number of priests increased to sixteen and he named himself Pontifex Maximus, or the supreme pontiff.[57] It was under this title, in which he had control and authorization over all political and religious affairs.[58] An example of the power of "Pontifex Maximus" was Julius Caesar's ability to change the calendar to 365 days, similar to the Egyptian calendar that existed two thousand years prior to Julius Caesar's implementation.[59]

The title of Pontifex Maximus gained new significance during the Christian era. The Roman Emperor Gratian (359- 383 AD) became the first Roman Emperor to relinquish the title. Since the reign of Julius Caesar it was a lifetime elected office.[60]Once Gratian

---

[55] pg. 167, Pontifex, The A. P. E., Vol.14, Grolier Incorporated, New York, 1967, Library Congress Catalog Card Number:67-10584
[56] Pg. 167, Pontifex, Ibid.
[57] pg. 167, Pontifex, Ibid.
[58] pg. 167, Pontifex, Ibid.
[59] pg. 167, Pontifex, Ibid.

relinquished the title, it then became the title of the Bishop of Rome, or the Pope of the Roman Catholic Church.[61] During his reign from 366-384 A.D., Pope Damasus (304-384 AD) became the first pope who received the title Pontifex Maximus.[62] Since then up until today, more than 1600 years later, the Pope still uses the name Pontifex Maximus, and this is evident today, when the Pope uses the name "Pontifex" for his Twitter ID.

After receiving the title of "Pontifex Maximus" in 378 A.D., Damasus sought to transform the early Roman Catholic Church away from the early Christian church established by the Lord Jesus Christ and the Apostles.[63] The reforms performed under the reign of Damasus transformed and further corrupted the Early Christian Church of the Apostles. The Early Christian church that the Apostles built eventually became corrupted by Constantine and his changes. Many of these changes signaled the creation of a more monarchical institution with the power and ability to control over civil and religious affairs. Damasus changed the official language of the liturgy from Greek to Latin.[64] Due to the change in official language, Pope Damasus exploited the advantage of mistranslation of the Bible texts from Greek to Latin. One of these biblical quotes is a staple verse that the Roman Catholic Church uses today to defend its primacy and sovereignty. In Matthew 16:18, the meaning of this quote is different from the original Greek translation concerning Jesus stating a

---

[60] pg. 167, Pontifex, Ibid.
[61] pg. 167, Pontifex, Ibid. ; pg.201 Hislop, Two Babylons,
[62] pg.202, Hislop, Two Babylons
[63] "Saint Damasus I." Microsoft® Student 2009 [DVD]. Redmond, WA: Microsoft Corporation,2008
[64] Saint Damasus I." Microsoft® Student 2009 [DVD]. Redmond, WA: Microsoft Corporation, 2008.

metaphor to describe how He is the Rock of the Church, and not Peter. In Latin, there is no distinction between *petra* or rock and *petro* meaning stone. Pope Damasus would also become the first Pope to claim to hold the two keys of Peter, which would be a reference to the following verse in Matthew 16:19, "And I will give unto thee the keys of the Kingdom of heaven: and whatsoever thou shalt bind on earth shall be bound in heaven: and whatsoever thou shalt loose on earth shall be loosed in heaven." This verse has been used by many Popes to proclaim authority over judgment decisions of life and death. However, this is far from the keys in which Christ gave to Peter. The Keys to the Kingdom of heaven actually represent the truth that is directed by the Holy Spirit. This is evident if you read the context of the quote, in Matthew 16:16 Peter answered Christ question asked in verse 15, "But whom say ye that I am?" Many people during this time still had no idea that Jesus Christ was the Son of God, the Good Father in heaven. Thus, in verse 16, Simon Peter, replies "Thou art the Christ, the Son of the living God." In verse 17, Jesus replies "Blessed art thou, Simon Barjona: for flesh and blood hath not revealed it unto thee, but my Father which is in heaven." Thus, the Holy Spirit worked through Peter and revealed to him the truth concerning Jesus Christ. Interestingly enough, if you read Matthew 16:12, you will realize that the whole conversation between Christ and Peter is happening after Christ warns the Apostles and His followers concerning the doctrines of the Pharisees and the Sadducees. In Matthew 16: 12, it states "Then understood they how that he bade them not beware of the leaven of the bread, but of the doctrine of the Pharisees and of the Sadducees." This warning ties in with the warning Christ gave to the Church of Pergamos, in Revelation 2:14, 15 concerning the doctrines of Balaam. In other words, committing spiritual fornication (mixing Biblical

Good Father, Bad Father

doctrines with Pagan doctrines) and eating food sacrificed to idols, which alludes to the Eucharist that had its pagan origins in Egypt. Also, Christ warns the Church of Pergamos of the doctrine of Nicolatians, which is a symbol of those doctrines implemented by Constantine and Pope Sylvester that sought power and control over Christian believers.[65] Furthermore, Damasus added more leaven to the bread of the biblical doctrines when he introduced into the Roman Catholic Church the veneration of the dead through setting up the veneration of the martyrs.[66] Pope Damasus was also key in the formation of the Vulgate Bible, which was the official Bible used many centuries within Roman Catholicism.

After Constantine and Damasus led the early Christian Church away from the original biblical principles and teachings into what is known today as Roman Catholicism, Pope Syricius continued to implement such changes. During his reign from 384-399 A.D. Syricius further developed the papacy as an authoritative and administrative power. Pope Syricius believed it was the prerogative of the Bishop of Rome to control all churches and through his decrees "he could bind in conscience all the faithful."[67] In other words, instead of using his position to bring people to the truth of God's words in the Bible, Syricius would use his words to unite and control the minds of others to conform to the Roman Catholic Church. One of the first things Syricius did while in office was to enact the celibacy of the

---

[65] "Saint Damasus I." Microsoft® Student 2009 [DVD]. Redmond, WA: Microsoft Corporation, 2008.
[66] "Saint Damasus I." Microsoft® Student 2009 [DVD]. Redmond, WA: Microsoft Corporation, 2008.
[67] "Saint Siricius." Microsoft® Student 2009 [DVD]. Redmond, WA: Microsoft Corporation, 2008.

Eliseo Santos

Clergy in 385 A.D.[68] This was the fulfilling of the prophetic warnings of Paul who in 1 Timothy ch.4, verses 1-3 speaking of the seducing spirits and doctrines of devils he includes:

Now the Spirit speaketh expressly, that in the latter times some shall depart from the faith, giving heed to seducing spirits, and doctrines of devils; Speaking lies in hypocrisy; having their conscience seared with a hot iron; Forbidding to marry, and commanding to abstain from meats, which God hath created to be received with thanksgiving of them which believe and know the truth.

The enforced priestly celibacy and virginity instituted by Syricius was part of what Paul refers to the "seducing spirits and doctrines of Devils." By introducing such doctrines Pope Syricius drastically veered the Roman Church off the road that Christ, His Apostles, and early Christians walked. All of these new doctrines and errors that have been instituted under the leadership of the Roman Church authority is what composes the Church of corruption called the Church of Pergamos, which is visually represented as a black horse, whose rider has sold out the way established on God's words and Ten Commandments. When speaking of the third seal and the black horse, the wheat and barley signify the words of God that have been sold for a cheap price and thus they have been changed. The wine and oil are symbols of the biblical doctrines and teachings that remain the same no matter how the Bible is ultimately changed. The wine and oil are preserved knowledge for future generations, who would read the Bible.

---

[68] pg. 202, The Two Babylons, Hislop

Good Father, Bad Father

In the fifth century A.D., the past pagan religious connotations made the word "pontiff" an appropriate title for the bishops of the Roman Catholic Church. [69] The Pope became Pontifex Maximus in the sense of being the high priest amongst the priests of the Roman Catholic Church. He controlled pagan religious ceremonies (public and occult), and political affairs (public and secret)[70] Thus the Roman Catholic Church became mixed and immersed in the political structure which existed in Rome since 746 B.C.

The greatest change that occurred from the early Christian church to the Roman Catholic Church was the creation of the mass. An important piece of the Roman Catholic Mass is the ceremony of the Eucharist, in which the communion wafer, or host is distributed during mass. For those of you not familiar with the communion wafer, here is a description from the American People's Encyclopedia, "In the Roman Catholic church, the host is a thin circular wafer of pressed unleavened flour on which is stamped some emblematic device, as the crucifixion, the lamb, or the letters, I.H.S."[71] This wafer is claimed to be the literal body of Christ and when the priest presents the host, the communion wafer ceases to be just any regular wafer and is then transformed into the literal body of Christ.[72] Thus, when the priest breaks the host he once again sacrifices the body of Christ. This in turn depreciates Christ's actual one-time infinite sacrifice on the cross on behalf of finite humanity. The perpetuation of the Eucharist causes people to lost sight of Christ's infinite sacrifice. It is only the one-time

---

[69] pg. 167, Pontifex, Ibid.
[70] pg. 167, Pontifex, Ibid.
[71] Pg.10-651, Host, The American Peoples Encyclopedia, Spencer Inc.,1958,Chicago,
[72] pg.10-651, host, Ibid.

infinite sacrifice of God that is necessary for salvation. In fact, it is the very act by which all human lives can be saved. The transmutation or (transubstantiation) of the communion wafer is what forms part of the Mysterium church doctrine. The American People's Encyclopedia clearly states, "Mass, the principal act of worship in the Roman Catholic Church. It is a ritual act, performed by a priest, and is considered in Roman Catholic theology to be a real sacrifice, the same as that offered by Jesus Christ on Calvary.[73]"

In his message to the Church of Pergamos, Jesus Christ plainly tells the church in Rev. 2:14 that the teaching of eating food sacrificed to idols, and to practice immorality are the "stumbling blocks" which cause Christians and many pagans to believe in a counterfeit Christian religion. Individuals practice immorality when they base their actions upon false principles, which counter the true principles of God and His Ten Commandments. To seek and obtain the eternal life, you must base your actions, thoughts, and life on the biblical principles of God and His Ten Commandments. He asks for His people to repent of their sins and stop eating food sacrificed to idols. Christ wants for all of the seven churches to remain faithful and solely established in the life, works, and words of Christ.

If you have not noticed, at the end of each message of the seven Churches, Jesus Christ gives you a glimpse of what life will be like in heaven. For all those who repent of their sins and follow His words and teachings that are found in the Bible, and believe that through His death and resurrection you are justified by faith if you pray to Him and seek forgiveness for wrong actions. To review, at the end of the

---

[73] Pg. 253, American Peoples Encyclopedia, Vol.12, Grolier Incorporated, New York, 1967,Library of Congress Catalog Card Number:67-10584

Good Father, Bad Father

church of Ephesus, Jesus says He will give fruits from the Tree of Life in Heaven only to those who overcome their personal sins and weaknesses. This is only achievable by maintaining and strengthening your faith in Christ, which includes Bible study, and learning Godly principles, and following God's Ten Commandments. At the end of His message to the Church of Smyrna in Revelation 2:11, Jesus says, "He that overcometh shall not be hurt of the second death." This signifies that those individuals who go to heaven will gain eternal life and won't be affected by God's judgment day over humanity. For the Church of Pergamos, Jesus promises to the redeemed and those who repent, "to Him that overcometh will I give to eat of the hidden manna, and will give him a white stone, and in the stone a new name written, which no man knoweth saving he that receiveth it." God here promises his redeemed will eat of the hidden manna, which is literal and also symbolic of the truth that has been occulted by the corrupt church of Pergamos, signified in the formation and development of the Roman Catholic Church. The white stone that every saved individual receives is a personal gift from God. It will have a name written that will be unique to you and God, and only the Good Father God and you will know your name, which creates a sense of enduring friendship with God as someone you can trust and another have an eternal personal bond with your Good Father, and Jesus Christ. As you continue to read about the last four of the seven churches, keep these promises in mind. God's promises are the important promises that each church has that leads to the much larger promise of eternal life. Therefore, let us repent and begin following the Will of God, found in the Bible and the Ten Commandments, for the Lord will come soon and make war with the sword of his mouth, which is the truth based on the Holy Word of God, and later on He Himself will come to put an end to evil, Satan, and this sinful planet.

During the time period of 313- 538 AD there were still many Christians who at this time kept the Sabbath in accordance with the words of Christ and Law of God. The Church of the Middle East and Persia faced opposition during this time from the Sassanid Kings, whose greatest complaint against those Christians was that they kept the 7th Day Sabbath, which was in direct opposition of their sun god. Sunday was separated for services to the god of the Persian Sassanid kings and Zoroastrianism. During the 40 year persecution of the Persian Sassanid King Shapur II, he stated, "They despise our sun-god. Did not Zoroaster, the sainted founder of our divine beliefs, institute Sunday one thousand years ago in honor of the sun and supplant the Sabbath of the Old Testament. Yet these Christians have divine services on Saturday."[74] During this time period the Church in Africa kept the Sabbath as told by Augustine who deplored the fact that in two neighboring churches in Africa one observes the Seventh-Day Sabbath, another fasted on it.[75] The Church of the East was still keeping the Seventh-Day Sabbath, "Mingana proves that in 370 AD, Abyssinian Christianity (a Sabbath Keeping Church) was so popular that its famous director, Musacus, traveled extensively in the East promoting the Church in Arabia, Persia, India, and China,".[76] According to Mingana, in the year 410, Isaac the Supreme director of the Church of the East held a world council, which some historians say was prompted by the visit of Musacus from the Abyssinian Church of Africa. There were delegates from 40 metropolitan

---

[74] pg. 83, 84, O'Leary, *The Syriac Church and Fathers*,
[75] pg.416, Dr. Peter Heylyn, *The History of the Sabbath*,
[76] p.308, *Truth Triumphant*, (footnote 27)

Good Father, Bad Father

divisions of the Eastern Church in attendance. In 411 A.D. a metropolitan director was appointed for the church in China. All of the churches of the East in Arabia, Persia, India, and China, all of them kept the Seventh-Day Sabbath. The Church of the East was not the only Christian Church keeping the Seventh-Day Sabbath. In Spain, Ambrose kept the 7th Day Sabbath in Milan, Italy and later on in Spain.[77]Evidence of Christian Seventh-Day Sabbath keeping in Spain, is found in the name of a small town located in the suburbs of Barcelona called, "Sabadell" because the town was originally inhabited by Christians who followed the 4th Commandment of God, which was kept by Christ and the Apostles. The Sabbath was also kept in Scotland and Ireland, as W.T. Skene states, "In this latter instance they seemed, to have followed a custom of which we find traces in the early monastic church of Ireland by which they held Saturday to be the Sabbath on which they rested from their labours."[78] Catholic Historian Bellesheim writes concerning the Celtic and Scottish Church, "We seem to see here an allusion to the custom, observed in the early monastic Church of Ireland, of keeping the day of rest on Saturday, or the Sabbath."[79] All of these historical facts are evidence that the Early Christian church kept the Seventh-Day Sabbath in accordance with the fourth Commandment and the teachings of Jesus Christ and the Apostles. This should dispel the idea that the Sabbath was made for just the Jews, but as Jesus said Himself, "The Sabbath was made for man, and not man for the Sabbath: Therefore the Son of Man is Lord also of the Sabbath," (Mark 2:27, 28). It is clearly evident in the words of Jesus that Sunday

---

[77] p.68, Truth Triumphant,

[78] pg. 96, W.T. Skene, *Adamnan's Life of St. Columba*, 1874,

[79] p.86,*History of the Catholic Church in Scotland*, Vol.1

worship was clearly not kept as much as compared with the Seventh-Day Sabbath. To convince more people to keep Sunday and follow Constantine's law, Pope Sylvester was the first to order the churches to fast on Saturday to bring disdain on the God ordained Seventh-Day Sabbath, when He rested from His work of Creation to spend time with Adam and Eve in Eden. Later on, Pope Innocent I (401-417 A.D.) enforced the fasting rule on the Sabbath.[80]

Due to this confusion that was introduced into the church of Pergamos, Jesus Christ, rebuked the church by "stating repent then, if not I will come to you soon and war against them with the sword of my mouth," (Rev.2:16). Jesus Christ made it clear early on that for the early church to follow the same precepts that their spiritual ancestors kept most importantly the 10 commandments that were given to Moses by God. When Jesus Christ mentioned the sword of his mouth, he is referring to the power of precision in which the Word of God can cut through lies, errors, and deceptions. Jesus Christ gives us the promise to those who are able to overcome spiritual errors in judgment and worship. Christians should follow only the Bible as the only source of spiritual doctrine. By following the Word of God in the Bible, Jesus will give you "the hidden manna" or the bread of life that refers to the many truths that will not only set us free from the chains of deception and manipulation, but also will lead you to eternal life that is found only through the grace of Jesus Christ.

---

[80] p. 44, Dr. Peter Heylyn, *History of the Sabbath*, Part 2,

Chapter 12: The Church of Thyatira and the 4th Seal

This leads to the fourth out of the seven churches, the church of Thyatira, which is composed of God's people during the broad time period of 538 to 1517 A.D. This Church covers the periods of the Dark Ages and Middle Ages, when Christianity, and Christian life, was under the direction of the iron rule of the Roman Church. Eventually the Papal chair had the political and religious authority of all Europe and the Middle East. This is the period that correlates with the 4th seal or the pale horse of death, which specifies the total spiritual, mental, and physical condition experienced by the church during this era. This is Jesus Christ's message to the Church of Thyatira and the description of the 4th seal:

> *"And unto the angel of the church in Thyatira write; These things saith the Son of God, who hath his eyes like unto a flame of fire, and his feet are like fine brass; I know thy works, charity, and service, and faith and thy patience, and thy works; and the last to be more than the first. Notwithstanding, I have a few things against thee because thou sufferest that woman Jezebel, which calleth herself prophetess, to teach and seduce my servants to commit fornication, and to eat things sacrificed unto idols. And I gave her space to repent of her fornication; and she repented not. Behold, I will cast her unto a bed, and*

Eliseo Santos

them that commit adultery with her into great tribulation, except they repent of their deeds. And I will kill her children with death; and all the churches shall know that I am he which searcheth the reins and hearts, and I will give unto every one of you according to your works, But unto you I say, and unto the rest in Thyatira, as many have not this doctrine, and which have not known the depths of Satan, as they speak; I will put upon you none other burden. But that which ye have already hold fast till I come. As he that overcometh, and keepeth my works unto the end, to him will I give power over the nations: And he shall rule them with a rod of iron; as the vessels of a potter shall they be broken to shivers: even as I received of my Father. And I will give him the morning star. He that hath an ear, let him hear what the Spirit saith unto the churches. – (Revelation 2:18-29; KJV)

"*And when he opened the fourth seal, I saw the voice of the fourth beast say, 'Come, and see. And I looked, and behold a pale horse; and his name that sat on him was Death, and hell followed with him. And power was given unto them over the fourth part of the earth, to kill with sword, and with hunger, and with death, and with the beasts of the earth,*" *(Revelation 6:7-8; KJV)*

The time period covered by the Church of Thyatira (538-1517 AD) was a time in which the Roman Catholic Church had a spiritual monopoly of error, and a monopoly on the mind and the ideas of the people. During this time, the principles and precepts of the Bible and Jesus Christ, were hidden by illiteracy and unfamiliarity with the Latin language. The rise in power of the Roman Church was sustained by hiding the truth of the Bible from the majority of the public. During these times slavery evolved to serfdom, where the common man was enslaved to nobles and lords, and they in turn were slaves to

Good Father, Bad Father

kings and Queens. Kings and Queens became slaves to the false king of kings, the Pope. Thus, nobles, lords, kings, and queens, did the bidding of the Pope and the Roman Catholic Church, often times against their will, at the pain of death and or having their kingdom removed from their hands, and given to a compliant Catholic candidate. Politically and spiritually, the Roman Catholic Church shocked the inhabitants of the known world by the violence, brutality, and immorality that was inconsistent with the Good Father and Jesus Christ of the Bible. It was more consistent with the Bad Father of lies and the Roman Empire. The Roman Catholic Church showed her true self in the many wars, persecutions, inquisitions, and cruel torture methods developed for the sole purpose of attacking those who went against the beliefs of the Roman Catholic Institution. The many inhabitants of the known world were cuffed in the chains of ignorance of God's love and Biblical Word, and thus the fear of the Papacy and the Roman Catholic Church pervaded society. The Words of life and light found in the Bible were surrounded by a depressing dim darkness.

The name Thyatira means (Sweet Savor of Labor, and the sacrifice of contrition or repentance). These two ideas form the Bad Father theology. First, the lie that man can be saved through their own works. The second, a man does not need to repent from their sins to be saved. During the Church of Thyatira, the Roman Catholic Church began to teach any human being could be saved if they go to Mass enough times and partake of the Eucharist. Many of the innocent people of this time were told to follow anything that the Pope and his priestly agents told them to do. Roman Catholicism became a type of Christianity that removes Jesus Christ and the significance of His works, which was His death, resurrection, and his current ministry in the Temple or sanctuary in heaven. Jesus Christ now hears the prayers of those who pray to him, asking forgiveness for their sins, and causing an inner transformation from sinner to a repentant human being via His infinite grace. The Roman Catholic system replaced the infinite works of Christ with the meaningless finite works of dead repetitive prayers and rituals. It's a Christianity that robs the human being of their direct connection with their Creator, Savior, and Comforter and replaces it with a Papal Caste system, a bureaucratic system of clergy, and a system of idols worship and mediation of dead saints. As Daniel prophesied in Daniel 8:11,12, "Yea, he magnified himself even to the prince of the host, and by him the daily sacrifice was taken away, and the place of his sanctuary was cast down. And a host was given him against the daily sacrifice by reason of transgression, and it cast down the truth to the ground; and it practiced, and prospered." In the words of Daniel, the Pope magnified himself to "the prince of the host", who is Jesus Christ. Christ, who took away the daily sacrifice of the Old Testament Tabernacle and Temple, and it was replaced with the infinite sacrifice of His body on the cross. The Papal system employs a world-wide system of priests who pretend to continue the Old Testament sacrifices by mixing paganism of Egypt and Babylon with Biblical themes of sacrifice and atonement for sins. This elaborate priesthood undermines the infinite power and grace of the priesthood of Jesus Christ, who is now in heaven hearing our prayers, pardoning sins of those who believe in Him as the resurrected Son of God.

In the same way in which Jesus Christ told Mary Magdalene to repent of her sins of adultery after she been forgiven by Jesus Christ, Jesus Christ also wants for those who profess His name, to stop committing spiritual adultery with the symbolic Jezebel or the Roman

Good Father, Bad Father

Catholic System. Jesus wants for Christians to repent of their sins and to seek God in the Holy Scriptures. Why go through all the unnecessary trouble of going to a confessional to confess your sins and wrong doing to a priest who commits at times greater sins before God than you? Why seek the priest who wrongly takes the place of God, when you can confess your sins in the comfort of your home directly to the genuine All –Mighty Creator, and Savior, Comforter, and have your sins instantly forgiven without the empty repetitive prayers and rituals? Why go to church for the stale communion wafer, when you can have the bread of life, by reading and studying the word of God? In Revelation 10:9, "John is asked to eat the little book" which is symbolic of learning and studying the Word of God and Bible Prophecy under the direction of the Holy Spirit. The purpose for learning and digesting the Words of God and Bible prophecy is to warn the people of the End Times and the 2nd Coming of Christ. Those who have digested the Word of God and Bible prophecy are given the responsibility to call people back to the Good Father before it's too late. God is calling on His people that are now in many different churches and denominations around the world, to leave the churches that do not clearly follow the Word of God, and The Ten Commandments, as Jesus followed and testified its unchanged significance. Only by following God in the Bible will it be a "lamp unto your feet" as it states in Psalm 119:105, because believing in Jesus Christ as the Son of God and His words in the Bible lead to eternal life.

Those who during this time period were not able to learn the truth concerning Roman Catholicism, but yet served God according to what they received as truth and did what was right in the spirit of truth, these individuals God will judge on whether or not they obeyed what they believed in their minds to be the Ten Commandments and the teachings of Christ. God will have mercy on many who lived during this period because of the fact that the Bible, the source of God's words and teachings was inaccessible to many during this time period.

There were two important Councils that brought about the removal of the Bible from the common people. In 1229 AD, in the Council of Toulouse, Pope Gregory IX stated, "We prohibit laymen possessing copies of the Old and New Testament… We forbid them most severely to have the above books in the popular vernacular. The lords of the districts shall carefully seek out the heretics in dwellings, hovels, and forests, and even their underground retreats shall be entirely wiped out."[81] The Roman Church Council of Tarragona in 1234 AD said "No one may possess the books of the Old and New Testaments in the Romance language, and if anyone possesses them he must turn them over to the local bishop within eight days after the promulgation of this decree, so that they may be burned."[82] God does not want you to follow the hooker Jezebel, who claims to be the most beautiful and fairest church of them all and hooks you with her captivating wine of doctrines. Jesus Christ own words describe this when he states in Rev. 2:20-23,

> *Notwithstanding I have a few things against thee, because thou sufferest that woman Jezebel, which calleth herself a prophetess, to teach and to seduce my servants to commit*

---

[81] Council Tolosanum, Pope Gregory IX, Anno. Chr. 1229, as quoted in National Sunday Law, Appendix 4, pg. 79, By A. Jan Marcussen

[82] D. Lortsch, Historie de la Bible en France, 1910, pg.14, as quoted in.pg. 79, Appendix 4, Ibid.

fornication, and to eat things sacrificed unto idols. And I gave her space to repent of her fornication; and she repented not. Behold, I will cast her into a bed, and them that commit adultery with her into great tribulation, except they repent of their deeds. And I will kill her children with death, and all churches shall know that I am he which searcheth the reins and hearts, and I will give unto everyone of you according to your works.

At the beginning of this time period, to further legitimize the new State religion, the emperor Justinian made a decree, which appointed the Bishop of Rome (The Pope) as the "Corrector of Heretics." Remember, heretic really means to choose who to worship and follow as a spiritual leader. By the Pope being named corrector of heretics, the Bible and the Words of God were no longer the standard by which a Christian made his decisions through his own will, choice, and study of the Bible. Through human means and influence, the Pope was now in charge of making the decisions concerning the faith and practice of Christianity. Because the Bible was the source of the genuine and true Christianity that Jesus and his disciples, practiced and endorsed, the Papacy sought to restrict public access to the Bible by making it a crime to have one in your home. If an individual was caught reading it, the individual was imprisoned and later burned at the stake. The Council of Toulouse in 1229 AD and the Council of Tarragona prohibited laymen from obtaining the copies of the Old and New Testaments. Anyone found in possession of a Bible was committed to death by burning at the stake. These Councils were in response to the spread of the truth that occurred through God's true people during this time, which were composed of the Albigenses and the Waldenses who were spreading the truth of the gospel through Europe during this time.

Due to this restriction of the word of God, Europe and the inhabitants entered into the Dark Ages, where the Bible-believing Christians were the most targeted group within that era. Because of the long length of time in which the time-period covered (remember this was during the era of Papal supremacy of 1260 prophetic days / actual years). There were many of God's people who were within the spiritual system of error and confusion. God took into account the dark times in which they lived where the light of truth, which was God's word, was covered up with the human error and confusion of the man of sin, the Pope. Since this segment of people within the Church of Thyatira, did not have access to the truth, yet they still believed and obeyed what they thought was true, Jesus accounts for them in his message in Thyatira in verses 24, and 25 when he says, "But to the rest of you in Thyatira, who do not hold this teaching, who have not learned what some call the deep things of Satan, to you I say, I do not lay upon you any other burden; only hold fast what you have, until I come." "The deep thing of Satan" in which Jesus was referring to was the Roman Catholic Church, the church that masquerades in the goodness and righteousness of Biblical Christianity to do the work of the Satan, the Bad Father of lies.

One of the many issues the Roman Catholic Papacy faced during this period was the schism within the Roman Catholic Church. Jesus summarized the schismatic situation faced by the Roman Catholic Church during this time by stating in Mark 3:23-26, "How can Satan cast out Satan? And if a kingdom be divided against itself, that kingdom cannot stand. And if a house be divided against itself, that house cannot stand. And if Satan rise up against himself, and be

Good Father, Bad Father

divided, he cannot stand, but hath an end." Jesus Christ explains what how Satan spiritually, mentally, and physically operates. In order to understand the significance of the words of Christ, you must understand that a key component of Satan's strategy against the Good Father God is to divide and conquer. The Bad Father Satan divides for the purpose of controlling both sides, and paints one side as a false good, (in other words a good mixed with evil) and paints another side as a false evil (in other words an evil mixed with good). The purpose of the false good and evil is to have people pick a choice that is not the true good (pure good), which is the Good Father, Jesus Christ, Biblical Christianity, and the Ten Commandments. The false good and evil also prevent people from seeing the true causes of death, destruction, and sin in the world. The pure evil of the Bad Father of lies and fallen angelic and greedy human accomplices are the ultimately the cause of all the evil in the world. During the Dark Ages and Middle-Ages, Satan utilized this method to attack humanity on the spiritual, mental, and physical plane. Satan used and still uses this methodology against humanity because if Satan can trick you into believing a lie (either a false good or false evil) then you give him power to control your mind and ultimately leads you to death and ruin. Satan uses this method against every human being on the planet and including the very people who swear allegiance to him. In order to convince people to swear to him, he has to one blind or distract them. Satan has to mix in a greater portion of truth with lies, so that an individual can accept him, or the false good or the false evil. To blind and distract, he manipulates people's emotions to bury their reasoning abilities under immediate feelings of happiness, security, etc. He usually ties people's emotions (happiness, and fear) to the physical realm so that he can heighten and develop an individual's greed. It is an individual's own greed for either physical possessions, money, power, drugs, liquor, sex, etc. that blinds and distracts him or her from rationally seeing the truth of Good Father and the Bad Father. Throughout the history of Israel, Satan has employed the use of foreign women to ensnare the men of Israel into not only fornication, but also idolatry, adultery, and to do things against the wishes of God. Jesus with the message for The Church of Thyatira uses the example of Jezebel, who was a harlot because she introduced the worship of Baal into Israel through her marriage to King Ahab of Israel. Jezebel manipulated her husband to install the worship of Baal amongst the people. All Satan has to do is to continue giving you whatever you want so that you don't start asking questions about what he is lying to you about.

Notice this process is the exact opposite of what the principles of the Good Father God, and Jesus Christ. In God's case, He wants you to see the truth and the truth originates and ends with Him and His words in the Bible. God does not sugar coat the truth with lies, but He dips the truth in the honey of the greater truth of the prophetic promises of God, which will never spoil or rot. For example, the Bad Father knows his end and the end of his earthly kingdom are near. Thus, he sugar coats the truth of the end of the world and the 2nd Coming of Christ with so many white coats of sugary lies, that the wholehearted truth of the 2nd coming of Christ is covered and indiscernible. God, on the other hand, covers the bread of life, the bitter truth of the Ten Commandments, the resurrection, and future persecution of God's people with the sweet natural, organic, and translucent honey, which is the truth of eternal life and the 2nd coming of Christ. 2nd Coming of Christ is good news because it is the revival of the Everlasting heavenly Kingdom that will be installed on the new earth for those who kept the Commandments of God, and the faith of Jesus. The 2nd Coming of Christ is an important piece of the true bread of life; if you are a Christian and don't believe in the 2nd Coming of God, then your faith is in vain. You can improve your faith dramatically by simply believing in the 2nd Coming of God. Thus, the bread of life that God offers He makes it known beforehand that it will be sweet now, but it will eventually become bitter when the world confronts you concerning your faith. In Matthew 5:10-12, Jesus Christ said all Christians at one point or another have to face a brief period of bitterness,

"Blessed are they which are persecuted for righteousness' sake: for theirs is the Kingdom of heaven. Blessed are ye, when men shall revile you, and persecute you, and shall say all manner of evil against you falsely, for my sake. Rejoice, and be exceeding glad: for great is your reward in heaven: for so persecuted they the prophets which were before you."

However, this bitterness is brief, when compared to the eternal sweetness of eternal life. It was for this reason, that Jesus Christ died for our sins, because He knew that it will be brief when compared to eternal life. Christ was aware that His brief and bitter experience with false accusations, pain, and death will yield eternal life for not only Himself, but for all those who follow His words, commandments, and example. Jesus Christ says in Matthew 10:37-39, "He that loveth father or mother more than me is not worthy of me: and he that loveth son or daughter more than me is not worthy of me. And he that taketh not his cross, and followeth after me, is not worthy of me. He that findeth his life shall lose it; and he that loseth his life for my sake shall find it." Here Christ explains that at times a true follower of

Christ not only will have to go against the world, but also his own family. In this case, it is by honoring God and His Commandments that you will honor your mother and father. For if you do the will of God, and seek eternal life, then how can you bring shame upon your parents? What will bring shame is the world and parents who neglect their responsibilities before God for instructing their children in the way of God. Keep in my mind that we are all children of the Good Father in heaven, and He loves each of His children with a love that human words fail to express. God would love for all families to join in Him heaven. But he knows that Satan takes the God's bread of life, and corrupts it, replacing the truth of eternal life, the 2nd coming of God, the eternal heavenly kingdom, and the new recreated earth with a counterfeit artificial processed sugar and sweetener, that hides the truth of the Ten commandments of God, the resurrection, and the future persecution of God's people. Those who partake of Satan's corruption of the bread of life will experience great bitterness in finding out that they were lied to and manipulated by Satan to their eventual 2nd death, which is eternal death from which no one will be resurrected from. Satan's prime objective today is to deceive and distract those inside and outside the God's true church. God's true church is the gathering of individuals who do the will of God on earth by keeping His authentic Ten Commandments, taking care of the sick and impoverished, and educating others with the truth of reality that is based on God's word found in the Bible.

For Satan, knowing his end is near, he seeks to deceive and take as many souls by leading them to death without them knowing of the salvation grace of Christ. The best way to do this was to impersonate the enemy and to control and limit the enemy. Satan did this with the creation of the Roman Catholic Church, by mixing God's principles

Good Father, Bad Father

with the traditions of Pagan Rome, ancient occult traditions, and pagan philosophy of other cultures. Satan mixed in the lies and errors of paganism with the one set of truthful beliefs in the face of the earth that reveal the reality concerning the Good and Bad father. The Bad father limits access to the Bible, which is the source of all truth and knowledge of reality.

The Roman Catholic Church also faced "fears" that affected its very existence. It actually feared small groups of Christians that existed outside the Roman Church and therefore did not recognize the Pope's authority. The various small groups that existed outside of the Roman Catholic serf system maintained the same peaceful and eternal truths that were preached by the Apostles and Jesus Christ. There were many independent pockets of Christianity that had not been corrupted by pagan reforms that occurred during the time of the Church of Pergamos. It was the pagan reforms introduced by Constantine and other popes, which plunged the majority of the Early Christian church into spiritual darkness. The sole authority and guide for these small groups of Christianity was the Word of God found in the Bible. Due to setting the Word of God as the only source of truth, they were able to understand how the events that were occurring in Europe with the development of the Roman Catholic Church correlated with a fulfillment of prophecy of Daniel 7 and 8, involving the arrival of the Little Horn power. Many during the era, of the Pergamos and Thyatira, saw how the Roman Catholic Church was the "Mystery of iniquity" spoken of by Paul in 2 Thessalonians 2:7, when he states:

Remember ye not, that when I was yet with you, I told the you these things? And now ye know what withholdeth that he might

> *be revealed in his time. For the mystery of iniquity doth already work; only he who now letteth will let, until he be taken out of the way. And then shall that Wicked be revealed, whom the Lord shall consume with the Spirit of his mouth, and shall destroy with the brightness of his coming: Even him, whose coming is after the working of Satan with all power and signs and lying wonders. And with all deceivableness of unrighteousness in them that perish; because they received not the love of the truth, that they might be saved. – 2 Thessalonians 2:5-10*

Paul here is describing a prophecy with two fulfillments. The first and symbolic fulfillment was the arrival of the Roman Catholic Papacy, created by Constantine when he mixed paganism with Biblical truths. The Roman Catholic Church became a false good, when in fact it is part of the true evil. In other words a good mixed with lies that hides great evils that are done in secret by the Higher-ranking Catholic leadership. Thus, the Mystery of iniquity, and the Little Horn of Daniel 7 and 8 refer to the arrival of the Papal System that is at variance with the teachings of God and the Apostles. When Paul states, "that the Mystery of iniquity doth already work," he is describing the precursor to the Roman Catholic Church which was the Roman Empire. As foretold in Daniel 7 and 8, from the Roman Empire would rise the Little Horn, or the Papacy, which would remain alive until the 2nd Coming of Christ. The 2nd and literal fulfillment of this prophecy is describing the events that are happening today in the Vatican and the Papal situation, and thus these events will be described in detail later.

For God, there is a clear difference between following the truth of His Word and Commandments that are found in the Bible, and following any other religious and spiritual leader that does not present the full truth contained within the Bible, but mixes truth with lies.

Good Father, Bad Father

Thus, God wants His People in these End Times to follow the Words of God, and His Commandments that have been preserved for well over 2,000 years for the sake of this generation that will witness the 2nd Coming of God and the End of the earth. To understand where you are today, in terms of Bible Prophecy and the grand picture of reality, it is important to review and become familiar with Papal History. To understand the truth you must see how Papal history correlates with the messages of Jesus Christ and the Apostles, and also the warnings of Daniel and the Prophets of the Old and New Testament.

The small groups, such as the Albigenses, arrived at the conclusion that the Papacy was part of the Anti-Christ system by reading their copies of the Holy Scriptures. They arrived at this conclusion and other accurate conclusions about the Papacy by studying and following the Word of God and Jesus Christ, who in Matthew 5:17-20 explicitly warned the future generations of Christians that 'He did not come to change the law of the God and His commandments but came to fulfill them' and validate them forever. Many Christians fail to realize that Jesus Christ died on the Cross for the law of the Good Father God to stand for eternity, via His one-time infinite sacrifice on the Cross. Jesus Christ, the infinite God, sacrificed Himself on the Cross, and withstood all types of humiliation so that He can not only save as many people as possible, but also pay the price of His own law, so that through Him many people can be saved. All the other pagan gods were not concerned with a law. They never would have come to earth to do the things Jesus Christ did for humanity. Thus, when the corruption of the early Christian Church began in 313 AD when Constantine introduced alternative pagan doctrines that undermined the law of God and the

Seventh-Day Sabbath, not all Christians at the time were in favor of such changes to the Ten Commandments of God. Thus many Christians hid in rural areas throughout Europe and continued to worship God in peace. One of these small communities was the community of the Albigenses.

The Albigenses (sometimes referred by many Catholic historians as the Cathars or Cathari) were a small community that lived in Southern France, in the town of Albi. This small group of people was converting many Catholics in their area to the authentic Biblical Christianity, practiced by Jesus Christ, the Apostles and the Early Christians of the Church of Ephesus and Smyrna. After 800 years living in peace in their native rural communities, the Bishop or leading priest in that area complained to Pope Innocent III.

The Roman Catholic Church considered the Albigenses on the same level as an army of invading soldiers, even though Albigenses were not engaged in physical war at all, nor accumulating weapons and soldiers to do battle. The Albigenses weapon was the pure words of God, whose origin was from the same Holy Scriptures that have been passed down through the generations. After sending missionaries to try and convince the Albigenses to return to the Roman Church, Pope Innocent III organized a crusade against the Albigenses. The Albigenses were able to overcome the missionaries of the Pope through a reliance on the Words of Truth only gained from the Holy Scriptures. The American Peoples Encyclopedia states the following when referring to Pope Innocent III's actions in dealing with the Albigenses, "He tried to quit the Albigenses by sending missionaries to them, but when they persisted in heresy he organized a crusade against them."[83] After sending the Crusades and shedding innocent

Good Father, Bad Father

Christian blood, Innocent III in 1215 AD called the Fourth Council of Lateran, and instituted rules for all Roman Catholics to attend confession once a year, and obligated Catholics to receive communion.[84] Innocent III also defined the doctrine of transubstantiation for future generations,[85]. Pope Innocent III acted not only of out of hatred, but more so out of fear of the truth of God and the Bible being known by the common people. The powerful truth of God found only in the Old and New Testaments turns individuals away from the falsehoods and deceptions of the Roman Catholic Church, and towards that true love of truth that emanates from the Good Father, and His Holy word.

As a result of their faith in God and His Words in the Bible, the Albigenses continued to grow and preach the word of God despite the Crusade of Innocent III. Due to the intolerance of the truth being spread and known by others, Pope Gregory IX would once again persecute the Albigenses. This pope at first used the tactics used in the 1st, 2nd, and 3rd century, which was to hunt down, capture, and publicly execute all Christians exactly as was done on and off in the first three centuries by the Roman Empire. However, this proved to be a waste of time on the part of the Roman Catholic Church. So they came up with a system of martial law, intimidation, and, interrogation, which they called the Inquisition. The Inquisition was used as a way to gather information about the whereabouts of the Albigenses through cruel torture tactics. The Inquisition would go from town to town through a given country where the Biblical Christianity was

---

[83] pg. 261-262, Innocent III, American People Encyclopedia, Grolier Incorporated, 1967
[84] Pg.262, Innocent III, Ibid.
[85] Pg.262, Innocent III, Ibid.

spreading. Officials of the Inquisition would first ask the people of a town a preliminary set of questions. The questions and responses were used to learn who were the Christians that did not submit to the authority of the Pope, and submitted to the Word of God found in the Holy Bible. Any and all Bibles were confiscated from the common people. In 1229 AD the Council of Toulouse and in 1234 AD the Council of Tarragona would prohibit the common man from owning the Bible because the Albigenses were an example of how a simple group of people can destroy the illusion of lies in which the Pope and other Roman leaders project without mercy to the common man. The truth in the hands of the Albigenses was a threat to papal authority. The truth is the Pope doesn't use the authority of the Divine truth of the Bible. God brings to those who submit to the truth of the Words of God the necessary help through the Holy Spirit and heavenly angels to direct their learning of the Bible and its many truths of reality. The authority of the Pope is gained from Satan himself as is told in Revelation 13:2. Using the authority of Satan's lies that hide the truth of God and the Bible, the papacy preferred to have all knowledge and learning concentrated in the minds of the priests, nobles, and higher echelons of society, especially concerning the Bible. The papacy preferred the common man to be uneducated and incapable of thinking about the problems of the world and their solutions. The Bible is the great equalizer for the common man. Most, if not all, of the solutions of the uneducated and common man can be found in Jesus Christ and the promise of eternal life. The accused Christian villagers would be then tortured to renounce their faith. If they did not recant, then they were publicly burned at the stake, or they died of starvation, or other injuries from their torture in prison. However, in reality, those who did die for the sake of Christ found the loop-pole of

Good Father, Bad Father

eternal life; if anyone loses their life for Christ sake or for the sake of keeping and following His teachings or commandments, then they will be rewarded with eternal life. Jesus states in Matthew 16:25, "For whosoever will save his life, shall lose it: and whosoever will lose his life for my sake shall find it." Once again the blood of the innocent was shed. Their only crime in the eyes of the Roman Catholic Church was to believe in the reality of God and Jesus Christ as told in the Bible. The torturous and murderous treatment of the Albigenses by the Pope and Roman Catholic leaders illustrates the fulfillment of the prophecy of Daniel 7 when referring to the Little Horn power. Daniel foretold close to 1700 years prior to the inquisition, that the Little Horn rose from the head of the dreadful and terrible beast of the Roman Empire. Daniel wrote, "As I looked, this horn made war with the saints, and prevailed over them until the Ancient of Days come," (Daniel 7:21). This quote shows how the Little Horn or the Papacy in the Vatican would be the church that would commit atrocious and unspeakable things to the Saints of God, who were blameless and did no wrong to deserve the treatment they received by the bloody hands of Roman Catholic leaders.

Unlike the Roman Empire, which was secular and pagan, the Roman Catholic Church would use the name of God and Christ as a cloak to veil their nefarious activities, especially killing innocent men, women, and children and Bible believing Christians. In the same way the beast of the field (a cow, bull, horse) eats large amounts of green grass from the field for nourishment, likewise the Roman Catholic Church of the Dark and Middle Ages fulfilled the prophetic symbolism of the 4th seal of the Pale Horse of Death and the prophetic symbolism of the beast by devouring large portions of God's people. In 1 Peter 1:23-24, Peter states, "Being born again, not of corruptible seed, but of incorruptible, by the Word of God, liveth and abideth forever. For all flesh is as grass, and all the glory of man as the flower of grass. The grass withereth, and the flower thereof falleth away." When John describes the Pale horse he describes that power was given to the Roman Catholic Church to kill a fourth part of the earth through "the sword, hunger, and death and the beasts of the earth." The Roman Catholic Church killed Christians to continue the existence of the false good it has created by mixing the Biblical teachings of God and the Pagan concepts of Satan. What made the Crusade against the Albigenses even more disturbing was this was a Crusade carried out not on a foreign threat, but on those who were peaceful French Christians. This was one of the worst crimes ever done in the past against the human family. Despite the deaths and innocent bloodshed caused by the Crusades against the Albigenses, their deaths would not be in vain. Their example of Christian living according to the Bible would forever impress many Christians throughout the world.

Thus, the Pope turned to new methods to fight against the Albigenses population that would forever change the history of Europe and the world. The American People's Encyclopedia, writes how unlike Americans today who enjoy the right of Habeas Corpus, during the Middle Ages, many Albigenses were wrongly detained, imprisoned, convicted and killed for merely expressing their beliefs, which were correct beliefs based upon the Word of God in the Bible.[86]The encyclopedia further states the following,:

---

[86] pg.263, Inquisition, The American Peoples Encyclopedia, Vol.10, Grolier Incorporated, New York, 1967, Library of Congress Catalog Card Number:67-10584

Good Father, Bad Father

The methods used by the Inquisition were comparable to those of civil courts at the time, but were barbaric according to modern standards. The defendant was denied counsel, testimony of heretics and excommunicates were admitted against him; cruel tortures were often used to extort a confession. Punishment took forms of imprisonment or death (usually by burning alive at the stake) with confiscation of the condemned's property in either case.[87]

All of these punishments were only due to the crime of learning freedom of thought, freedom of speech, and freedom of conscience, all of which are important for any Christian to love God with all their heart, mind, and soul. Without these freedoms, you and everyone else cannot be a Christian. The Albigenses, learned to live as though God and Him alone, was the only one who gives these freedoms to mankind and the only Judge who can take them away. The Pope exerted influence over the populace of the time by labeling individuals, who recognized their freedom under Christ, as "heretics." The word heretics comes from the Greek word *Hairesis* which means "to decide for oneself." In actuality it was the Roman Catholic Popes and leadership that decided for themselves to change God's law and edit the Ten Commandments. It was also they who decided for themselves to mix in ancient forms of sun worship with real Biblical Christianity. It was also the Roman Catholic leadership who decided for themselves to benefit from lying to the public, and to continue to benefit from that lying, they defamed and detained the heretics to inflict pain and death. Daniel in the Old testament foretold the torture and gruesome deaths experienced in the Dark and Middle Ages by The Albigenses and other groups that were following the meaning of

---

[87] pg.264, Inquisition, The Medieval, Inquisition, Ibid.

scripture. Daniel states concerning the Little Horn in Daniel 7:21, "I behold, and the same horn made war with the saints, and prevailed against them." Here the Holy Spirit, briefly and concisely explains the events that would occur in the Middle and Dark Ages to God's people. Remember, Peter said that all scriptural interpretation should lead you to one conclusion and therefore it is not private, (2 Peter 1:19-21). God wrote the Bible to be understood by everyone and wrote it so that everyone can be on the same page and arrive at the same conclusions. In order to do so, these Christians under the guidance of the Holy Spirit were led to essential truths of the world and God. Some of these essential truths of the Bible are the existence of Good and Evil. According to the infallible words of the Bible, these essential truths show that Satan exists in the world and that the Roman Catholic Church is part of an anti-Christ system, and true salvation is only found in the Words of Jesus Christ that are found in the Bible. The love of God exhibited by the Albigenses to God and their fellow men was not the same as the fierce hatred displayed by Roman Catholic sympathizers. Roman Catholic Church would only continue to kill Christians without the mercy of Christ. The lack of patience and sympathy on the part of the Roman Catholic Church was evident in the repulsively gruesome torture techniques that would be developed by the Church during this time period.

During the broad time period of Thyatira, The Roman Catholic Church had become the Little Horn of Daniel 7, 8 and The Sea Beast of Revelation 13. In order to fully understand why the Bible would label the Roman Catholic Church as Babylon in the Book of Revelation you must understand who is Jesus Christ according to the Bible and understand His current role after He ascended into heaven

Chapter 13: Christ, The Holy High Priest and Sole Mediator of Humanity

The Apostle Peter writes in his first letter, 1 Peter 1:18-19, "Forasmuch as ye know that ye were not redeemed with corruptible things, as silver and gold, from your vain conversation received by tradition from your fathers; But with the precious blood of Christ, as of a lamb without blemish and without spot," (KJV). The precious blood of Christ is what cleans the mind, body, and soul from all impurities of sin that accumulates during an individual's life. This precious blood of Christ cannot be the literal drinking of wine. The bloodshed of the infinite God on the Cross covers all the finite sins of any individual that seeks forgiveness and repentance from God. Peter goes on to say in 1 Peter 2:24, "He himself bore our sins in his body on the cross that we might die to sins and live to righteousness. By his wounds you have been healed." There are two important points in these two quotes that counter the need for the continuation of the mass sacrifice via transubstantiation of the wafer into the "body and blood" of Christ. In the first quote, the point of emphasis is the precious blood of Christ continues to clean us of all our sins. The precious blood of Christ is imperishable because it flowed from the God of Infinite Life, which was further demonstrated with the resurrection of Christ. Because Christ resurrected, we can pray with confidence and seek forgiveness of our sins and repent from our wrong courses of actions that eventually cause pain, suffering, and death to us and others in society. When you pray to God in Christ's name, the precious blood of Christ, covers your sins in the heavenly temple or sanctuary, where He is currently listening to the prayers of all those who pray in his name. The 2nd point, which is crucial to understand, is that Christ's sacrifice covers the sins of past and future humanity on the cross. When you recognize the significance of the death of the infinite God in the finite human form of Christ, you are called by Peter "to die to sin," which is the process of repentance, and "live to righteousness," which is to observe the law of righteousness found in the Ten Commandments. Then the sins that you and I commit today are pardonable only if we recognize Christ as our savior.

Another group of verses in the Bible explains why God and Jesus Christ do not favor the continuation of the transubstantiation and the sacrifice that is performed at Mass. Paul in his Letters to the Romans and Hebrews brings up many good points about why partaking of the Communion is not a good idea for any believer of Jesus Christ. Paul in Romans 6: 9-10 states, "Knowing that Christ being raised from the dead, dieth no more; death hath no more dominion over him. For in that he died, he died unto sin once; but in that he liveth, he liveth unto God." If Paul states that Christ being raised from the dead, no longer dies, then how can it be true that the Roman Catholic priest has the ability to turn the Communion wafer into the body and blood of Christ, then, in essence reenact the crucifixion of Christ during mass? The Roman Catholic priest can't make such a claim, because Jesus is

Good Father, Bad Father

still alive after His resurrection, in heaven hearing the prayers of humanity. The Book of Hebrews explains the purpose of Jesus Christ after the resurrection, which was to become the High Priest of humanity and intercede for humanity in front of the Good Father in the heavenly Temple. Paul in Hebrews 2:17-18 explains the purpose of Christ's life on earth:"Wherefore in all things it behooved him to be made like unto his brethren, that he might be merciful and faithful high priest in things pertaining to God, to make reconciliation for the sins of the people. For in that he himself hath suffered being tempted, he is able to succor them that are tempted." Therefore, Christ living an eternity before the creation of the earth without sin, came to earth and became human to experience everything you experience, and identify with all the problems in which a human being suffers as a result of the enemy Satan. God did this in order to share a closer connection with His creation. By being motivated by His love for His Creation, Christ paid the price of sin, which is death, so that His death can cover all the death penalties and sins of every human being that believes in Him and that He is really the Son of God. Therefore, if that is the case, then only Christ can hear our confessions and intercede on our behalf before God because He is still the only one to die and resurrect three days later. Paul in Hebrews 3:1 alludes to the fact that only Christ can take on the office High Priest, "Wherefore, holy brethren, partakers of the heavenly calling consider the Apostle and High Priest of our profession, Christ Jesus." Therefore, the only true way to have your sins forgiven is through Christ and no one else. Paul reiterates this point in Hebrews 4:14-16,

> *"Seeing then that we have a great high priest, that is passed into the heavens, Jesus the Son of God, let us hold fast our*

profession. For we have not an high priest which cannot be touched with the feeling our infirmities; but was in all points tempted like as we are, yet without sin. Let us therefore come boldly, unto the throne of grace, that we may obtain mercy, and find grace to help in the time of need."

How do you approach the throne of grace, you may ask? You do so, via prayer. Prayer is when you address the God of the universe, the Good Father. You bring your petitions before Him by praying through Jesus Christ and His name.

Will God forgive your sins? Paul states in Hebrews 7:25,26, "Wherefore he is able also to save them to the uttermost that come unto God by him, seeing he ever liveth to make intercession for them. For such an high priest became us, who is holy, harmless, undefiled, separate from sinners, and made higher than the heavens." Paul, who is writing the letter, is a perfect example of just how powerful is the power of redemption through Jesus Christ. Paul at one time was a bounty hunter for the leaders of the synagogue to catch those who have accepted Christianity. After witnessing Christ after the ascension into heaven, he was made blind and had his eyesight restored by Ananias (Acts 9:21). After his conversion and baptism, he became the Apostle to the Gentiles and had a significant role in the growth of the early church. So in Paul's life you see just how powerful redemptive grace is in turning a man, who sought to bring others to death, to someone who now seeks to bring others to eternal life with Christ. Paul, who once took joy in persecuting, later on took joy being persecuted for proclaiming the word of Christ. Therefore, by believing in Christ as the Son of God, then you can also pray to Him and seek forgiveness for your past sins and repenting of them. The

Good Father, Bad Father

first and most important step towards eternal life is believing in Jesus Christ as the Son of God, who is now in heaven hearing your prayers.

Therefore, why do human priests exist, if Jesus Christ can more than cover your sins through His one-time and infinite sacrifice on the cross? Daniel 8:11-12 tells us that, when speaking of the Papacy,

> *"Yea, he magnified himself even to the prince of the host, and by him the daily sacrifice was taken away, and the place of his sanctuary was cast down. And an host was given him against the daily sacrifice by reason of transgression, it cast down the truth to the ground; and it practiced, and prospered."*

Therefore, the reason why human priests still exist today is via transgression, and presumption. The human priest blocks the way Christ established on earth and in heaven, for the salvation of those who believe in Christ. In this sense, the human priest is an anti-Christ, in the sense he opposes and counteracts Christ's heavenly priesthood. Paul speaks of Christ's priesthood in Hebrews 7:27, "Who needeth not daily, as those high priests, to offer up sacrifice, first for his own sins, and then for the people's: for this he did once, when he offered up himself." Thus, the human priesthood system of a daily sacrifice was upgraded by God to a more perfect system whereby the Son of God, Jesus Christ, becomes both the sacrifice and the high-priest. Only Jesus Christ can be considered both the sacrifice and the High-priest because He himself is infinite alongside God the Father. Paul summarizes these conclusions about Christ by stating in Hebrews 8:1,2, "Now of the things which we have spoken this is the sum: We have such an high priest, who is set on the right hand of the throne of the Majesty in the heavens. A minister of the sanctuary, and of the true tabernacle, which the Lord pitched, and not man." It was the realization of these Biblical truths that led to a movement to reform the Roman Catholic Church and its doctrines, rituals, and traditions. This would movement would forever be known as the Protestant Reformation.

Chapter 14: The Church of Sardis and the 5th Seal

What marked the end of the Church of Thyatira and the beginning of the Church of Sardis was Martin Luther's actions that started a process to bring back the authority and appreciation of the Word of God back to the common people and this occurred from 1517-1755. The series of calls for reforms by Martin Luther and other reformers would be called the Protestant reformation. The man who history would point to as the beginner of the Protestant reformation would be Martin Luther. It would be during the Church of Sardis and the fifth seal, which would be the Church of the Protestant Reformation. The name "Sardis" means renewal, and during this time period there was the renewal of the doctrines and teachings of the Bible brought about by the Protestant reforms that were done by many reformers. The following is the message of the Church of Sardis and the fifth seal:

And unto the angel of the Church in Sardis write; These things saith he that hath the seven Spirits of God, and the seven stars; I know thy works, that thou hast a name that thou livest, and art dead. Be watchful, and strengthen the things which remain, that are ready to die; for I have not found thy works perfect before God. Remember therefore how thou hast received and heard, and hold fast, and repent. If therefore thou shalt not watch, I come on thee as a thief, and thou shalt not know what hour I will come upon thee. Thou hast a few names even in Sardis which have not defiled their garments; and they shall walk with me in white; for they are worthy. He that overcometh, the same shall be clothed in white raiment; and I will not blot out his name out of the book of life, but I will confess his name before my Father, and before his angels. He that hath an ear, let him hear what the Spirit saith unto the churches. - Revelation 3:1-6

And when he had opened the fifth seal, I saw under the altar the souls of them that were slain for the word of God, and for the testimony which they held: And they cried with a loud voice, saying, How long, O Lord, holy and true, dost thou not judge and avenge our blood on them that dwell on the earth? And white robes were given unto every one of them; and it was said unto them, that they should rest for a little season, until their fellow servants also and their brethren, that should be killed as they were, should be fulfilled. - Revelation 6:9-11

After more than 400 years without the Bible in the hands of the common people, Europe and the known world were in great spiritual darkness. The Protestant Reformation took God's people out of the spiritual darkness of the Dark and Middle ages. The many individual reforms of the Protestant reformers were similar to small candles that slowly lit a dark world in which Christ's church spent well-over a millennium. God and Christ's church became accustomed to the darkness. Therefore, the lights of the Protestant Reformation had to come at a gradual pace until all the lights of the Protestant Reformation were combined to restore the full brightness of light that emanated from the Early Christian Church of Ephesus. Similarly, each individual Protestant reform was not perfect in the eyes of God, even though they brought to light an important truth. The problem

Good Father, Bad Father

with each individual protestant reform, and the Church that resulted from it, was that it was still a mixture of truth and falsehood. Keep in mind, for more than 1000 years the Roman Catholic Church has been mixing the pure Biblical doctrines of God with the lies of paganism. The individual Protestant reforms were still polluted with the spiritual doctrines of the Roman church. The Protestant reforms were a step in the right direction because they helped clean a lot of the spiritual doctrines and clarified a lot of what was being said in the Bible in terms of salvation through Christ alone, Bible prophecy, and the Papal system being the Anti-Christ system. Despite this, many of the Protestant reforms still held onto one falsehood, which was Sunday worship. This falsehood is not Biblical, but it is a mark and blemish of the Roman Catholic system. In 1868, Monsignor Louis Segur spoke about the problem that the Protestant churches face. He states "The observance of Sunday by the Protestants is an homage they pay, in spite of themselves, to the authority of the [Catholic] Church."[88] As Christ stated earlier in His message to the Church of Sardis, the individual Protestant reforms were not perfect in the eyes of God. The failure to abide by God's 7th Day-Sabbath (Saturday) will eventually come to haunt the Protestants who continued to believe and teach Sunday worship.

But despite this in the mercy of God, He asked this Church of Sardis to be "watchful, and strengthen what remained and that was at the point of death," because the Roman Catholic church in retaliation launched a counter-reformation using the Jesuits, who would secretly infiltrate and control all Protestant Churches and bring them back into

---

[88] Monsignor Louis Segur, *Plain Talk about the Protestantism of Today* (1868), p.213, excerpt from pg. 147, The Secret Terrorists, By Bill Hughes, 2002.)

the hands of the Pope. These Jesuits, would be as what Jesus said in Matthew 23:27, 28, "Woe unto you, scribes and Pharisees, hypocrites! For ye are like unto whited sepulchers, which indeed appear beautiful outward, but are within ye are full of dead men's bones, and of all uncleanness. Even so ye also outwardly appear righteous unto men, but within ye are full of hypocrisy and iniquity." The Jesuits launched a new era of inquisitions and persecutions on account of the spread of the Bible and its many biblical truths. The Jesuit's Counter Reformation resulted in many more martyrs who died for the name of Jesus Christ and the truth of His Holy Bible, which is evident in the fifth seal and the souls under the altar. The Jesuit led counter-reformation evident in the inquisition and persecution of God's people is still going on today and will continue in the near future under different pretexts and more modern technology.

Chapter 15: Martin Luther and the Dawn of the Protestant Reformation

Martin Luther put into words and had the courage to express the words that many noble and intelligent men throughout the Middle-Ages wanted to say of the Roman Catholic institution, that it was a horrible scam. The actions of the Pope and the papal office throughout the Middle-Ages have put into question for many the existence of God and the authenticity of the Bible. Martin Luther and all the reformers of the Protestant Reformation would forever restore the authenticity of God and His Holy word found in the Bible. The American People's encyclopedia states concerning Luther's critical critique of the Roman Catholic Church:

> *"All-high minded men recognized that much was amiss in the church. The enforcement of clerical celibacy in the eleventh century had resulted in widespread clerical concubinage. The attempt to finance the Papacy as an international institution had led to making merchandise of spiritual goods. Partly a result of the gold drawn to Rome, the Parish clergy were miserably supported and the local parishes were grossly neglected. Popular superstition was rife as to the cult of the Saints, the miraculous power of relics, and the merit of pilgrimage to holy sites,."*[89]

---

[89] pg. 32 Luther, MartinAPE-Vol.12-Grolier Incorporated-New

Thus, Martin Luther and the other reformers had brought to light many of the false and pagan doctrines within the Roman Catholic Church because they were not found in the Bible. The Bible that was hidden for many years served as a light for many Roman Catholics during this time and it led them out of the Roman Catholic Church.

What separated Luther from other contemporary reformers is that "Luther attacked the Church on the doctrines and also the life of Church.[90] " Martin Luther considered the fundamental abuse of Roman Catholic Church's power was 'the attempt of man to put himself right with God through his own good deeds and by appropriating the good deeds of the saints,"[91] In other words, Christ and His unique salvation become irrelevant to those who were inside the Roman Catholic System, and prayed to saints on their behalf instead of praying directly to Christ. According to Luther, if any man or woman is to enjoy God's salvation, only available through the prayers to Jesus Christ, then they must realize that they are saved due to God's favor even though man remains unworthy.[92] Martin Luther touched a biblical doctrine that was not taught by the Roman Church at the time, and that doctrine was the justification by faith, which means if we believe in the Jesus Christ as the Son of God and that He died and resurrected to cover the sins of mankind then Christ accepts us if we believe and have faith in him. It is based on this faith that will determine our future actions and how we live our lives in accordance with the Ten Commandments, which is the guide for humanity to live according to the heavenly-principles. This principle is summed in the

---

York, 1967, Library Congress Catalog Card Number: 67-10584
[90] pg,32. Martin Luther, Ibid.
[91] pg,32. Martin Luther, Ibid.
[92] pg,32. Martin Luther, Ibid.

words of Christ in John 3:16, "For God so loved the world, that he gave his only begotten Son, that whosoever believeth in him should not perish, but have everlasting life." It is our belief and faith in God that should continually direct us to pray and seek forgiveness of our sins in Jesus Christ and lead us to embrace the Words of the Old and New Testament.

Martin Luther's strong commitment and trust in the Word of God brought cultivated the necessary confidence and conviction, which he and other reformers needed to confront the pope on many of the injustices of the time.[93] The Papal practice of Indulgence or the sale of notes that pardon sins was by far one of the most anti-Christian things the Roman Church has done, along with the slaughter of whole genuine communities of Christianity. To sell sin forgiveness notes is to profit from lies about God's salvation, no different from the Pharisees and Sadducees during the time of Christ.[94] These forgiveness notes were at first given to people who participated in the Crusades or Inquisition, or any activity in which the Roman Catholic Church would gain from the sins of its followers.[95] Therefore those who were contributors to the continual success of the Roman Church were given false credits, which could be redeemed for the apparent forgiveness of penalties and sins against God in this life and after death[96] . The American People's Encyclopedia mentions how the Church used this virtual ethical credit system to control the actions and behavior of the public so that they supported anything that was made by the Papacy:

---

[93] pg,32. Martin Luther, Ibid.
[94] pg,32. Martin Luther, Ibid.
[95] pg,32. Martin Luther, Ibid.
[96] pg,32. Martin Luther, Ibid.

> *Originally indulgences remitted penalties imposed by the Church; they were acquired by going on a crusade or contributing to a crusade, or to any expense of the Church. In return the Pope, would transfer to the contributor, some of the merits of Christ and the Saints who were believed to have been better than they needed to be for their own salvation and had thereby accumulated some superfluous credits which could be made available to others. The indulgences were later extended to cover the penalties not only on earth but of purgatory, and some indulgences offered not only to remission of penalties but also of sins.* – [97]

The sale of indulgences by the Roman Catholic Church really was the tipping of all the evil the Church had done during the Dark and Middle Ages. On two occasions, Jesus forcefully chased out the money changers out of the temple because they were selling salvation and the forgiveness of sins at an exorbitant price. The Pharisees and Sadducees gained and did not distribute their earnings to those who most needed it within their community. Jesus also said that it is only through Him and Him alone in which anyone can be saved, in John 14: 6, "I am the way, the truth, and the life: no man cometh unto the Father, but by me." If you read the words of Paul in Romans 5:17, 18, you will clearly see why the sale of forgiveness notes by the Roman Catholic Church was so wrong. Paul states, "For if by one man's offence death reigned by one; much more they which receive abundance of grace and of the gift of righteousness shall reign in life by one, Jesus Christ. Therefore, as by the offence of one judgment came upon all men to condemnation; even so by the righteousness of

---

[97] pg,32. Martin Luther, Ibid.

Good Father, Bad Father

one the free gift came upon all men unto justification of life." Therefore, when the Roman Catholic Church sold the false claim that by buying an indulgence (sin forgiveness note) then your sins will be forgiven in heaven, it was scamming the uneducated populace of Europe at the time. Keep in mind, the Bible was still forbidden in the hands of the people in their local language. Thus, the Roman Catholic Church exploited the people of their hard-earned money through for their own sake.

The question is what did the Roman Catholic Church do with all the money raised from the sale of indulgences? The most likely answer is that it funded the trips to the New World to extend the Inquisition and also it funded more inquisitions in and throughout Europe. The Roman Catholic Church used the money from the sales of indulgences to finance a system whereby through the doctrine of discovery[98], they would kill, subjugate, and enslave whole communities of freeborn indigenous people native in the lands of Africa, North and South America, and Indonesia. Also, keep in mind that many monasteries served as community banks throughout the Dark ages. Thus, the sales of indulgences aided the Roman Church revenues at the spiritual expense of the people. Throughout the centuries, the influence of the bad father of lies, and the Roman Catholic Church created a religion that had many confusing concepts and ideas that entangled truth with lies. What made matters worse was that the Bible was banned from the public for 400-500 years before an independently published Bible was printed in a local language.[99] The general public of the Middle Ages had no stable foundation for their Christian faith. Therefore, many continued to believe what they were

---

[98] See notes section at the End of the book
[99] See notes section at the End of the book

being told in the hopes of growing closer with God. The reformers and the Protestant reformation brought back hope for many people because now they could worship God and learn about God without having anything to deal with an evil and corrupt institution that the Roman Catholic Church had become. The Roman Church had created a for-profit enterprise around a false system of salvation that was not of God. The leaders of the Roman Church were able to get away with this fraud of indulgences because the people did not have access to the Bible. However, God seeing the great injustice being done, lifted the Protestant Reformers to put an end of such practices and expose the evil of the Roman Catholic Church. God foretold the evil practices of the Roman Church during Middle-Ages using the Prophets of the Old Testament. At least 2000 years beforehand, in the prophecies of Daniel 7:25, it states when speaking of the Little Horn Roman Catholic Pope, "And he shall speak great words against the Most High, and shall wear out the saints of the Most High, and think to change times, and laws." Through Martin Luther and other reformers, the people during the time period of the Church of Sardis became aware that they were being lied to about a great many things. When the Bible reached their hands and they heard or read the Word of God, they learned Jesus was the only way to be saved. Through Christ, all that was needed was to pray in His name, and seek forgiveness for sins. A sign of overcoming sin and to live a life of righteousness is to separate yourself from sin and to do the will of the Good Father, which is found in the law and many lessons from the Bible. The people became aware that they did not need to go to the Roman Catholic Church and hassle with a priest to find salvation. They could find it in commune with Jesus in the comfort of their home with their family, and did not need to go to an extravagant church. What Martin

Good Father, Bad Father

Luther did was truly a rare accomplishment in challenging the Church's authority. The people found their new hope in the words of the Bible and they found the truth, which would be the only authority they would need.

In the Holy Scriptures, God's plan of salvation showed how Jesus Christ was prophesized to be the one-time infinite sacrifice for a lost and sinful finite human race. The Biblical prophecies would also point to the Little Horn of Daniel, the beast of Revelation 13, the Whore of Revelation 17, and the anti-Christ all pointed to the Roman Catholic Papacy and the Vatican as the source of all the evil in the physical world. These points, based on the Bible and history, would prove the Protestant reformers and Martin Luther were correct. The Bible proved to be the Holy-Inspired Word of God that was given to mankind out of the love and mercy of the Good Heavenly father. A sign of this truth is that the Roman Catholic Church has been an institution with close to 1700 years of existence as foretold in the prophecies of the Little Horn in Daniel 7 and 8, whose end is foretold to occur at the 2nd Coming of Jesus Christ. The following quote from the American People's encyclopedia encapsulates Martin Luther's defrocking of infallible authority, and revealing the true infallible authority was the Word of God in the Bible. The A.P.E. States:

> *When Luther's views were condemned by scholar commissioned by Pope Leo X to make a reply, Luther retorted by denying the infallibility of the Pope and even of a general council of the Church... [...] He was even allowed to debate in public at Leipzig in 1519 against the redoubtable Dr. John Eck. Again Luther asserted that popes and councils are not infallible. The sole infallible authority is the Scripture. The Papacy is of human rather than of divine institution,*[100]

Luther had unmasked the fraudulent spiritual authority that the Pope and the Roman Catholic Church claimed to have exercised. The idea of infallibility or the ability of always being right, proceeds from God and God alone. The Pope wrongly considers himself to be one with God. Therefore, the Pope considers himself always correct, even in disputes against the Protestant Reformation. The Pope even erroneously presumes to be correct in discrepancies between God's word and the words of the papacy. God and Jesus Christ do not and will not change their principles and their Commandments. God and Jesus Christ know they're right because they have already prophesied the future without evil in the universe. The Pope can't come close in justifying his claims, because he is only a man. Paul talks about Christ's immutable character and nature, when he states "Jesus Christ the same yesterday, and today and forever." The shameful lie of the sale of indulgences and also the many other lies concerning God and His Bible is what maintained the illusion of power of the Roman Catholic Church throughout the Dark and Middle-Ages. The basis of the power of the Roman Catholic Church was not the Love of God, but the greed of Satan for the destruction of souls through spiritual confusion and manipulation.

Due to Luther and other reformers who defended the truth, Protestantism grew throughout Europe. The name Protestant was not used until 1529 at the Diet of Speyer, as a designation for nobles who protested the policies of the Roman Church. [101]Within ten years the truths in which Luther and others revealed were gaining ground and also many princes converted to the understanding of Christianity that was solely based on the Word of God.[102] The American Peoples

---

[100] pg,33. Martin Luther, Ibid.
[101] Pg.296, Protestantism, A.P.E- Vol.15,

Encyclopedia states, "The Word Protestant arose at the Diet of Speyer, 1529, as a designation of the Lutheran princes who protested against the decree the diet requiring that Catholic minorities to be tolerated in Lutheran territories although Lutheran minorities were not to be tolerated in Catholic territories,"[103] Even though this name "Protestant" was not used until the late 1600-1700's, it did not become popular during the 16th century. The reformers preferred to be called the Evangelicals, which comes from the Greek word *Evangelion*, which means "good news.[104] " The term is still used today to denote protestant groups who don't agree with the Roman Catholic Institution. The difference between Protestants and Catholics came down to the authority of the word of God compared with the lack of scriptural authority, especially on faith and morals that is found within the Papacy. The American People's Encyclopedia states the following on the struggle between Good and evil:

Perhaps the most basic difference between the theologies of the two branches of Christianity is that Protestantism believes that Christ's office as the only unique mediator between God and men (1 Tim. 2:15); precludes any mediatorship on the part of the Church, so that historic Protestantism considers generally that the visible church has no teaching authority [...] and that grace of salvation cannot come through the instrumentality of sacramental rites or a priesthood," [105]

---

[102] pg.296,Protestantism, Ibid.
[103] pg.296,Protestantism, Ibid.
[104] pg.296,Protestantism, Ibid.
[105] Pg. 59, Christianity, Vol.5, American Peoples Encyclopedia, Grolier Incorporated, New York, NY 1967

Therefore the central point in the spiritual war between the Good Father and Bad Father is over the truth of the scriptural authority of the Bible versus the scriptural authority of the Roman Catholic Church. The difference in scriptural authority highlights the importance of proper Biblical interpretation especially of portions of the Bible such as in parts of Revelation where some prophecies of the Bible are given in metaphors and symbols. If you ask sincerely and earnestly for the Holy Spirit to reveal to you, the truth concerning Bible Prophecy, then the Holy Spirit will lead you to the truth. To make sure you are more receptive for the Holy Spirit, it is best you keep the Ten Commandments of God and repent of any sins. Jesus Christ said in the Book of John 14:15-17, "If ye love me, keep my commandments. And I shall pray to the Father, he shall give you another comforter, That He may abide with you forever. Even the Spirit, of truth, whom the world cannot receive, because it seeth him not, neither knoweth him. But ye knoweth him, because he dwelleth with you, and shall be in you." Here Jesus promises He will send the Holy Spirit to those who sincerely ask for his name. Also, keep in mind, that even Eve, who was deceived by Satan, was saved. This is an example of how far ranging is God's love for his children of Creation. In 1 Tim. 2:15, "Notwithstanding she shall be saved in childbearing, if they continue in faith, and charity and holiness with sobriety."

Once you understand, the Bible and its prophecies via the mercy of the Holy Spirit it becomes easier to proclaim these verses to others. In the same way God and Jesus Christ spoke and taught in parables, and symbols, the Bible and its prophets always have used a concordance of symbols, allegory, and parables to give a message to the people. For many of these symbols, allegories, and parables they

Good Father, Bad Father

are explained within the context of the Bible passage in which they are found. Also, at times an angel of God explicitly states the meaning of certain symbols to help the people understand and prevent them from making false interpretations. When dealing with Bible prophecy it is important to understand the many levels of truth in which God is trying to tell a human being through not only history, but also the literal and plain interpretation of the words in context using the symbols employed in the Bible. For example, when interpreting Daniel and Revelation you can be sure if an interpretation of a symbol, or metaphor is correct if there are multiple places in the Bible where you find the same or similar use of a symbol, or metaphor.

For example the beast of Revelation 13 that comes out of the sea, or the sea of peoples that composed Europe and the Middle East. The beast is also used in Daniel 4, as a symbol of a King who makes himself to be like a god. The reason why the beast is interpreted in such a way is because the King of Babylon Nebuchadnezzar after being revealed the Dream of the statue in Daniel 2, he seeks to become like a god and change his fate in Daniel 3. Remember in Daniel 2, God had revealed to King Nebuchadnezzar via Daniel the Kingdoms that will reign over the earth after the fall of Babylon, and Daniel stated that the King Nebuchadnezzar was represented as the head of Gold, and then Medo & Persia were represented as the chest and arms of silver; Greece was the thighs of bronze; and Rome the legs of Iron and then Rome became mixed with clay at its feet and toes symbol of the Roman Catholic Church. In Daniel 3, you will read how King Nebuchadnezzar after receiving this revelation from God, then made his own statute that was of pure gold and asked all of Babylon to bow down and worship it. Everyone did as the King asked except the Three Hebrew youths, who were thrown into the fire and were not harmed because they followed the 2nd Commandment of God that forbade the worship of statues. In Daniel Ch. 4, God punishes and humbles the King of Babylon by changing His mind to the mind of a beast and He spent 7 years outside eating grass of the field. Therefore, the beast here is also used as a symbol to denote a king or leader who sought to become like a god. Therefore, when you review the history of the leaders of Medo-Persia, Greece, Rome, and of the Roman Catholic Church many of them claimed to be descendants of the gods or one with the pagan gods. In Revelation 13, you see this literal interpretation of beast of Daniel 4 is used to describe the Roman Catholic Church, whose king, the pope, speaks blasphemies because he pretends to be like a god. A sign of this blasphemous presumption of the Pope is that he believes he is infallible, when in fact he is a fallible human sinner, like everyone else. Peter gives us clarity on the issue of biblical interpretation and scriptural authority when he states the following in 2 Peter 1:16-21:

> *"For we have not followed cunningly devised fables, when we made known unto you the power and cunning of our Lord Jesus Christ, but were eyewitnesses of his majesty. For he received from God the Father honour and glory, when there came such a voice to him from the excellent glory, "This is my beloved Son, in whom I am well pleased. And this voice which came from heaven we heard, when we were with him in the holy mount. We have also a more sure word of prophecy; whereunto ye do well that ye take heed, as unto a light that shineth in a dark place, until the day dawn, and the day star rise in your hearts. Knowing this first, that no prophecy of the scripture is of any private interpretation. For the prophecy came not in old time by the will of man; but holy men of God spake as they were moved by the Holy Ghost (2 Peter 1:16-21, KJV).*

Good Father, Bad Father

Therefore, when it comes to scriptural authority it comes from the Holy Spirit, and not the Church. How do you know if you are doing what God asks of you and therefore know that you are being led by the Holy Spirit? The only way to make sure you're being led by the Holy Spirit is to faithfully keep the Ten Commandments of God in the same way, Jesus Christ Our God and Creator, kept them on Earth to seek repentance of all the sins in your life. Therefore you can be sure that the Roman Catholic Church is not being led by the Holy Spirit, but it is being led by the Bad Father because the Roman Church still reveres its own false Ten Commandments in which they switched the 7th Day Sabbath to the 1st day of the week Sunday and it removed God's original 2nd commandment banning the idol worship. Thus, due to the removal of the 2nd commandment, the Roman Catholic Church has introduced an influx of worship of statutes, idols, and saints, throughout its history. Instead of being the Church that reflects the values of the Creator and triune God, the Roman Catholic Church became a church that reflected the values of ancient pagan polytheism and sun worship mixed with biblical concepts, people, and themes.

The Protestant reforms posed a threat to the spiritual and temporal authority of the Roman Catholic Church. The America People's Encyclopedia states concerning how the Roman Catholic Church ruled during the medieval centuries, "Medieval Catholicism heightened the emphasis upon the church as an institution, since it had temporal sovereignty, vast possessions, political power throughout Europe, and all the insignia of secular dominion."[106] It was with this temporal authority, the Roman Catholic Church sought to impose its

---

[106] pg.74, Church, APE-Vol.5-Grolier Incorporated, New York, Copyright 1967, Library of Congress Catalog Card Number:67-10584

hybrid pagan and Christian belief system on the public. With fear of the Pope rather than the love of God, many innocent Roman Catholics became loyal to lies rather than the truth of the Bible found in the Law and prophets of God. A sign of its papal temporal and spiritual authority was the implementation of the Gregorian calendar, named after Pope Gregory XIII, which is still in use today. The Gregorian calendar is a mixture of the Babylonian lunar calendar and its 13 months translated into 52-weeks spread out over 12 months of 365 solar days. Another great change that came with the Gregorian calendar is the changing New Year's Day from April 1st to January 1st. The change was made after millennia, people celebrated the start of a New Year to coincide with spring and it was moved to the dead of winter. At the time the Gregorian calendar was implemented in 1582, only England and other Protestant communities, nations, the North American Colonies did not observe the Gregorian calendar until later on. It would not be until 1752 then England would again recognize the Papacy and thus it would implement New Year's Day. The change of New Year's Day would also come after 1752 for the American Colonies."[107]

Another sign of the temporal authority of Roman Catholic Church is found in the prophecy of the Little Horn of Daniel 7. In Daniel 7:25, Daniel under the direction of the Holy Spirit wrote, "He shall speak words against the Most High, and shall wear out the Saints of the Most High, and shall think to change the times and the laws; and they shall be given into his hand for a time, two times, and half a time." During the time period of the church of Sardis, the people clearly saw the fulfillment of the Prophecy of the Little Horn of

---

[107] New Year's Day, pg.441, APE, Vol.13, 1967, New York

Daniel 7:25. The prophecy of the "Little Horn" of Daniel 7 and 8 was fulfilled in the papacy, located in the smallest political state in the world known as the Vatican. This Little Horn that is located at the Vatican speaks words against the Most High, The Good Father God, in a matter of ways. Martin Luther unveiled the fact the pope did not have any scriptural authority. The Pope being an individual, could not impose his private interpretation of scripture on other individuals. It would be via the Holy Spirit alone that will lead those who honestly and sincerely are seeking the truth and are seeking the eternal life that only Jesus Christ can bestow on those who are faithful to Him and His words, and do His will on the planet. The claim of papal infallibility would be another word spoken against the Most High, because only God and His words found in the Bible are infallible. A signal of God's infallibility is Bible prophecy, which ultimately foretells of the 2nd Coming of Jesus Christ and the End of the World as we know it.

Another sign of the degree to which the Papacy does things contrary to God, at the most important time for repentance, is the Pope himself proclaims the authority to elevate dead human beings to the Pantheon of false gods, which are then called either "Saint" or "Blessed." In Greek mythology, there were more than 30,000 deities and other mythical beings.[108] Today, the Roman Catholic Church has a pantheon of more than 10,000 "Saints" and "Blessed" people, who the church encourages its members to pray to instead of praying only to our Lord and Savior Jesus Christ.[109] Many of the Roman Catholic saints are patron saints for towns, cities, dioceses, and archdioceses. There are also many patron saints for different types of jobs,

---

[108] pg.232, Mythology, Vol.13, APE, New York, 1967

[109] http://saints.sqpn.com

professions, weather conditions, and even patron saints for health ailments and animals. Many of these patron saints reveal how much pagan superstition has entered into the Roman Catholic Church during the Dark and Middle-Ages, even in Modern-Times. For example, there are patron saints for bailiffs, accountants, and even some patron saints to help avoid thunderstorms, hail storms, or protect against a host of common health problems, such headaches, hangovers, common cold, and cancer. There are also specific patron saints for specific Roman Catholic secret societies, such as the Jesuits, the Order of St. Lazarus, the Teutonic knights, the Franciscan order, the Order of the Garter, and the Order of the Golden Militia. There are even patron saints for those rejected by religious orders and to protect and work against enemies of religion[110]. Many Roman Catholics pray to many of these various patron saints. There are many more patron saints that cover over 6,000 different categories. This demonstrates how "these patron saints" are not actually alive and are still very much dead. Leaders within the Roman Catholic Church attribute miracles linked to demons to these Saints, who can make themselves appear to be benevolent for the sake of giving credence to the lie of the immortality of the soul. Because these patron saints are dead and have not yet been resurrected, when prayers are made to these patron saints, many innocent Roman Catholics are unaware that they are praying to the Bad father and his demons. If you consider yourself a Christian, then it is best to lift all prayers to Jesus Christ. Christ, who is the One with the Good Father and is alive today. Jesus hears our prayers in heaven because He has resurrected and returned to the eternal life.

---

[110] http://saints.sqpn.com

Good Father, Bad Father

The overwhelming response to the reformers Hussites, Wycliffe, and Martin Luther were unprecedented. The Renaissance movement was sweeping throughout Europe, and along with it was the Protestant reformation. The Papacy had only recently started the expansion and conquest of the new world, and in Europe they were facing a greater threat to the Church. To address the growing truths of the Protestant Reformation, the church sought to use the strategies used during medieval times to contain the Albigenses and other groups that were preaching the Word of God straight from the Holy Bible. However the group that usually carried out the inquisitions was already busy abroad in the New World carrying out their own inquisition of the native indigenous peoples of America, Africa, and Asia in the New World that would not submit to the foreign authority of the Roman Church. The papacy needed another important religious group to lead the counter-reformation. The group the church turned to was the Jesuit.

Chapter 16: The Jesuits and the Counter- Reformation

There is no other group within the Roman Catholic Church that has caused so much death, deception, and disaster than the Jesuits. The beginning of the Jesuits is intertwined with the life of the founder of the order, Ignatius of Loyola (1491-1556). The Jesuits would become the Pope's personal army of priests ready to obey his orders, and obey his word over the Word of God. In 1538, they decided to officially form a permanent religious organization within the Roman Church.[111] Ignatius Loyola and the Jesuits developed a comprehensive plan for the activities of the order. They also devised an evil formula for how the order could help the Pope and the Roman Catholic Church gain control of the whole world.[112] The intended purpose of the Jesuit order was expressed in their plan of activities, which included a pledge to do whatever the Pope may command, to work such as spreading the presence and influence of the Roman Catholic Church throughout the world in foreign missions, and work towards the education of youth to develop potential recruits in the future for the order. In educating the youth the Jesuit Order would create a

---

[111] pg.506, Jesuits, American Peoples Encyclopedia, Vol.10, Grolier Incorporated, 1967
[112] pg.506, Jesuits, Ibid.

future generation of individuals who would be sympathetic toward the Pope and Roman Catholic Church, without knowing what the Pope and Jesuits do in secret. [113]The Jesuits' plan of activities for their order was presented by Ignatius Loyola to Pope Paul III, who personally liked the idea of creating the Jesuits considering the rapid spread of Protestantism was largely unchecked at the time.[114] However, there was immediate opposition to the Jesuit's plan from Cardinals who were part of other religious orders within the Church.[115] Despite the early opposition to the approval of this group, the Society of Jesus was officially recognized as a Catholic order on Sept.27, 1540 via a papal bull which recognized the Jesuits.[116]

Similar to the different hierarchies in different ancient occult pagan societies, such as Mithraism, the Jesuits had developed a sophisticated internal structure for its organization.[117] The Jesuits are divided into four classes: novices, scholastics, coadjutors, and professed fathers.[118] In the novice class of the Society of Jesus, the initiate undergoes a short period of trial as a postulate as in when entering and joining any cult or secret society. During the initial two years, the novice spends most of his time involved in the spiritual exercises. Prayer, reading, and meditation, are all parts of the Jesuits spiritual exercises. The Jesuits spiritual exercises were a set of a controlled movements and experiences in which an individual's mind is controlled and broken down and reshaped by a Jesuit Superior for the purpose of building absolute obedience.[119] If for some reason the

---

[113] pg.506, Jesuits, Ibid.
[114] pg.505, Jesuits, Ibid.
[115] pg.505, Jesuits, Ibid.
[116] pg.506, Jesuits, Ibid.
[117] pg.506, Jesuits, Ibid.
[118] pg.506, Jesuits, Ibid.

Jesuit chooses to leave the society his mind and imagination would be scarred due to the previous spiritual exercises. These spiritual exercises resemble in many cases eastern mysticism, found in many branches of Hinduism. The spiritual exercises involved performances of certain Catholic dogmas and precepts, where an emphasis on every sense is taken note in order to leave an impression of Roman Catholicism on various portions of the brain. Such spiritual exercises would ingrain the idea of Roman Catholicism as an impulse and memory, rather than a truth with a stream of logic and reasoning. Edmond Paris described the phenomena as controlled-auto suggestion, which is used to program any individual with irrational behaviors that will take long time to overcome. [120]Therefore, with this information in mind, the Jesuit Spiritual Exercises were actually the principles of psychology that came into play in the 20th and 21st century in the formation of television and Hollywood. The principles of the Jesuit Spiritual exercises have even been used in marketing to the masses by making products that call to people's pride and desires. Such massive consumer advertising ultimately is used to develop people's irrational greed to gratify their senses and appetites. Jesus Christ, had the best solution for this when he stated in Matthew 6:31-33, "Therefore, take no thought, saying, What shall we eat? or, What shall we drink? Or, Wherewithal shall be clothed?" (For after all these things do the Gentiles seek;) for your heavenly Father knoweth that ye have need of all these things. But seek ye first the Kingdom of God,

---

[119] pg. 25, 34-35, H. Boehmer, - Les Jesuites (Armand, Colin, Paris, 1910) as quoted in pg. 30 The Secret History of The Jesuits, By Edmond Paris, Chick Publications

[120] pg.30, The Secret History of the Jesuits, by Edmond Paris, Chick Publications,

and his righteousness; and all these things shall added unto you." For Christ, what is most important is not who has the most money, or it isn't who has the best food supplies, or who wears the best clothes. By trusting in God, and seeking to develop His Character in your own life is to seek the Kingdom of God and strengthen your relationship with the Good Father. When you strengthen yourself with the Good Father, then the enemy Bad Father would seek to drive you off the path you're on with Jesus Christ.

The coadjutors are ordained priests, who out of some flaw in character, ability, or health necessary are not able to meet the high rigorous standards of professed father.[121] The class of coadjutors is most important in the realm of espionage, and infiltration into other organizations. The Jesuit General and all other high provincial officials within the Jesuit order are professed fathers. The Professed fathers are required to take and retake the oaths of chastity, poverty, and obedience, and also take an additional vow of allegiance to the pope.[122]

Besides their typical vows, there is an extreme secret oath taken by some Jesuits. This core inner group of the Jesuits takes a blood oath similar to other occult satanic secret societies. An excerpt from the Jesuits extreme oath, highlights how the Jesuits only serve the purpose of deceiving, torturing, and killing those Protestants individuals who speak the truth concerning God, His word, and Ten Commandments. The Jesuits were created to oppose any Protestants that openly opposed papal authority. The most egregious part of this extreme oath is the following:

---

[121] pg. 506, Jesuits, Ibid.
[122] pg. 506, Jesuits, Ibid.

Good Father, Bad Father

I will spare neither age, sex, or condition, and that I will hang, burn, waste, boil, flay, strangle, and bury alive these infamous heretics; rip up the stomachs and wombs of their women, and crush their infants' heads against the walls in order to annihilate their execrable race. That when the same cannot be done openly, I will secretly use the poisonous cup, the strangulation cord, the steel of the poniard, or the leaden bullet, regardless of honor, rank, dignity, or authority of persons, whatever maybe their condition in life, either public or private, as I at any time may be directed so to do by any agents of the Pope or superior of the Brotherhood of the Holy Father of the Society of Jesus. In confirmation, of which I hereby dedicate my life, soul, and all corporal powers, and with the dagger which I now receive I will subscribe my name written in my blood in testimony thereof; and should I prove false or weaken in my determination, may my brethren and fellow soldiers of the militia of the Pope cut off my hands and feet and my throat from ear to ear, my belly opened and sulphur burned therein with all the punishment that can be inflicted upon me on earth and my soul shall be tortured by demons in eternal hell forever. —[123]

The Jesuits as a group would become what Jesus foretold in Matthew 23:25-28,:

Woe unto you, scribes and Pharisees, hypocrites! For ye make clean the outside of the cup and the platter, but within they are full of extortion and excess. Thou blind Pharisee, cleanse first that which is within the cup and platter, that the outside may be clean also. Woe, to you scribes and Pharisees, hypocrites! For ye are like unto a whited sepulchers, which indeed appear beautiful, but are within full of dead men's bones of all

---

[123] From U.S. Congressional Record – House, February 15, 1913, Pg. 3216, and Edwin A. Sherman, The Engineer Corps of Hell, or Rome's Sapper's and Miners, Private Subsciption,1883, pg. 118-124

> *uncleanliness. Even so ye also outwardly appear righteous to men, but within you are full of hypocrisy and iniquity, (Matt 23:25-28, KJV).*

These words of Christ were symbolic of not only many religious leaders, like the Gnostics, but also popes, cardinals, bishops, and priests, especially of the Jesuit order. Many of these religious leaders do evil in secret using the name of God (Jesus) in public. To use the name of "Jesus," the Jesuits use the name of God in vain, especially when they seek to do evil in secret. This is taking the Lord's name in vain, which not only breaks God's Ten Commandments, but also the Roman Catholic Commandments as well, "Thou shalt not take the name of the Lord thy God in vain; for the Lord will not hold him guiltless that taketh His name in vain," (Exodus 20:7).

Once the Jesuits were officially recognized, the papacy made another move in response to the growing popularity of Protestantism. At the end of the 12th and early 13th century, the Roman Catholic Church created Roman tribunals that dealt with cases of "heresy."[124] The Roman tribunals were called the Roman Inquisition, which were created by not so Innocent III to stifle the Albigenses in the 13th century. Due to the spread of Protestantism in the 16th century, Paul III reorganized the "Roman Inquisition" into a new department within the Vatican called "The Holy Office of the Inquisition." This new office was created to be the supreme doctrinal tribunal that would be in charge of carrying out persecution, torture, and death of any Christian group that recognizes God's authority via the Holy Scriptures over the authority of the papacy.[125] This office has

---

[124] pg.264, Inquisition, APE-Vol.10, Grolier Incorporated, 1967,
[125] pg.264, Inquisition, Ibid.

continued to exist in modern-times under the shortened name, "the Holy Office" that at one time was led by Cardinal Ratzinger. Popes throughout history have used the Jesuits and the Holy Office of the Inquisition to plan, organize, and execute the inquisition on a global scale.[126] The inquisition was one of the most horrible things that the Roman Catholic Church was part of in the 16th and 17th centuries.[127] This would be the beginning of the Roman Catholic Church's worldwide inquisition on native peoples who had not yet learned about Christ. The inquisition extended to the New World and the Spanish colonies and for a period of time to Portuguese colonies.[128] After nearly two centuries of intermittent Inquisitions, the Inquisition has become the prime and sublime example of religious persecution and cruel injustice in the name of religion.[129] The Inquisition only achieved the selfish desires of the Pope and Roman church hierarchy to continue to reign unopposed. The office of the papacy being the seat of the anti-Christ, is no surprise that the popes were opposed to the Light of Truth, of the Bible and thus committed all of this bloodshed to satisfy their greedy thirst for power and global control.

---

[126] pg.264, Inquisition, Ibid.
[127] See Notes at the end of the book
[128] pg.264, Inquisition, Ibid.
[129] pg.264, Inquisition, Ibid.

Chapter 17: The Inquisition

In response to the growing popularity of the truth of Bible-based Protestantism, and with it the spread of the Bible in the local language, the Papal hierarchy during this time called for major inquisitions in many countries throughout Europe. Two major inquisitions that occurred during the era of the Church of Sardis was the infamous Spanish Inquisition and the other was the French Inquisition. During this time period, there were many martyrs, who in knowing and learning the Biblical truths believed in the reality of Jesus Christ and His resurrection. This allowed the martyrs with confidence to stand for the truth, even though it may cost them their lives. By having their eyes set on Christ and following His example, they were able to gain eternal life. The 5th seal, speaks of the Souls under the Altar that died for the Word of God, and cried out to Him, "How long, O Lord, holy and true, dost thou not judge and avenge our blood on them that dwell on the earth?" The 5th seal and the Souls under the altar allude to the widespread amount of martyrs during the period of the Church of Sardis in 1517-1755. John in Revelation 20:4 reveals the future fate of these souls,

> *"And I saw thrones, and they sat upon them, and judgment was given unto them: and I saw the souls of them that were beheaded for the witness of Jesus, and for the Word of God,*

> *and which had not worshipped the beast, neither his image, neither had received his mark upon their foreheads, or in their hands; and they lived and reigned with Christ a thousand years."*

Thus, the living souls who died for Christ and His Word, were later on resurrected to eternal life.

All the inquisitions in general followed a process. The Papal hierarchy would first send an envoy to the leading monarch in an area where Protestantism was spreading. Usually, the monarch in question would accept the inquisition in their territory at the pain of death and/or removal of their Kingdom.[130] The same methods would be employed to carry out the Spanish inquisition as in the early 13th century.[131] There were attempts made by the agents of the inquisition to bring back the accused back to the Catholic faith and renounce the truth of the Bible, and their faith in Christ. This was usually done through some of the most gruesome torture techniques created to inflict unnecessary pain on a victim, whose only crime in the eyes of the Roman Church was to believe in God and His Word. The issue at the heart of the inquisition was either to choose to continue in an illegitimate faith in the Papal throne and their human laws, or to continue in the true faith in Jesus Christ and His Commandments for eternal life found in the Bible. If the accused individual rejected the attempts to recant their faith in Jesus Christ and His Holy words, then the agents of the inquisitions would hand over the prisoner to the civil power for the execution of the sentence, which often times was death by being burned alive at the stake or being beheaded.[132] The 'auto da

---

[130] pg.264, Inquisition, A.P.E-Vol.10, Grolier Incorporated, 1967,

[131] pg.264, Inquisition, Ibid.

Good Father, Bad Father

fe,' which was the Portuguese name for the Act of Faith, was the official name of the ceremony in which those who were sentenced to death by the inquisition would be paraded around their communities and the whole town would come to see a neighbor or a loved one in their community be burned alive.[133] The people would see the flames escalate and engulf the innocent follower of Jesus Christ. The people would smell the awful odor of roasted human flesh. They would hear the cries of pain and agony of a human being who had not killed, robbed, or raped anyone. The martyrs only wanted to continue in the love of truth, wisdom and understanding that only Jesus Christ and the Holy Spirit can give. In the words of God, they found the reality that was hidden from them by the Church during the Middle Ages. They came to realize the bleak reality and the true character of the Papacy, that it was the Mother of all the Harlots, as in the words of God through John the Revelator in Ch.17 verses 1-2, "Come, I will show you the judgment of the great harlot, who is seated upon many waters, with whom the Kings of the Earth have committed fornication; and with the wine of whose fornication the dwellers of the earth have become drunk."

During the Spanish and French inquisition humanity saw an example for future generations of the results of shameless public interaction between the great Harlot, the Roman Catholic Church, and the civil authorities and Kings. God's people were represented by the clean Virgin Woman from Rev.12. In the same way, Jesus is betrothed to a clean virgin woman symbolic of all of God's people throughout time. The bad father, Satan, copies Jesus and creates his

---

[132] pg. 264, Inquisition, Ibid.

[133] pg. 264, Inquisition, Ibid.

own church of many of God's people entrapped in the anti-Christ system through lies concerning God, His law, and His Bible. The clean virgin woman from Revelation 12 is a metaphor of those individuals throughout the generations who have become saved in Christ and believing in Him and His promises of eternal life. The bad father, Satan, inebriates his Church with false doctrines and then he passes and even induces his followers to drink the cup of wine, which includes supporting the unjust and atrocious deaths of the followers of Jesus Christ, who are the enemies of the bad father and his whore. In Revelation 17: verse 5 and 6, John describes this whore drinking wine that includes the blood of the followers of Jesus Christ, "on her forehead was written a name of mystery: 'Babylon the great, mother of harlots and of earth's abominations.' And I saw the woman, drunk with the blood of the saints and the blood of the martyrs of Jesus." This passage is pretty clear and straightforward of what the Bible and God thinks about the leadership of the Roman Catholic Church, who has killed many of His innocent followers and children throughout the centuries.

Thus, those who refused to drink the wine of this whore were burned for exercising their free will that did not submit to peer-pressure or popular opinion. The fornication between the Roman Catholic Papacy and the monarchs of Spain and other European countries led to a win-win for the Roman Church and the civil government at the expense of many martyred Protestants, who died in front of their eyes. The Protestants that died for the Word of God during this time period are best described by Paul in 1 Thessalonians 4:14, "For if we believe that Jesus died and rose again, even so them also which sleep in Jesus will God bring with him." The Spanish inquisition was a way for the Pope to exercise his spiritual and temporal authority and for the Spanish monarchs to profit from the deaths of Christians. The American Peoples Encyclopedia states, "Strongly influenced by, the civil power, the Spanish Inquisition became a political instrument used as a means of getting rid of political foes and of securing coveted wealth, and was often guilty of cruelties that are today considered inhuman.[134] " According to the words of Christ, those that died in the faith of Jesus were in a better position than those who lived with the riches gained via evil means. In Mark 8:36, Christ says, "For what shall it profit a man, if he shall gain the whole world, and lose his own soul?" Through possessing a greed for power and wealth, the Papal hierarchy and the monarchs profited from the inquisition by keeping the property and wealth of the martyred Protestants. The members of the papal hierarchy and monarchs who benefited from the deaths of innocent people would according to Christ lose their own souls for the sake of riches and property that they will not be able to take with them to the grave. Thus, those that believe in Jesus Christ and died for His name's sake actually got the reward of eternal life and the riches of heaven. Jesus Christ's quote from Luke 6:22-24 can summarize what occurred during the time of the Inquisition throughout Europe,

> *"Blessed are ye, when men shall hate you, and when they shall separate you from their company, and shall reproach you and cast out your name as evil, for the Son of Man's sake. Rejoice ye in that day, and leap for joy: for, behold, your reward is in heaven: for in the like manner did their fathers unto the prophets. But woe unto you that are rich! For ye have already received your consolation."*

---

[134] pg. 264, Inquisition, Ibid.

Therefore, the Protestants that died in the faith and the love of Christ and His Words will receive the reward of eternal life for believing in Christ unto death, and those who lived and kept the possessions of the dead Protestants received their consolation.

The 2nd major inquisition was in France, where Papal Crusades and the inquisition occurred in the late 12th and 13th century against the innocent Albigenses. Now, during the time of the Church of Sardis from the early 16th- mid 18th century, a new group of people drew the ire of the Vatican. This group was the Huguenots, who were composed of many French Protestants, many of whom were Calvinists from 16th- 18th centuries. John Calvin, a French clergyman who found the truth concerning the Bible, God, and the salvation only found in Jesus Christ, drew many French Middle Class and nobility to Biblical Christianity and the gospel of Christ.[135] The French Kingdom during most of the first half of the 16th century was ruled and controlled by the reign of Francis I (1515-1547).[136] Francis I was at first tolerant of the beliefs of the Protestants, but however things changed towards the end of the reign in which resulted in widespread persecution of the Huguenots throughout France.[137] After the death of Francis I, his son Henry II, developed a tribunal to carry out the activities of the inquisition which were to search and burn all innocent Bible-believing Christians otherwise known as heretics. Due to the widespread persecutions of Christian Protestants, especially in France, they fled from their homes, families, communities, and nations and found a safe haven in Geneva, Switzerland.[138] The persecutions

---

[135] Pg.50,Huguenot, Ibid.
[136] Pg.50,Huguenot, Ibid.
[137] Pg.50,Huguenot, Ibid.
[138] Pg.50,Huguenot, Ibid.

Good Father, Bad Father

during the Church of Sardis helped spread the Protestant movement in many other areas throughout the world, especially the New World.

Similar to the early persecutions of the early Christians of the Church of Ephesus and Smyrna churches, the persecution and the deaths of Christians led to the increase of Christians. In 1559, a National Evangelical Church was created in France.[139] With the French royal families support, on Aug.24, 1572 the bloodiest day for French Christians would be forever memorialized as "St. Bartholomew Massacre." On that horrible day and in the days that followed, there were widespread deaths of many French Protestants, especially of Protestant nobles. The leaders of the Protestant movement in France at the time were Protestant nobles. Many French Protestants died in their faith in Jesus Christ and their hope of eternal life. The survivors of the massacre later organized an independent church for all Protestants, but it was independent from any nobility and the Royal monarch in terms of leadership.[140] The reformed Church had reorganized its power structure on a representative basis largely independent of the nobles and the crown, which in the past, had an important part in the French Protestant movement.[141] After the reorganization, the Huguenots were now a political party as well as a religious movement.[142]

Henry IV, who was a Protestant sympathizer, accepted Catholicism in order to bring an end war in 1598, by the Edict of Nantes.[143] The Edict granted Protestants religious liberty and full

---

[139] Pg.50,Huguenot, Ibid.
[140] Pg.50,Huguenot, Ibid.
[141] Pg.50,Huguenot, Ibid.
[142] Pg.50,Huguenot, Ibid.
[143] Pg.50,Huguenot, Ibid.

exercise of other rights of citizenship.[144] This sounds good however in the 1650's Louis XIV would revoke the Edict of Nantes and thus causing another campaign of persecution against the Protestants. When the Edict of Nantes was revoked there was another exodus of Protestant French nobles and the most useful French citizens to other countries that were havens for Protestants such as Prussia, Scotland, Netherlands, and to the English Colonies in North America.[145] It would not be until the French Revolution in the late 18th century, when Protestants in France would be given equality and the name Huguenots would no longer be used."[146]

After the renewed onslaught of the Roman Catholic Church through the Jesuits and the inquisitions of the 16th, 17th, and early 18th centuries, there came a break as much of Protestantism flourished without any restraint, and the Word of God and the Bible became deeply embedded within society. Thus, the Love of God, and truth spread throughout all classes of society. Out of the darkness of the Middle-Ages, the Protestant reforms created a society that valued Biblical morals and cherished Holy integrity. As a result of the majority of the people valuing Biblical Christian values, many countries, nations, and peoples prospered as a whole. The time was approaching for the Church of Philadelphia, a Church of brotherly love in which would display the Love of Christ and love of Truth.

---

[144] Pg.50,Huguenot, Ibid.
[145] Pg.50,Huguenot, Ibid.
[146] Pg.50,Huguenot, Ibid.

Chapter 18: The Church of Philadelphia and the 6th Seal

The sixth church is the church of Philadelphia, which existed from 1755-1844 AD. The Church of Philadelphia correlates with the 6th seal. The 6th seal is composed of great signs of a destructive earthquake, the darkening of the sky, and falling stars, and other signs, which will occur at the 2nd Coming of Christ. Some of these great signs before the 2nd Coming of Christ actually took place during the same time as the Church of Philadelphia, which occurred towards the end of the tribulation of the 1260 prophetic years. The remaining signs include the sky opening up as a scroll and the mountains and islands moving out of their places. Another remaining sign that is on its way to being fulfilled is the kings and leaders of the world hiding in underground bases that exist today, and begging for the rocks to fall on them, so they can die and not see the 2nd Coming of Christ.

After experiencing the height of its power for more than 1,200 years, the Roman Catholic authority of the Pope subsided until it suffered its mortal wound to its authority. When the seventh seal is opened, it occurs when Christ says the words "It is done." Christ having the Key of David, to open and shutteth, ends His ministry in the Most Holy Place in the Heavenly sanctuary or Temple of God. The 7th seal signifies the end of His ministry in the Most Holy Place in heaven, which means Jesus will stop hearing and pardoning sins in preparation for the 2nd Coming of Christ. Then those who dwell in heaven will make a short trip to earth with Jesus Christ and the heavenly angels. They will make this short trip to bring back to heaven those on earth who are still found in the Book of Life.

The name of this Church, Philadelphia is derived from a city in Asia minor originally built by Attalus II for his brother Eumenes. Thus, this city was the first city to be named "Philadelphia." It is interesting that the modern-day city of Philadelphia in America arose in importance near the same time frame of the Church of Philadelphia. The message for the Church of Philadelphia and the sixth seal state the following:

And to the angel of the church in Philadelphia write; These things saith he that is holy, he that is true, he that hath the key of David, he that openeth, and no man shutteth; and shutteth, and no man openeth; I know thy works: behold, I have set before thee an open door, and no man can shut it,: for thou hast little strength, and kept my word, and hast not denied my name. Behold, I will make them of the synagogue of Satan, which say they are Jews, are not, but do lie,; behold, I will make them to come and worship before thy feet, and to know that I have loved thee,. Because thou hast kept the word of my patience, I will also will keep thee from the hour of temptation, which shall come upon all the world, to try them that dwell upon the earth. Behold, I come quickly: hold that fast which thou hast, that no man take thy crown. Him that overcometh will I make a pillar in the temple of my God, and he shall go no more out: and I will write my name of God, and the name of the city of my God, which is new Jerusalem, which cometh down out of heaven from my God: and I will write upon him my new name. He that hath an ear, let him hear what the Spirit saith unto the churches. – (Revelation 3:7-13, KJV)

> *And I beheld, when he had opened the sixth seal, and, lo, there was a great earthquake; and the sun became black as sackcloth of hair, and the moon became as blood; And the stars of heaven fell unto the earth, even as a fig tree casteth her untimely figs, when she is shaken of a mighty wind. And the heaven departed as a scroll, when it is rolled together; and every mountain and island were moved out of their places. And the kings of the earth, and the great men, and the rich men, and the chief captains, and the mighty men, and every bondman, and every free man, hid themselves in the dens and in the rocks of the mountains; And said to the mountains and rocks, Fall on us, and hide us from the face of him that sitteth on the throne, and from the wrath of the Lamb: For the great day of his wrath is come; and who shall be able to stand? - (Revelation 6:12-17).*

Jesus in the message of the Church of Philadelphia speaks of the door which no man can open or close, which refers to the door to the Most Holy Place in the Temple / Sanctuary in Heaven. Once Christ enters in the Most Holy Place it marks the beginning of the End Times. Christ begins the work of the investigative judgment to review and finalize the decisions for eternal life or death for those that died with faith in God and Christ. The same process will be done over all those living with faith. The sinner living in the End Times is to believe in Jesus Christ and His words, and not take the Mark of the Beast, or the enforced National Sunday Law. The Church of Philadelphia or the Church of "Brotherly love" was a church that was able to thrive because of the mortal wound of the beast or the Roman Catholic Church received during the French Revolution.

Aside from this, the Jesuits were also banned throughout Europe. This allowed for the Rise of many new Protestant institutions such as

Bible Societies, and Protestant missionaries, who unlike the Roman Catholic ambassadors, did not kill, steal, or covet the natural resources of the indigenous natives of India, Africa, and South America. To definitely mark the beginning of the End Times, then God sent three very strange signs to heaven and earth that made people wake up to the existence of God. These signs were the Lisbon earthquake, the Dark Day of New England, and the Night of Falling Stars. These were important signs of the rapidly approaching End Times. All of these signs ushered in the end of both the 1260-day prophecy and the 2300-day prophecy of Daniel. 7, 8, and 9. The 2300-day prophecy was the center of a new Protestant religious movement that helped revive the complete restoration of the truths of the Bible. Remember how each individual Protestant reform was like a small individual candlelight that was part of a much larger light of truth found in the Bible. There along came God's church that will be a remnant. This Church will combine all the Protestant reforms into one church. The remaining two reforms that were left of this church was the Biblical truth about the Seventh- Day Sabbath and the Biblical truth about the Holy Sanctuary. Jesus Christ now hears all the prayers of everyone who prays and seeks forgiveness for their sins against God and seeks to follow His teachings that are found in the Bible.

Chapter 19: Signs of the End Times

During the time period of the Church of Philadelphia, there were three important supernatural events that took place that were signals to the world of the quickly approaching End Times. These three signs were the Lisbon Earthquake, the Dark Day of New England, and the Falling Stars.

Thus, it was apparent to everyone living at the time that the solemn and supernatural events that took place in Lisbon were a sign of the approaching End Times and the 2nd Coming of Christ. Many readers of the Bible were keenly awakened by the widespread devastation of the Great Lisbon Earthquake. Matthew 24:7, Jesus warns of the signs of the End Times would be the following "For nation will rise against nation, and kingdom against kingdom: and there shall be famines, and pestilences, and earthquakes, in divers places." Keep in mind, during this time Colonial America was preparing to rise against Great Britain and the French Revolution, all occurred and many more revolutions spread throughout Europe and South America during the time period of 1755- 1844. The American Encyclopedia gives the following account of the Great Lisbon Earthquake:

> *Regarded as the most notable earthquake of history, was the Lisbon earthquake of November 1, 1755. There were two*

Eliseo Santos

> *violent shocks, one a little before 10 A.M. and another at noon, the first one being the greatest. It was All Saints' Day, and thousands of people were congregated in the churches, which were destroyed and many people were killed. Deaths in Lisbon alone were 50,000 out of a population 235,000. Thousands of additional causalities occurred in other towns of Portugal, and in Spain, Morocco, and Algeria, the shock being felt over an area of nearly 1.5 million square miles. Within six minutes in Lisbon, all large public buildings were ruined and 15,000 houses out of 20,000 made uninhabitable and Fires completed the destruction. A large tsunami resulted from the main shock. The great wave, variously estimated at 16 to 50 feet high, engulfed the shore for a half-mile. Bridges and walls were wrecked, ships torn from their moorings, and many people washed away to sea. In the West Indies 3540 miles away, the waves were 12 feet high.*[147]

The scale of destruction of the earthquake was on par with that of the 2011 Japan earthquake that caused similar widespread destruction in Japan. Imagine, within the span of six minutes, if 21% of the population of a major modern-city suddenly died. Now imagine if 75% of all the housing was suddenly made uninhabitable. This is why the earthquake of Lisbon was significant and was remembered for its widespread destruction. This earthquake is a microcosm of the destruction that will take place on a global level as the world makes its final rejection of God and His blameless principles in favor of fallible human principles.

The widespread supernatural destruction that was witnessed in Lisbon caused many secular poets, philosophers, and writers to reevaluate their atheist positions. Voltaire, whose dramas and plays before the Lisbon earthquake were about to be performed at the

---

[147] pg.13, American Peoples Encyclopedia, Vol. 7, Earthquake, Grolier Incorporated, New York

Good Father, Bad Father

opening of the theater at Lausanne, were after the Lisbon earthquake postponed. One writer commenting on the motive for the postponement states, referring to the Lisbon earthquake, "The earthquake had made all one thoughtful. They mistrusted their love of the drama, and filled the churches instead."[148] Voltaire and others, while not being fully familiar with the Bible started to think of the biblical concepts such as the End Times, the Last Judgment, and the meaning of these Biblical truths for humanity. The values of freedom of speech, thought, and conscience that come from the pure Biblical teachings of God are rapidly eroding in favor of man uniting around the fallible principles of mankind. The fallible human principles gravitate toward the implicit idea of a man trying to become like a god, but at the same time deny the existence of the one true All-mighty God. In actuality, this is the maxim of satanic philosophy. Satan will one day put his teachings to practice when he reveals to himself using the appearance of Jesus Christ, instead of his own natural appearance. The second important idea that we all must recognize or acknowledge, is the idea of the Creator God, and the idea everything you see, including yourself is ultimately attributable to the God's creation. The third important idea to recognize is the Bible is the basis of all truth of reality. The Bible was created out of the mercy and love of God the Creator, so that His people can get to know God and His will, revealed in the Ten Commandments and Bible prophecy. The final idea to recognize is that because you are living in these End Times, you have to first and foremost spiritually prepare, and then mentally and physically prepare yourselves for the 2nd Coming of Jesus Christ, who will put an end to evil on the planet. Therefore, if

---

[148] Tallentyre, "Life of Voltaire" – pg. 319 as quoted in Our Day in the Light of Prophecy, pg. 81)

Eliseo Santos

you wish to attain eternal life, first and foremost, you must believe in Jesus Christ as your Resurrected Savior and advocate in heaven. Then you should take time out of the day to seek God in prayer, and read and study the Bible. Applying the lessons learned from the Bible in your daily life will help prepare you to live eternally with God the creator.

After the great earthquake of the sixth seal, there came the supernatural events that occurred when the sun became covered with darkness. When did this happen, you may ask? It occurred on May 19, 1780, during the Dark Day of New England. Imagine it's a bright sunny day in May, and then suddenly at noon the sky and the sun become enshrouded in a deep darkness. This is what actually occurred during the Dark Day of New England. There are many accounts that verified the supernatural nature of events that occurred on that day. An article for the Boston Gazette and Country Journal of May 29, 1780, gives an hour by hour account of what occurred that day from the witnesses of men who worked at that time in liberal education,

> *About eleven o'clock the darkness was such as to demand our attention, and put us upon making observations. At half past eleven, in a room with three windows, twenty-four panes each, all open toward the southeast and south, large print could not be read by persons of good eyes. About twelve o'clock, the windows being still open, a candle cast a shade so well defined on the wall, as that profiles were taken with as much ease as they could have been in the night. About one o'clock, a glint of light, which had continued to this time in the east, shut in, and the darkness was greater than it had been for any time before... We dined about two, the windows all open, and two candles burning on the table. In the time of the greatest darkness some of the ....fowls went to their roost. Cocks crowed in answer to one another as they commonly do in the night. Woodcocks, which are night birds, whistled as they do*

Good Father, Bad Father

only in the dark. Frogs peeped. In short, there was the appearance of mid-night at noonday. About three o'clock the light in the west increased, the motion of the clouds [became] more quick, their color higher and more brasey than at any time before. There appeared to be quick flashes of coruscations, not unlike the aurora borealis... At half past four our company, which had passed an unexpected night very cheerfully together, broke up. – [149]

The account presents the very unique and unusual events that occurred on that day in New England. This account is further corroborated by the following account written by the President of Yale College at the time, Timothy Dwight, who wrote about that dark day in May and how it affected the Connecticut state legislature.

"The legislature of Connecticut was then in session at Hartford. A very general opinion prevailed that the day of judgment was at hands. The House of Representatives, being unable to transact their business, adjourned. A proposal to adjourn the council [a second legistlative-body called the Governor's council], was under consideration. When the opinion of Colonel Davenport was asked, he answered, "I am against an adjournment. The day of Judgment is either approaching or it is not. If it is not, there is no cause for adjournment,; if it is, I choose to be found doing my duty. I wish therefore that candles may be brought.'" [150]

Therefore, this is an event that did occur and it is in the record of the Connecticut Statehouse, and Massachusetts Statehouse. If the supernatural earthquake of Lisbon was an example of the quick and sudden destruction that is approaching for the whole world, this event

---

[149] Our Day In the Light of Prophecy - pg. 88
[150] Barber, "Connecticut Historical Collection," P. 403. as quoted in Our Day In The Light of Prophecy, pg. 90

Eliseo Santos

is an example of the darkness which is covering the whole world during these End Times.

The final sign of the sixth seal that has already occurred is the day of the falling stars, which occurred on November 13, 1833. Imagine, looking up in the sky and then suddenly seeing what appears to be many bright stars that are falling from the sky. However, it is unlike a shooting star which only briefly passes by, it is continuous throughout a major portion of the night. As if, the stars and everything in the sky was falling from the heavens. This is a description of what occurred on November 13, 1833, from the Popular Astronomy, "The Boston observer, Olmstead, compared them, at the moment of maximum, to half the number of flakes which we perceive in the air during an ordinary shower of snow."[151] Thus, an estimate of how grandiose this event really was is to imagine stars falling at approximate rate of 34,600 stars an hour, which was an estimate made by Professor Denison Olmstead from Yale's Astronomy department. Here is another description of the event from Professor Olmstead, who wrote in the American Journal of Science

> *"Though there was no moon, when we first observed them, their brilliancy was so great that we could, at times, read common-sized print without much difficulty, and the light which they afforded was much whiter than that of the moon, in the clearest and coldest night, when the ground is covered with snow. The air itself, the face of the earth as far as the very countenances of men, wore the aspect and hue of death, occasioned by the continued, pallid glare of these countless meteors, which in all their grandeur flamed 'lawless through*

---

[151] Flammarion, Popular Astronomy, p. 536, as quoted in pg, Ibid.

> *the sky. [...] The sanguine flood rolled a broad slaughter o'er the plains of heaven, and nature's self did seem to totter on the brink of time! [...] There was scarcely a space in the firmament which was not filled at every instant with these falling stars, nor on it could you in general perceive any particular differences in appearance; still at times they seemed to shower down in groups – calling to mind the fig tree, casting her untimely figs when shaken by a mighty wind."* [152]

Therefore, you can see that this event was amazing to even Professors of Astronomy at the time, who were accustomed to seeing celestial phenomena on a regular basis. Another Yale Professor, Alexander Twining from the Civil Engineer department, gave the following description of the event

> *Had they held on their course unabated for three seconds longer, half a continent must, to all appearance, have been involved in unheard-of calamity. But that almighty Being who made the world, and knew its dangers, gave it also its armature – endowing the atmospheric medium around it with protecting, no less than with life-sustaining, properties [...] Considered as one of the rare and wonderful displays of the Creator's preserving care, as well as the terrible magnitude and power of His agencies, it is not meet that such occurrences as those of November 13 should leave no more solid and permanent effect upon the human mind than the impression of a splendid scene.* [153]

Olmstead and Twining both describe an event that was supernatural. Olmstead's description even uses John's description of a

---

[152] American Journal of Science, Volume XXV(1834), p. 382, as quoted in pg, 97,98 Ibid.
[153] American Journal of Science, Vol. XXVI (1834), pg. 351 as quoted in ODLP pg. 96).

fig tree casting her untimely figs, validating John's prophecy in the Book of Revelation of the Falling Stars event more than 1700 years before it occurred. John's detailed and accurate explanation of the event that occurred on November 13, 1833, even caught the attention of a writer for the New York Journal of Commerce, who wrote on Nov. 14, 1833, "No philosopher or scholar has told or recorded an event like that of yesterday morning. A prophet eighteen hundred years ago foretold it exactly, if we will be at the trouble of understanding stars falling to mean falling stars."[154] The event was not only visible over the skies of North America, but also over the skies of Europe during that night. British scientific writer Thomas Milner wrote in "The Gallery of Nature," "In many districts, the mass of the population were terror-struck, and the more enlightened were awed at contemplating so vivid a picture of the apocalyptic image – that of the stars of heaven falling to the earth, even as a fig tree casting her untimely figs, when she is shaken of a mighty wind."[155] Four different contemporary writers from that time who witnessed the event on the night of November 12-13,1833 used the example of the plain-stated words from John's prophecy of the sixth seal.

John's description of the events in the sixth seal matches with what Jesus said in His sermon on the Mount of Olives in Matthew 24: verse 29. Christ described the events that marked the beginning of the sixth seal, and the beginning of the End Times. Jesus said to His Apostles, "Immediately after the tribulation of those days the sun shall be darkened, and the moon shall not give her light, and the stars shall fall from heaven, and the powers of the heavens shall be

---

[154] Our Day In the Light of Prophecy, pg. 97
[155] pg. 140, Thomas Milner, *The Gallery of Nature,* (London, 1852), as quoted on pg. 99, Our Day in the Light of Prophecy

shaken." Christ, then gave the Apostles a glimpse of His 2nd Coming in verses 30 and 31,

> *"And then shall appear the sign of the Son of man in heaven: and then shall all the tribes of the earth mourn, and they shall see the Son of man coming in the clouds of heaven with power and great glory. And he shall send his angels with a great sound of a trumpet, and they shall gather together his elect, from the four winds, from one end of heaven to the other."*

Christ then uses the parable of a fig tree to describe how by seeing the leaves growing from the fig tree you will know the summer is coming soon, likewise if you see these extraordinarily unique signs and events occurring then you know that the 2nd return of Christ is quickly approaching. Christ states in Matthew 24:32-39,

> *Now learn a parable of the fig tree; When his branch is yet tender, and putteth forth leaves, ye know that summer is nigh: So likewise ye, when ye shall see all these things, know that it is near, even at the doors. Verily, I say unto you, This generation shall not pass, till all things be fulfilled. Heaven and earth shall pass away, but my words shall not pass away. But of that day and hour knoweth, no man, no, not the angels of heaven, but my Father only. But as the days of Noah, were, so shall also the coming of the Son of Man be. For as the days of Noah were, so shall also the Coming of Son of man be. For as in the days that were before the flood, they were eating, and drinking, marrying and giving in marriage, until the day that Noah entered into the ark. And they knew not until the flood came, and took them all away; so shall also the coming of the Son of man be.*

Eliseo Santos

The Words of Christ here pertained not only to the times of the Apostles and the destruction of Jerusalem and its Temple in the year 70 A.D., but it also pertains to our current generation which is close to witnessing the awesome presence and grandiose glory of the Jesus Christ with all the angels of heaven.

Therefore, Christ's words bring to light three important lessons that are important for all Christians and non-Christians living today in the world. The first is to recognize the signs of the End Times and how the world is slowly being polarized between those who are faithful to God and His Words in the Bible, His Ten Commandments, and Bible Prophecy, the rest who are not. The second lesson is to prepare for the 2nd Coming of Jesus Christ. This preparation should encompass the whole being, spiritual, mental, and physical. In order to highlight this lesson, Christ uses the example of Noah, who prepared for the flood as the Lord God instructed to do so. The first step a person should take in preparing for the 2nd Coming of Christ is to believe in Jesus Christ, His death on the cross, His resurrection, and His ability to forgive any and all sins confessed to Him in prayer. Also, it is important to study your Bibles, and for every individual to have a firm and thorough understanding of the Words of God in the Old and New Testament. However, many men and women who did not believe in the approaching flood and were busy eating and drinking, getting married as if they would grow old together and see their grandchildren, when in fact they were approaching cataclysm and disaster. Therefore, along with preparation the third important lesson is to do the work that God wants done in these End Times, which is to primarily spread the good news of Jesus Christ, His 2nd Coming, and receive something this world will never give you, eternal life.

Chapter 20: The End of the 1260-Day Prophecy

In order to understand the time period of the Church of Philadelphia and thus the End Times it is best to review the two major time prophecies of the Bible. During the church of "Brotherly Love," the two long-standing prophecies of Daniel are fulfilled. The 1st fulfilled prophecy is the 1260-day prophecy of Papal supremacy and the 2nd is the 2300-day prophecy concerning the Heavenly Sanctuary Temple. These two prophecies, like brothers, would support each other in proving the existence of God and His love for us through the creation of the world and the Words of the Bible. The first major End-Time prophecy concerns the reign of the Roman Catholic Church through the Dark and Middle ages up until the Modern Age. Christ referred to this prophecy in Matthew 24:29 "Immediately after the tribulation of those days shall the sun be darkened, and the moon shall not give her light, and the stars shall fall from heaven, and the powers of the heavens shall be shaken." The time period of 1260 days is spoken of many times in the Bible especially in the Book of Revelation. To best review the prophecy of the 1260 days or 1260 actual years, it is best to review Revelation Ch. 12 and Ch.13.

The first place in the Book of Revelation where you find a detailed history of the Papacy is in Revelation Ch. 12. John first speaks of "a woman clothed with the sun, and the moon, and upon her head a crown of twelve stars," (Rev. 12:1). The woman is a representation of God's people throughout the ages, first composed of the people of Israel and later on Bible-believing Christians. This is described as being a woman with a child, "travailing in birth, and pained to be delivered," (Revelation 12:2). This represents the people of God during the period of the early Church of Ephesus and Smyrna, which was a church that experienced great pain to be born due to all the opposition this church received from the Romans, occultists, and the Gnostics. John then describes "Satan as a great red dragon who has seven heads and ten horns with seven crowns upon his heads," (Rev.12: 3). John continues to elaborate on Satan "whose tail brought down one-third of the stars in heaven." John refers to how Satan brought down one-third of God's bright angels to rebel against their heavenly and kind Good Father. It was the lying tale instead of the tail of the dragon that brought down one-third of God's angels. Satan in developing lying tales of fables, stories, and gossip about God, brought down one–third of the angels of heaven all of whom experienced the joys of eternal life and all of whom became ungrateful about having it after believing Satan's lies.

According to Revelation 12:4, it appears Satan anticipated Christ's arrival on earth, and thus sought to do all he could to kill Jesus. He also sought to kill and confuse early Christian believers. In the next verse, John explains the life of Jesus Christ, who is described "as a man child, who was to rule all nations with a rod of iron: and her child was caught up unto God, and to his throne." Following the resurrection and the ascension of Christ into heaven, Satan's devious plans to persecute and destroy the woman, caused God's pure church, to flee and hide in the wilderness during the Dark and Middle Ages, better described in the Bible as the 1260 prophetic days, which are

Good Father, Bad Father

1260 years, (Revelation 12:6). This prophetic period started in 538 A.D. and ended in 1798 A.D. with Napoleon and arresting the Pope Pius VI. In Revelation 12:7-9, recaps the history between the dragon, Satan, his fallen angels, against Michael, and the heavenly angels. Two key points within these verses is that first Satan did not prevail or will never prevail against God or Michael, whose name is a representation of Jesus, (He who is Like God). Another important point to take note is that the Devil, the Bad Father of lies "deceiveth the whole world," (Rev. 12:9). In other words, the Bad Father through lies about God and heaven that have become considered truth, while the real truth about God and heaven has been considered lies. In verse Rev. 12:10, we read the following, "And I heard a loud voice saying in heaven, 'Now is come salvation, and strength, and the kingdom of our God, and the power of his Christ: for the accuser of our brethren is cast down, which accused them before our God day and night.'" Satan continues to relentlessly cause all human beings to sin against God and does not rest from developing new lies that are convenient to believe in and distract the people from realizing the infinite benefits of believing and doing the will of God and His commandments.

Also, remember John 15:9-10, "As the Father have loved me, so have I loved you: continue in my love. If you keep my commandments, you shall abide in my love; even as I have kept my Father's commandments, and abide in his love." It is a sincere and continued faith in God and belief in His glorious promises that causes people to keep in faith His law and Ten Commandments. Because of this system of salvation, then any human being, no matter their previous past history will able to win their cases before God through the mediation of only Jesus Christ. Revelation 12:11, reaffirms that it is only through Jesus Christ in which anyone can gain the victory over

Satan, "And they overcame him [Satan] with the blood of the Lamb, and by the word of their testimony; and they loved not their lives unto death." In other words, since Satan's process is a continuous process of accusations of sins before God, then you have to rely continually on God and His infinite grace to overcome the steady streams of temptations that Satan will throw at you any given day. Satan seeks to embed himself in the minds of many people and seeks to operate them without them being aware of his existence. Thus, you have to continually be active doing the Will of God on earth, in teaching others the truth about Jesus Christ and by helping those who need food, shelter, and the basic necessities of life.

    Some sins are more complex than others to overcome. Thus, some sins require more time to overcome than other sins because of the addictive nature of some sins that take a toll on the mind and body. Once you separate yourself from the sins you have done for many years, then you start to experience withdrawal effects because by continually sinning it affects the mind, body, and soul. However, there is good news that not only do you have Jesus Christ on your side, He will help you recover and overcome all the effects of sin in your life. Luckily, God gave every human being brains that are neuro-plastic meaning they are capable of change. There is no greater way to glorify God than to say that you overcame a sin, in order to follow Jesus Christ. An example of this Christian transformation was the Apostle Paul, who was previously a bounty hunter, who upon experiencing the glory of Christ converted and became one of the best writers in the New Testament. Another good example of Christian transformation in the Old Testament was Moses, who lived in Egypt and surrounded by sin and even killed a man. Moses repented of his sins, and left Egypt to live a new life in the desert in Midian. Moses

Good Father, Bad Father

lived 40 years in Egypt and it took Moses another 40 years before He could stand in the presence of God. Another method that purifies individuals is when they face persecution for the God's namesake. There will come a time in the future when many Christians will be persecuted for Jesus Christ's name sake, and the experience will help purify those who undergo it. In order to best prepare for the times of Christian persecution, it's best to study your Bible. Make sure you're aware of, and know for certain, all the doctrines that are taught by the Bible and those that are taught by mankind. Every Christian individual will have to give an account for their faith in Jesus Christ, and they themselves have to be able to defend their position against others who will seek to get them to renounce their faith during the times of persecution. When confronted by these situations it is best to focus on Jesus Christ, and His life, especially the closing scenes when He died on the cross and resurrected. Christ says in John 11:25, "I am the resurrection, and the life: he that believeth in me, though he were dead, yet shall He live. And whosoever liveth and believeth in me shall never die. Believest thou this?" Let us all believe as fully as we can in the promises of Jesus and let a sign of our belief be reflected in our actions such in proclaiming the Word of God and keeping His commandments.

Revelation 12:12, states something that is even more true today than yesterday when following upon the previous verse, "Therefore rejoice, ye heavens, and ye that dwell in them. Woe to the inhabiters of the earth and of the sea! For the devil is come down unto you, having great wrath, because he knoweth that he hath but a short time." Satan is aware of that the End is coming near for him and for his transgressions of power. He follows his own principles of Evil and keeps this truth to himself and his fallen angels and does not say this to his many followers, who believe Satan's tale about having control of the planet for 1,000 years via the New World Order. John gives another recap of Satan in verses 13, and 14. John describes how he was cast down to earth and chased the Church that brought forth Christianity and thus God's true Church hid in the wilderness for a time, times, and half a time. Therefore, by restating the same information in a different way, John equates the time period of 1260 prophetic days with time, times, and half a time, which is a period of three and a half prophetic years. Thus, three and half years is equal to 42 prophetic months and when you multiply 42 months by 30 days then you wind up with 1260 prophetic days. Keep in mind, this number is in prophetic terms and thus to convert to actual time you have to apply the rule of a prophetic day equals an actual year, (Eze.4: 5,6). This is how to understand the 1260-year prophecy.

As a recap the prophecy began in 538 A.D. when the Justinian decree gave Pope Vigilius at the time temporal power and the spiritual title of "Corrector of heretics." Keep in mind, that in Daniel 7:8 He states concerning the Little Horn, "I considered the horns, and, behold, there came up among them another little horn, before whom there were three of the first horns plucked up by the roots: and, behold, in this horn were the eyes of a man, and a mouth speaking great things." In Daniel 7:23:24, you find Daniel repeats the same information using different words,

> *"Thus he said, the fourth beast shall be the fourth kingdom upon the earth, which shall be diverse from all kingdoms, and shall devour the whole earth, and shall tread it down, and break it in pieces. And the ten horns out of this kingdom are ten kings that shall arise; and another shall rise after them;*

Good Father, Bad Father

and he shall be diverse from the first, and he shall subdue three kings."

The three kings that were subdued were the Kings of the Vandals, Ostrogoths, and Heruli. The last of the three kings that was subdued was the King of the Ostrogoths, which from 537 – June 538 had control of Rome up until Justinian's general Belisarius and his forces permanently brought the Ostrogoths out of Rome. With the Ostrogoths out of Rome, then Pope Vigilius began his reign under the protection of Belisarius[156]. We know it is 538 A.D. and not 537 A.D. because in 538 A.D. Pope Vigilius rose to the Papal chair after the previous Pope Silverius was deposed by the General Belisarius in 537 A.D. for showing sympathy to the enemy[157]. This year is significant because from this year onward the Pope would be involved in secular, political affairs and would eventually gain human authority in both the religious and political spheres of influence.[158]

Now that you know the start date of the 1260 year prophecy of Papal supremacy, all you have to do is add 1260 years to 538 AD and you end up in 1798 AD. What significant event happened in 1798 A.D.? Whatever it was, under the implications of the 1260 year prophecy of Papal Supremacy, there should be have been an event in 1798 A.D. that caused the Pope to lose his power and authority in the political and religious world. Sure enough, there was such an event in 1798 and that occurred when, Napoleon sent His General Berthier to Rome to arrest the Pope. Once Berthier removed the Pope from the

---

[156] "History of the Christian Church", Vol. III, p. 327 as quoted from Our Day In The Light of Prophecy, pg. 135
[157] American Peoples Encyclopedia, Vigilius, pg.104, Grolier incorporated, New York, 1970 and ODLP pg. 135
[158] ODLP-pg. 137

Papal throne and from Italy, General Berthier proclaimed a new Roman Republic. Therefore, the 1260-year prophecy in which Daniel wrote at least 500 years before the birth of Christ, proves the existence of the all-mighty and all-knowing God, who through the Holy Spirit made available to Daniel all of the prophecies and their symbols that found in the Book of Daniel and the Bible. Thus, it is by knowing the validity of these Biblical prophecies that you can say for certain God does exist. Therefore, you must prepare for His long-awaited 2nd Coming, which will put an end to the evil of this world. How can you be certain that the 1260 days of prophecy ended in 1798? Well, if you take a look at a periodical from that time period then it will put aside any and all doubts. The Philological Society of London produced "The European Magazine and London Review." Vol.33 of their magazine covered the events from January to June 1798 and had several first-hand accounts of the arrest of Pope Pius VI by Napoleon's General Belisarius. An important part of the magazine article is that the magazine transcribes a dispatch made by General Berthier informing the French Directorate of their success in removing Pope Pius VI from the Papal throne and from exercising his power. His dispatch read:

> *Head – Quarters at the Capitol, Feb. 15*
>
> *"Citizen Directors,*
>
> *"The French army has been at the Capitol to render homage to the great men of the fairest times in Rome. The Roman people have declared their resumption of those rights which have been usurped from them, and have demanded from me the protection of the French Republic – Rome is free.*

"Health and Respect,

Alex, Berthier." [159]

This dispatch is a sign of what the Bible calls the mortal wound of the beast in Revelation 13:3, when the 1st beast of Revelation 13 goes through a period of time when it has lost its political dominion that it wielded for 1260 years. John writes in Revelation 13:3, "And I saw one of his heads as it were wounded to death; and his deadly wound was healed: and all the world wondered after the beast." John not only foretold the mortal wound of the Papal authority, but also its resurgence from death. The Pope's mortal wound began to heal first through Pope Pius VII, when Napoleon gave power back to the Pope, albeit without the same reverence that the Papacy had during the 1260-year period. Since then the Papacy has been in a state of rehabilitation of restoring the temporal and political power that it wielded during the 1260-year period. In 1929, a major sign of the Vatican healing its mortal wound was the Treaty of Lateran between the Vatican and the Italian Republic under Mussolini. In 1933, the Pope would also sign a Concordat with Nazi Germany. These were signs of its return to the field of temporal and political power. Under Popes John Paul II, Benedict XVI, and Francis, the papacy would display to the world its temporal and political power and "the world wondered after the beast" as the Papacy became popular on the global stage. Later on you will see how these Popes fit in to the discussion of who will be the last Pope to be alive when Jesus Christ returns, which the Bible alludes to in Rev. 17:11.

---

[159] "The European Magazine and London Review", Vol.33, March 1798, pg. 208-209

Eliseo Santos

Now that we are aware of the significance of the 1260-year prophecy, and how it correlates with the 42 prophetic months and the "times, time, and half a time," when you continue reading Revelation 12: 15-16, "And the serpent cast out of his mouth water as a flood after the woman, that he might cause her to be carried away of the flood. And the earth, helped the woman, and the earth opened her mouth, and swallowed up the flood, which the dragon cast out of his mouth." This quote is describing the history of what occurred during the Church of Sardis when many Protestants left Europe because of widespread persecutions and inquisitions against Protestants and they left Europe and went to New World where it was less populated or lack of water existed. Therefore the earth, or the ground with soil, here is a symbol of a location that is not heavily populated, and water here is a symbol of "peoples, and multitudes, and nations, tongues," (Rev. 17:15). Because the woman, or God's Church escaped into the New World, according to John, "the dragon was wroth with the woman, and went to make war with the remnant of her seed, which keep the commandments of God, and have the testimony of Jesus Christ," (Rev. 12:17) Therefore, through God's help and mercy many of God's people were able to flee the dragon who was in Europe, and they were able find peace in the New World, primarily North America, where many Protestants found a home in America. The main reason why Protestantism during the Church of Philadelphia was able to thrive was because of the deadly mortal wound that the Papacy received in 1798 when the Pope Pius VI was arrested and removed from the Papal chair. To explain the motivations behind such a remarkable action, you will first need to know understand the disavowal of the Jesuit Order from the Roman Catholic Church.

Chapter 21: Suppression of the Jesuit Order

By Napoleon and His French army removing the Pope from power, the Roman Catholic Church received a mortal wound. Right before the mortal wound, the Roman Church was undergoing an important conflict with its most well-known and nefarious order, The Jesuits. Throughout the latter period the Church of Sardis, the Jesuits were gaining more power and influence within the Roman Church and society. There were not only becoming rich by developing schemes to swindle money and natural resources from the indigenous natives of the New World Colonies, but also the Jesuits were involved in taking money away from the Monarchs of various European countries. The Jesuits were quickly becoming the Pharisees of the new modern age and sought to bring under their control as many people as possible.

In the aftermath of the Lisbon Earthquake, the Portuguese Prime Minister Sebastiao Jose De Carvalho y Mello, also known as the Marquis de Pombal(1699-1782), gained greater influence in the Portugal government by naming himself Prime Minister during the reign of Joseph I. After the devastation in Lisbon, the Marquis de Pombal sought to fix all the political and financial problems that Portugal suffered after the devastating earthquake. He started the recovery effort to restore the City of Lisbon to its previous state. Again, imagine today if a major city experiences a sudden loss of approximately 20%-25% of the population and suddenly 75% of all housing is made inhospitable. Imagine all the people who as a result of the Lisbon earthquake were suddenly injured, and homeless and without adequate food, clothing, and shelter. Pombal after seeing the destruction of Lisbon took an active role in burying the dead, as well as helping the survivors in the coping and rebuilding process. With this new found power and influence, and still affected by the devastation, Marquis de Pombal sought to begin important projects to restore the city of Lisbon and country of Portugal. These projects included to bring the aristocracy under his control and also to remove the Jesuits from Portugal and its colonies. Pombal sought the religious reform as a measure to restore morality within Portugal and remove the corrupt religious leaders, who at the time had great power and control over the minds of the people.

For The Jesuits, their veil of darkness and sheep's clothing were coming off. Many started to see them for what they really were, wolves in sheep's clothing. Previously, between 1750-1753, Spain and Portugal agreed to a treaty for redrawing the borders of their colonies in South America. Portugal received the territory east of the Uruguay River and which is now Modern-day Brazil and Uruguay. Apparently after the treaty was made, the Jesuits who were working in the Portugal side crossed over to the Spain territory. The Jesuits then armed the native Guaranis and led them using guerrilla warfare techniques against Portugal.[160] Portugal relinquished parts of the land to the Jesuits who then returned portions to Spain. This incident and other acts of immorality by the Jesuits undermined the Portuguese monarchy and government. In seeking God after a time of great

---

[160] pg. 96 The Secret History of The Jesuits, Edmond Paris, Chick Publications

Good Father, Bad Father

devastation and misery that arose in Portugal, on September 19th, 1757, Marquis De Pombal removed three Jesuit Priests who worked as confessors for the Royal court and replaced them with ordinary priests. He also published many pamphlets speaking out against the immorality and injustices committed by the Jesuits. He wrote to Pope Benedict XIV stating that the cause for removing the Jesuits' from the Royal Court was due to the Jesuit's commercial enterprise ventures, using Portugal land and resources, were getting in the way of the commercial plans of Portugal and for its national prosperity, especially after the Great Lisbon earthquake,[161] Therefore, you see that the Jesuits' plan in action for taking over a monarchy was to economically limit the monarchy and thereby the country. Thus, the Jesuits like a parasite and leech would attach itself to a monarchy or country until it grew big enough so that the monarchy and the country became dependent on the Jesuits. Therefore, the Jesuits also made it their goal to gain economic control of a monarchy and a country.

Colonial expansion became very lucrative for the monarchies that were involved in acquiring new land and natural resources overseas in the New World. The business of colonial expansion became so lucrative that the Jesuits would seek a piece of the action. However, the Jesuits were so motivated by greed for money that they began to infringe upon the rights of other monarchs and commercial business owners for earning money. Thus, the monarchs and many among the nobility wanted to remove the Jesuits out of the way, and confiscate their accumulated wealth and property. Unlike, other religious orders within the Roman Catholic Church that took their oath of poverty

---

[161] pg. 335, G.B., Nicolini, History of The Jesuits: Their Origin, Progress, Doctrines, and Design, London, Henry G. Bohn, York Street, Covent Garden, 1854

very seriously because they sincerely and earnestly wanted to follow the example of Jesus Christ and the Apostles, the Jesuits used their oath of poverty as an excuse to ask and in some cases take large sums of money with no intention of paying it back as promised. French writer, Pierre Dominique, writes in his *La Politique des Jesuites*,

> *"The Fathers became involved too much in affairs which had nothing to do with religion, in commerce, exchange, as liquidators of bankruptcies. The Roman College, which should have remained the intellectual and moral model of all Jesuit colleges had cloth made in huge quantities at Macerata and sold it in fairs at a low price. Their centers in India, Antilles, Mexico, and Brazil soon started trading in colonial products. At Martinique, a procurator created vast plantations which were cultivated by negro slaves."* [162]

M.Martin who was the general commander of Pondicherry, India wrote the following concerning the commercial enterprises of the Jesuits up until the Mid-Eighteenth century.

> *"It is certain, that after the Dutch, the Jesuits are the largest and richest traders in India, richer than even than the English, than the Portuguese themselves, who have brought them there...Those disguised Jesuits intrigue everywhere. The secret correspondence they keep amongst themselves, apprises them of the merchandises that ought to be bought or sold, and to what nation, in order to make a more considerable profit; so that those disguised Jesuits are of immense advantage to the Society, and are only responsible to the Order represented by*

---

[162] Pierre Dominique, op.cit., pp.190-191. as quoted pg. 96 The Secret History of The Jesuits,Edmond Paris, Chick Publications

Good Father, Bad Father

> *other Jesuits, who overrun the world under the true habit of St. Ignatius, and who possess the confidence, the secrets, and the orders of their chiefs in Europe. Those Jesuits, disguised, and dispersed all over the earth, know each other by signals, like freemasons, and act all upon the same plan. They send merchandise to other disguised Jesuits, who, having the goods from first hand, realize considerable profits for the order. However, this traffic is highly prejudicial to the interest of France. I have written about it to the Company (of India), but under Louis XIV. I have received orders very precise, and often repeated, to grant and advance to those fathers all that they may ask. And Father Tashard alone owes at this moment more than 450,000 francs to the Company (of India)".[163]*

As an example of the mindset of the Jesuits, they did not deny their ambition was set on making money and profiting from the sale of produce using land acquired through the subjection of the indigenous population. It seems that the Jesuits excuse themselves of the "sin" in business, "when they state, "The ecclesiastical law has never forbidden the sale of produce of one's own domains."[164] This shows that the name they use for their society of "Jesus," is used in vain. Paul states the root of the matter in 1 Thessalonians 6:10, "For the love of money is the root of all evil: which while some coveted after, they have erred from the faith and pierced themselves with many sorrows." The Jesuit Order, much like the Knights Templar, were involved in the protection of Catholic Christians in the New World, and this was especially the case for those who were in Paraguay. The Jesuits missionaries received the authority of Spanish kings to begin selling the produce of the ground that was cultivated

---

[163] Voyage de Duquensne Chef d'escadre, tom. XXXV. P. 15. – as quoted in *History of the Jesuits*, Pg. 337

[164] Voyage de Duquensne Chef d'escadre, tom. XXXV. P. 15. As quoted in "History of the Jesuits, Pg. 337,

by Jesuit novices and other Jesuit missionaries[165]. The Jesuits earned so much profits that eventually they entered the banking business and eventually owned the major banking houses of South America during the 17th and 18th centuries[166]. One of these banking houses owned by Jesuit Lavallette went bankrupt for more than two million and a half francs, which was an exorbitant amount of money for that day and age.[167] Keep in mind, the Jesuit order acquired most of their wealth from confiscating the money and property from the many Christians they persecuted and put to death during the French and Spanish inquisitions eventually ended up in the hands of the Monarchy and in the hands the Roman Catholic hierarchy,[168].

After the attempted regicide of King Joseph I of Portugal, was eventually tied to Jesuit conspirators, Portugal took decisive measures to remove the Jesuits from Portugal. Pombal and the King Joseph approved of a decree on the 1st of September 1759, which expelled the Jesuits from all the lands of Portugal (including the colonies of Portugal) and brought them to ships and sent them to Italy. The Bishops of Portugal took control over all Jesuit teaching and other activities they were obliged to do in Portugal.[169] After all of Europe saw the events unfold in Portugal that revoked the Jesuits of their special status, other monarchs and governments sought to bring to justice the Jesuits, for the crime of using the name of Jesus to kill other Christians. Also many monarchs and businessmen were tired of the Jesuits trying to gain and profit from unjust business practices that

---

[165] Cret. Vol. V p. 171 as quoted on pg. 337,ibid
[166] pg. 337, ibid.
[167] pg. 337,ibid.
[168] Pg. 264, American Peoples Encyclopedia, Inquisition, Vol.10, 1967
[169] Pg. 342, "History of the Jesuits", G.B. Nicolini

undermined the well-being of others for the sake elevating their order and the Roman Church. The Jesuits during the late-middle Ages came to represent what Christ said "They shall put you out of the synagogues; yea, the time cometh, that whosoever killeth you will think that he doeth God service. And these things they will do unto you, because they have not known the Father nor me," (John 16:2-3.) Like the Pharisees and other Jewish religious leaders accumulated lots of wealth from the manipulation of their followers, so did the Jesuits accumulate lots of wealth. The Jesuits piggybacked on the Papal influence and control over the minds of the monarchies and other governments to then control of the people and resources of the kingdom.

After the repeated and continued calls for the suppression of the Jesuit order, on account of the monarchs, on July 23, 1773, Pope Clement XIV issued a brief, calling for the immediate suppression of the Jesuit order in all Catholic localities. Like Clement V, who worked with the King of France to suppress and abolish the Knights Templars in the early 14th century, Clement XIV bowed to the desires of the major Catholic monarchies of Spain, France, Portugal, Naples, and Parma to suppress the Jesuit order. In the beginning of this "Brief for the Call and Suppression of the Order of the Jesuits")[170], you read Clement XIV's words in describing the Jesuits and their actions. There are several important points about Clement XIV's brief for permanent suppression of the Jesuits that confirm the evil of the Jesuit order, as shown in their extreme oath. Towards the beginning of the brief when he takes responsibility for all Roman Catholic religious orders, he also mentions the following which is significant when

---

[170] Pg. 387, Ibid.

describing the suppression of the Jesuits, "so the bond of mutual charity requires that we be equally ready and disposed to pluck up and destroy even the things which are most agreeable to us, and of which we cannot deprive ourselves without the highest regret and the most pungent sorrow.[171] " The language in which Clement XIV uses "to pluck up and destroy," is a similar to the language used to describe the Little Horn power of Daniel Ch. 7 and 8. Daniel 7:8 states when symbolically describing Roman Papacy, the Little Horn "I considered the horns, and behold, there came up among them another little horn, before whom there were three of the first horns plucked up by the roots: and behold, in this horn were eyes like the eyes of man, and a mouth speaking great things," (Dan. 7:8, KJV). The significance of Clement XIV words is that he implicitly identified himself as the "Little Horn" which is a prophetic symbol of how the Vatican, the smallest independent state in the world, will also be the strongest and most influential state with the power to set up kings and or destroy them.

Clement XIV confirms many of the problems in which other authors and historians have attributed to the Jesuits. Clement XIV states that within the heart of the Jesuits there was sown "diverse seeds of discord and dissension not only amongst themselves but with regular orders, secular clergy, the academies, universities, public schools, even the Princes of the state in which they were received[172] Clement XIV clarifies the areas in which he received the most complaints concerning the Jesuit order. He states that dissentions and disputes arose concerning the nature of their vows, the time of admission to them, and concerning the absolute authority of the

---

[171] Pg. 389, Ibid.
[172] pg. 390, Ibid.,

Good Father, Bad Father

General of the Jesuit order.[173] Clement XIV confirms the extreme satanic nature of the extreme oath of Jesuits that is taken by a core group of Jesuits. He writes, "On the contrary, very violent disputes arose on all sides concerning the doctrine of the Society, which many represented as contrary to the orthodox faith and to sound morals."[174] By the Jesuits going against Biblical principles and morals, the Jesuits became a tool in the Bad Father's hands to continue to cultivate greed and lying amongst their members to the point where they themselves would do anything, including killing, stealing, and wickedly deceiving for the greater good of their own order and the Roman Catholic church. Clement XIV continues to explain and confirm the great wealth in which Jesuits accumulated for their order. He states

> *"The dissensions among themselves, and with others, grew everyday more animated; the accusations against the Society were multiplied without number, and especially with that insatiable avidity of temporal possessions with which it was reproached. Hence the rise not only of those well-known troubles which brought so much care and solicitude upon the Holy See, but also of the resolutions which certain sovereigns took against the said order,"*[175].

Thus, the trouble in which the Jesuits have caused in different countries are really true, so much so that the Jesuits in their fifth general congregation of the Company of Jesus, stated "the said society would prevent the effect of these precious goods, and expose them to the most imminent dangers, if it concerned itself with

---

[173] pg. 390, 391, Ibid.,
[174] pg. 392, Ibid.,
[175] pg. 392, Ibid.,

temporal matters, and which relate to political affairs and the administration of government,"[176] Throughout their history, the Jesuits have used the name of Jesus in order to overthrow governments and assassinate any leaders Catholic or Protestant if they dared get in their way of achieving control of all the world and resources, even if it meant killing their Papal leaders, such as Clement XIV. Clement XIV frankly admits that the Jesuits continued to get involved in the politics of a nation even after the Jesuits themselves resolved to "abstain from all appearance of evil" and to forbid any interference in "any manner whatever in public affairs, even though they be thereto invited, or to deviate from the institute, through entreaty, persuasion, or any motive whatsoever."[177] Also the intervention of a myriad of Popes in the affairs of the Jesuits (Urban VII, Clement IX, X, XI, and XII, and Alexander VII, and VIII, Innocent X, XII, and XIII and Benedict XIV) was of no avail to maintain trust of the Roman Church with other monarchs and political leaders.[178] Clement XIV reveals the problems the Jesuits caused the Roman Church with their secular affairs and missions, in which due to the interference of the Jesuits caused strife with other Catholic religious orders, and also within other communities in Europe, Africa, and America. The Jesuit's interference of politics even led to what he describes as "the revolts and intestine troubles in some Catholic states," and also attacks on the Roman Catholic Church and priests in Asia, and Europe.[179]

---

[176] pg. 393, Ibid.,
[177] pg. 394, Ibid.
[178] pg. 394, Ibid
[179] Pg. 394- 395, Ibid.,.

Despite the problems in which Clement XIV enumerates against the Jesuits, he fails to recognize how the Roman Catholic Church is guilty of the same evils committed by the Jesuits, even before the Order was approved by Loyola in 1540. Clement XIV's tone throughout this brief for the suppression of the Jesuits is that of the Roman Church distancing herself from the evils of her Jesuit children, while ignoring that she herself has committed many of the same evils committed by the Jesuits. Clement XIV states when speaking about the resolution made by the Catholic Kings of France, Spain, Portugal, and Sicily, to expel and drive the Jesuits from their Kingdoms because they were "persuaded that there remained no other remedy to so great evils; and this step was necessary in order to prevent the Christians from rising one against another, and from massacring each other in the very bosom of our common mother the Holy Church."[180] The words of Clement XIV here does not take into account the centuries of Christian bloodshed caused by the Roman Catholic Church before the existence of the Jesuits in terms of the persecutions, Crusades, and inquisitions, against the Bible-believing Christians who were labeled as "heretics" by the Roman Church. During the period of 1260 days from 538-1798 A.D., the Roman Catholic Church fulfilled Bible Prophecy in Daniel 7:21, Daniel 8:24 when it persecuted, tortured, and killed Bible-believing Christians, such as the Waldenses, Albigenses, Huguenots, and Sabbath-keepers.

After the measures taken by the Kings of France, Spain, Portugal, and Sicily against the Jesuits, they urged Clement XIII and later Clement XIV to absolutely abolish the Jesuit order for the good of the Roman Catholic Church, and to reestablish its trust and credibility

---

[180] pg. 396, Ibid.

with other monarchs and political partners. Therefore after repeated calls and measures taken by the Kings of France, Spain, Portugal, and Sicily, and other governments of Europe against the Jesuits, Clement XIV spoke the fateful words, "the fate of a society classed among the mendicant orders, both by its institute and by its privileges; after – a mature deliberation, we do, out of our certain knowledge, and the fullness of apostolical power, suppress and abolish the said company,"[181] . So that there is no confusion on what he means, Clement XIV continued to explain the extent of the order of suppression of the Jesuits,

> *"we deprive it of all activity whatever, of its houses, schools, colleges, hospitals, lands, and in short, every other place whatsoever, in what-ever kingdom or province they may be situated; we abrogate and annul its privileges, indults, general, or particular, the tenor, whereof is, and is taken to be fully and as amply, expressed in the present Brief as if the same were inserted word for word, in whatever clauses, form or decree, or under whatever sanction their privileges may have been conceived."*[182]

Clement XIV with this brief shuts down all the operations of the Jesuit Order and all of their work is suddenly and dramatically terminated. Concerning the authority of the Superior General, provincials, and other superiors within the ranks of the Jesuit Order, Clement XIV "annulled and extinguished, of what nature whatsoever the said authority may be, as well in things spiritual as temporal,"[183] The most instrumental group within the Roman Catholic Church was

---

[181] pg. 398, Ibid.
[182] pg. 398, Ibid.
[183] Pg. 398, Ibid.

forever removed of their ability to work for the Papacy. Clement XIV's brief was thought of to be the nail in the coffin for the Jesuits. However, at the time of this briefing, there were many Jesuits who felt betrayed by the Roman Catholic Church and they felt they were a scapegoat for the source of all the evils of the Roman Church. Thus, the Jesuits sought revenge on their very own Papal leaders, after they were expelled from the Church.

Through God's intervention, the suppression of the Jesuits is what led to the peaceful time period and growth of the Protestant Church in America. Since the Church of Ephesus, during the Times of the Roman Empire, Biblical Christianity has been the constant target for persecution by Roman Emperors and the Roman Catholic Papacy. Even after 1,750 years of on and off persecution of the Bible-believing Christians, the Bad father Satan was still unable to silence the Bible and the Holy Spirit that moved with many people throughout this period. Even after 256 years since the Martin Luther started the Protestant Reformation in 1517 AD to the Jesuit's suppression in 1773 AD, the Bible-Believing Protestant Church has still grown despite the persecutions, inquisitions, and disinformation that were set in place by the Jesuits.

Now that they were abolished and suppressed, the Jesuits' primary target became the Roman Catholic Church and not the Protestants. The Jesuits sought revenge even if it meant attacking their own church and their own leader the Pope. The Jesuits at first appeared to submit to the brief for the suppression and abolishment of the Order, but many Jesuits at first reacted in a typical Jesuit fashion by writing many publications against the Roman Church and the Pope, knowing full well how corrupt was the Roman Church[184]. The techniques the

Jesuits used to spark rebellions against Protestant monarchs was now being employed against the Pope who expelled them from the Roman Church. Other Jesuits sought to kill the same Pope that condemned them, Clement XIV. When the death of Clement XIV occurred fourteen months later, the Jesuits became the party that was attributed with the murder. The following is a excerpt that summarizes the opinion of the Jesuits during mid- 1770's in Europe, "The Jesuits, in principle at least, were no more; but Clement XIV knew very well that, by signing their death warrant, he was signing his own as well: "This suppression is done at last," he exclaimed, "and I am not sorry about it... I would do it again if it was not done already; but this suppression will kill me."[185] It was later confirmed that on September 22, 1774, Pope Clement XIV died via poisoning and thus an implicit confirmation that the Jesuits killed their Pope in retaliation for the destruction of the Jesuit order.

The suppression of the Jesuits would aid in the growth of Protestantism in America and abroad. God foretold long ago in the Book of Daniel, that there would come a time period where the Little Horn would display to the world its true character and greed for power and control over all people, most especially Bible-believing Christians. In the words of Daniel 8:24, "And his power shall be mighty, but not by his own power: and he shall destroy wonderfully, and shall prosper, and practice, and shall destroy the mighty and the holy people." Daniel also foretold how God's Bible-believing

---

[184] pg.365, J.Huber, Les Jesuites, Sandoz et Fischbacher, Paris, 1875. as quoted pg. 101, The Secret History of the Jesuits,

[185] p. 313, Caraccioli: "Vie du Pape Clement XIV" (Desaut, Paris 1776, as written on pg. 101, Ibid.)

Christians, shall "instruct many: yet they shall fall by the sword, and by flame, by captivity, and by spoil,"(Dan.8:33). The Papacy throughout the Middle Ages have relied upon civil governments and religious order like the Jesuits to carry the bloodshed of the Protestants. The end of the Jesuit order eventually was the writing of the wall that the end of the 1260 years of overt papal political authority was quickly approaching. In 1798, Pope Pius VI would suffer the Papal mortal wound as a result of Napoleon and the French Revolution.

Chapter 22: Revelation 11 and the French Revolution

After the Jesuits were expelled and suppressed in several Kingdoms such as Spain, France, Portugal, and others, the monarchs of these Kingdoms never foresaw a scenario where their peaceful kingdoms would once again be brought to conflict, and strife. The monarchs never thought that their own subjects would turn against them. The monarchs did not think they would die at the hands of an angry mob. Well, that is what exactly happened during the French Revolution. France was at times a great help for the Pope, such as when France helped the Pope with the suppression of the Knights Templar in the early 14th century. In the late 18th century, France became the enemy of not only the Pope, but of all of Europe.

Before explaining how France fits in with the prophetic message of Revelation 11, it is important to understand the symbols that John uses in Revelation 11 to describe the French Revolution. In Revelation 11, John describes the importance of the two witnesses and their significance to the Church of Philadelphia. Before John begins talking about the two witnesses John states the following,

> *"And there was given me a reed like unto a rod and the angel stood saying 'Rise, and measure the Temple of God, and the altar, and them that worship therein,'" But the Court which is without the temple leave out, and measure it not; for it is given*

Eliseo Santos

unto the Gentiles; and the holy city shall they tread under foot forty and two months," (Rev.11: 1,2).

Previously in Rev. 10, John receives a vision where the angel gives him the message that

"But, in the days of the voice of the seventh angel, when he shall begin to sound, the mystery of God should be finished, as he hath declared to the prophets. And the voice which I heard from the heaven spake unto me again, and said, 'Go and take the little book which is open in the hand of the angel which standeth upon the sea and upon the earth'. And I went unto the angel, and said unto him, 'Give me the little book. And he said unto me 'take it, and eat it up; and it shall make thy belly bitter, but it shall be in thy mouth sweet as honey.' And I took the little book out the angel's hand, and ate it up; and it was in my mouth sweet as honey: and as soon as I had eaten it, my belly was bitter. And he said unto me, 'Thou must prophesy again before many peoples, and nations, and tongues, and kings'." - Rev.10:7-11

In the days of the seventh angel or in the days of the final church of Laodecia, and in the final trumpet of the seventh angel, God's people will have to once again prophesize as they did in the early Church of Ephesus of the Apostles. The Bible symbolically represents this as John eating a "little book" as a sign of studying and internalizing the Word of God and the Bible. This was symbolically also shown to the prophet Ezekiel 2:9 -3:3. After this then the angel asks John to measure the Temple of God and those within the temple worshiping God. The angel asks John to not measure the court that without the Temple of God, because as he says it is given to "The Gentiles" for 42 months. What does John possibly mean in these two verses? First, remember that the 42 months, is equal to the 1260 years of prophecy of Papal Supremacy where God's people during these years was under the subjection and control of the Roman Church. During this era, in the Church of Thyatira and Sardis many Gentiles, who were previously Roman Catholics, became Protestants on account of the Protestant Reformation and many of them left the Roman Catholic Church. So the angel is stating symbolically that the people within the Temple of God is the End-Time Remnant of the Gentiles, which are also the people from the Revelation 10 that John says that they will have to prophesize once again as the Apostles of Christ once did.

The previous stated explanation was important in explaining the following verses of Revelation 11:verses 3- 13,

And I will give power unto my two witnesses, they shall prophesy a thousand two hundred and sixty days, clothed in sackcloth. These are the two olive trees, and the two candlesticks standing before the God of the earth. And if any man will hurt them, fire proceedeth out of their mouth, and devoureth their enemies: and if any man will hurt them, he must in this manner be killed. These have power to shut heaven, that it rain not in the days of their prophecy: and have power over waters to turn them to blood, and to smite the earth with all plagues, as often they will. And when they shall have finished their testimony the beast that ascendeth out the bottomless pit shall make war against them, and shall overcome them, and kill them. And their dead bodies shall lie in the street of the great city, which spiritually is called Sodom and Egypt, where also our Lord was crucified. And they of the people and kindreds and tongues and nations shall see their dead bodies three days and an half, and shall not suffer their dead bodies to be put into graves. And they that dwell upon the earth, shall rejoice over them, and make merry, and shall send

> *gifts one to another; because these two prophets tormented them that dwelt on the earth. And after three days and a half the Spirit of life from God entered into them, and they stood upon their feet,; and great fear fell upon them which saw them. And they heard a great voice from heaven saying unto them, Come up hither. And they ascended up to heaven in a cloud; and their enemies beheld them, And the same hour was a great earthquake, and the tenth part of the city-fell, and in the earthquake were slain of men seven thousand: and the remnant were affrighted, and gave glory to the God of heaven.*
> *– Revelation 11:3-13.*

There are several key important biblical symbols that are being used by John here to describe a specific message. First, John uses the symbolic language of two witnesses, two olive trees, two lamp stands, and the two prophets that all relate to the Word of God and Bible prophecy found in the Old Testament and New Testament. Keep in mind, that an official witness always produces a testament where he describes his or her testimony. Therefore, the two witnesses have the testimony of God, especially found in the Bible prophecy. When John states in Revelation 11 verse 3, " that the two witnesses will prophesy for a thousand two hundred and threescore days covered in sackcloth," John is stating how the Bible and the correct interpretation of the 1260 years prophecy will be revealed after the time period has been come to an end. The following verses 5 and 6 are key to understanding the correct interpretation. If any man hurts the two witnesses or destroys the Bible, the infinite wisdom and understanding that leads to eternal life, then the individual all but guarantees his death will be in the same manner in which he uses to destroy the Bible, typically by fire. The reason for the existence of the Bible is it is the only official connection in which all human beings

Good Father, Bad Father

can learn about God and the principles and commandments that lead to eternal life.

By rejecting the many infinitely valuable truths found in the Bible, then they opened themselves to accept the lies of the Bad Father. To accept the lies of Satan is to accept that for the remainder of life you will be lied to, because you are rejecting the only person who can help, God. The following verse continues to explain the power of the Bible to "shut heaven, that it not rain in the days of their prophecy," which means that during the 1260 days prophecy no one was able to understand the 1260 year prophecy until God allows it to be understood. First, God reveals the depth of knowledge and understanding of the Bible to his faithful and loyal servants, who are humble and acknowledge their weaknesses and their need to be close to the God of salvation to gain eternal life. In the remainder of verse six when it states that the Bible "have power over the waters to turn them to blood and smite the earth as often they will" John, is describing that is our current generation we will see widespread chaos, death, and destruction, when the plagues of the Revelation start to fall on the inhabitants on the planet, who accepted the mark of the beast and rejected the Love of God revealed in the Bible and His Ten Commandments. Remember from earlier that "waters" is a symbol of peoples, multitudes, and nations, and tongues, (Rev. 17:15).

As an example of the accuracy of bible prophecy, to prove that the Bible is not joking around when it says these things it states that after the Bible's 1260 years of prophecy, then "the beast of the bottomless pit, shall ascend out of the bottomless pit and shall make war against them, and shall overcome them, and kill them," (Revelation 11:7). The beast of the bottomless pit, is a symbol of Satan, remember that Satan seeks to become like God and therefore qualifies with the definition of a beast given in Daniel 3 and 4. The bottomless pit here signifies that Satan is king of the symbolic underworld, of the demons and also all the unbiblical spiritual ideas that lead to death and ruin. In these End Times, after 1798, Satan began a campaign throughout the 19th century to symbolically destroy the Bible without actually burning it. He did achieve some of this in the modern-era through the theoretical science of evolution, which destroys an individual's belief in the Creation of God. Once you don't believe in the creation of God, then you won't believe God rested from creation on the Sabbath day. Thus, in believing God as a creator and it allows an individual to understand of the Seal of the Ten Commandments, which is the fourth commandment that gives the name and title God as the Creator, and His territory being the heavens and the earth. In the same way human laws are approved by a seal, which has the official title of authority, and the place in which the title is valid, God in the 4th Commandment places His seal of authority by telling you His official title, The Lord God and area where the title is valid, all that is in the heavens, earth, and sea.

Now in verse 8, the beginning of this secular attack on the Bible was during the French revolution. The age of reason caused a frenzy amongst the inhabitants of France that caused them to burn The Bible and throw them out of their homes. People were killing priests, and other ministers of religion. Also, an angry French mob decided to kill Louis XVI and his wife Marie Antoinette in 1793. Henceforth, France would remain a republic without a monarchy. The French revolution was a microcosm of the events that will occur throughout the world in the final End Times when mankind makes its final rejection of God and His principles, and thus rejecting the divine light of truth, and justice mankind will rapidly degenerate into children of the Bad

Good Father, Bad Father

Father, who will control their minds to continually seek to do evil. Verses 9-11 of Revelation 11continue to describe the scenes witnessed in the French Revolution more than 1700 after John witnessed them and wrote them down after His Holy prophetic vision. John even gives a specific detailed mini-prophecy that was just for the French Revolution in verse 9 and 11,

> *"And they of the people and kindreds and tongues and nations shall see their dead bodies three days and an half, and shall not suffer their dead bodies to be put in graves. [...] And after three days and a half the Spirit of life from God entered into them, and they stood upon their feet; and great fear fell upon them which saw them."*

This mini-prophecy tailored to the events of the French revolution stated that in 3 days and a half, which if you apply the prophetic day per actual year rule, translates to 3 years and a half when the Word of God would be dead and it will rise again to life meaning that there would be a revival of the Word of God. This did in fact take place in November 1793, when the members of the French convention passed a decree that abolished religion in France. Thus, the French government in banning all forms of religion they actually killed the Word of God. W.H. Hutton wrote in "Age of Revolution," "On Nov. 26, 1793, the Convention, of which seventeen bishops and some clergy were members, decreed the abolition of all religion."[186] When this occurred, many people thought the abolition of religion validated the age of reason and scientific thought, and many thought the Bible would be a book of the past. But much to the surprise of the

---

[186] pg. 156, W.H Hutton, "Age of Revolution," as quoted in Our Day in the Light of Prophecy, pg.140

Eliseo Santos

contemporary observers of events, exactly 3 years and a half later on June 17, 1797, the French government reinstated religion after they saw the disastrous consequences of the abolition of religion had on society. Despite proclaiming to live in the age of enlightened human reasoning, the people reverted to the uncivilized standard of society, rather than the civilized society they proclaimed. Instead of living in a society of enlightened intellectuals, France became where the people became savages in every sense of the word.

From that point onward, the Bible would be taken more seriously especially after many saw how the Bible foresaw the French escapade into atheism and how their attempt to live in a society without God, was foretold by God 1700 hundred years before they even existed. The Bible became the foundation of new movements to evangelize the world with the words of truth, grace, and eternal life of the Bible. The first of these movements was that of the Bible societies and the movement to translate and send as many Bibles as possible to every region and corner of the earth. This movement began as soon as the events of French Revolution and the end of Daniel's 1260 year prophecy of Papal dominion ended in 1798. In 1804, the British Bible society and also the Foreign Bible society began studying and sharing the Words of eternal life with as many people as possible. Gone was the stigma of having and reading the Bible as many people both men of science, and politics, were reading and studying their Bibles on a routine basis. G.S. Faber wrote in His "Dissertation on the Prophecies," wrote the following description of the revival of the Bible from death, like the risen savior Jesus Christ,

> *"The stupendous endeavors of a one gigantic community to convey the Scriptures in every language to every part of the*

globe may well deserve to be considered as an eminent sign even of these eventful times. Unless I be much mistaken, such endeavors are preparatory to the final grand diffusion of Christianity, which is the theme of so many inspired prophets, and which cannot be very far distant in the present day." [187]

This quote encapsulates the Church of Philadelphia being the church of "brotherly love." Like the love of God to tell the truth of God to others, and keep the Commandments of God, this revival on Christianity showcased a society that was primarily based on the Love of God, the prosperity and peace that existed amongst many people, who shared the Word of God and spent time with one another learning about the many prophecies in the Bible.

Another important bible-based movement that started after the mortal wound of the Papal government, was the beginning the Protestant based missions to other countries. With the papacy losing its temporal and religious authority to persecute the people of God, now the People of God were free to roam the earth and proclaim the glory of God without any negative consequences. The fear of speaking and proclaiming one's thoughts and ideas as during the Middle Ages disappeared and now mankind had access to faster and increasingly affordable means of transportation via ships. With all these conditions, the People of God were ripe to yield a bountiful harvest for the real Lord of Lords and King of Kings, Jesus Christ. Dr. D.L. Leonard, commented on the revival of Protestant evangelism and missionary trips abroad that brought the message of Jesus Christ in a

---

[187] p. 406, G.S Faber, D.D., "Dissertation on the Prophecies," Vol. II, (1844) as quoted on pg. 308 of Our Day In The Light of Prophecy

peaceful and loving way to human brothers and sisters all around the world. He states,

> *The closing years of the eighteenth century constitute in the history of Protestant missions an epoch indeed, since they witnessed nothing less than a revolution, a renaissance, and effectual and manifold ending of the old, a substantial inauguration of the new. It was then that for the first time since the apostolic period, occurred an outburst of general missionary zeal and activity. Beginning in Great Britain, it soon spread to the Continent and across the Atlantic. It was no more push of fervor, but a mighty tide set in, which from that day to this day has been steadily rising and spreading.*[188]

Now that you have seen the workings of God in Europe with the French Revolution and the Papal wound, let us return to America and briefly review how God has worked in His providence with the Church of Philadelphia during the American Revolution.

---

[188] p. 69, Dr. D.L. Leonard, "A Hundred Years of Missions," on pg. 308 Our Day in the Light of Prophecy

Chapter 23: Protestantism and the 2nd Beast of Revelation

The persecution of the Church of Sardis led many of God's people away from Europe to the wide and open plains of North America. Throughout the 16th, 17th, and 18th centuries, many European Protestants would find peace and safety from oppression here in the shores of the North America and other parts of the world such as South Africa, and Australia. These Protestants were thankful for God for delivering them out of the persecution of the Roman Catholic Church and the Church of England. Many who grew up in the time period of the Church of Sardis would live in the era of the Church of Philadelphia, where they lived to see and believe in independence and freedom. There were few places in Europe where independence and freedom was guaranteed to Protestants. In the American Colonies they would gain a better appreciation of independence and freedom. Especially those who fled the persecutions and inquisitions of the Roman Catholic Church and other governments who would follow in the so-called example of intolerance and oppression established by Satan and his church. This is unlike the principles of patience and love found established by God and found within His church.

Two examples of Protestant settlers, who believed in religious freedom and freedom of conscience, were Roger Williams and William Penn. These two individuals felt strongly that no human being should be coerced into the religious beliefs of another, and they believed that every human being is given the ability to discern truth from lies, and justice from injustice. The convictions of their beliefs were a key component of their leadership as early governors of the colonies of Rhode Island, and Pennsylvania.

Roger Williams, and William Penn founded colonies that not only reflected Protestant values, but also included the liberties and freedoms that were later incorporated into the United States Constitution. Roger Williams, founded Rhode Island, after witnessing the same problems within the Puritan establishment in Massachusetts that were found in the Roman Catholic Church and the Church of England. The major problem witnessed by Roger Williams was the unholy mixture of church and state that caused unjust oppression of those who did not agree with the Puritan principles. The Puritans forced people to go to church and even publicly whipped those who fell asleep in church. Despite trying to live Godly lives, which is a noble purpose, the Puritans failed to take into account the importance of an individual's free will and conscience. Roger Williams questioned The Puritan's form of government and its practices. In 1636, Roger Williams escaped the colony and founded his own colony. Williams' government set a precedent in not interfering with religion. The people of Rhode Island were free to worship God according to their conscience, and the people were not forced to attend church. The Pilgrims and Puritans of Massachusetts bay, despite seeing the value of religious freedom for themselves, they did not give it to others. For example, Roman Catholics and Jews were banned from Massachusetts in the early days of the Colonial period.[189]

---

[189] American Adventures, New Edition, Volume One, A Nation Conceived and Dedicated pg. 28

Good Father, Bad Father

William Penn, another English settler, who became a Quaker after witnessing how the Quakers heroically stayed back and took care of those who fell ill and victim to the spread of the "black plague" of 1665. William Penn, would run into the trouble for upholding the Quaker beliefs in peace, non-violence, and honesty in all areas of life. They were against unfair treatment against individuals, and thus they actively volunteered to the help the sick and help those in prison. After being arrested three times and going through horrific conditions in the Tower of London, he asked the king for a favor. His father was a wealthy Navy hero and the current King at the time Charles II owed William Penn's father a large sum of money. William Penn asked the King for a plot of land in the rapidly growing colonies instead of his father's money. After receiving the deed to Pennsylvania, Penn would become its first governor. One of the revolutionary things that Penn did was create a Charter of Liberties for Pennsylvania, which later on became the framework for the U.S. Constitution. The Charter of Liberties stated that lawmakers of the colony would be elected by male citizens who resided at the colony. Thus, it would not behoove the residents to make laws that enforce or give favor to one religion. Penn's Charter of Liberties also protected freedom of religion and speech, as well as ensured a trial by jury of peers for any accusation of a crime. [190]

Roger Williams and William Penn both created governments that were repugnant to the mixture of Church and State and by creating the governments that were not involved in religion. The truths based on the eternal values of liberty of conscience, which includes freedom of speech, thought, and religion, proceed from the Good Father God of

---

[190] American Adventures, New Edition, Volume One, A Nation Conceived and Dedicated pg. 29-30

the Bible. Paul sums the principle of freedom in the Bible in Galatians 5:1, "Stand fast therefore in the liberty wherewith Christ hath made us free, and be not entangled again with the yoke of bondage." In Christ, you are given the truth that not only frees you from the yoke of bondage, which are your sins, but also gives you the truth of a better eternal life in His Heavenly Kingdom. In heaven, every act is done of out the love for God and His greatness and mercy.

New churches would be formed from the group of religious individuals who saw that a key component of God's Word was missing with in a church's religious teachings and services. Thus, in America came many other religious movements that sought to establish Protestant churches here in America. In the same way Church of England left the Roman Catholic Church, many other religious movements sought to leave the Church of England for its resemblance to the tyranny of the Roman Catholic Church. Two of these religious groups were the Pilgrims, and the Protestant Puritans. A key mark that identified these religious groups descendants of the Roman Church was that all of them continued to keep the Sunday observance, instead of the Word of God and His Ten Commandments. These churches have spent so much time in darkness that they started to act like the Roman Church of intolerance and persecution. The men and women of God raised up during the Times of Sardis, were ultimately useful in the spread of Biblical Christianity and its principles.

Many of the enemies of these authoritative churches sought and found a better way of life in the North American colonies and colonies established in other regions. It is from this group of Protestants that saw in Colonial America a better way of life of freedom and independence. Many sought to only listen to God and

Good Father, Bad Father

His Holy Word, even though their enforcement of the religion suffered.

> "For more than two centuries the humbler Protestant sects had sent up the cry to heaven for freedom to worship God. To the panting for this freedom half the American states owed their existence, and all but one or two their increase in free population. The immense majority of the inhabitants of the thirteen colonies were Protestant dissenters; and, from end to end of their continent, from the rivers of Maine and the hills of New Hampshire to the mountain valleys of Tennessee and the borders of Georgia, one voice called to the other that there should be no connection of the Church with the State, no establishment of any one form of religion by the civil power; that "all men have a natural and unalienable right to worship God according to the dictates of their own consciences and understandings." With this great idea the colonies had travailed for a century and a half; and now, not as revolutionary, not as destructive, but simply as giving utterance to the thought of the nation, the states stood up in succession, in the presence of one another and before God and the world, to bear their witness in favor of restoring independence to conscience and the mind. The establishment of liberty of conscience, which brought with it liberty of speech and of the press, was, in the several states, the fruit not of philosophy, but of the love of Protestantism for the open Bible...But from the beginning the Church no longer formed a part of the State; and religion, ceasing to be a servant of the government, or an instrument of dominion, became a life in the soul. Public worship was voluntarily sustained. Nowhere was persecution for religious opinion so nearly at an end as in America, and nowhere was there so religious a people.[191]

---

[191] pp. 119-122, Bancroft's History of the United States, Vol. V., as quoted in pg.375, Romanism: A Menace To The Nation, By Jeremiah J. Crowley, The Menace Publishing Co., 1912
"Tenure

Eliseo Santos

It would be from this historical background in which the founding fathers would write their constitution and would seek come up with a civil equivalent to God's immutable law, the Ten Commandments, by forming the Bill of Rights or the first Ten Amendments of the U.S. Constitution. The eternal truths of freedom and independence were the principles of God would later on be included in the U.S. Constitution and its bill of rights. The United States became one of the first governments in the world to not recognize the Papacy in their Constitution. This would be found in the 1st amendment and the establishment clause, "Congress shall make no law respecting an establishment of religion, or prohibiting the free exercise thereof." Such a government would make it very difficult for the Papacy to proclaim a universal entitlement and sovereignty. Rev. P.A. Baart, a supporter of Roman Catholic Canon wrote the following about the United States,:

> *Each of the 13 thirteen colonies, before the revolution of 1776, recognized some form of Protestantism as its state church, and several levied taxes for the support of the authorized worship. To prevent contention, the constitution of the United States, in its first amendment, prohibits the recognition of a state religion, though it intends that all forms of Christianity shall be protected from disturbance in worship and in property. Because of this constitutional prohibition, the government of the United States does not recognize the Catholic Church as such, nor can the Church as such become incorporated.* [192]

---

[192] "Tenure of Catholic Church Property in the United States of America" section 19 as quoted on pg.356, Romanism:A Menace to The Nation, By F. Jeremiah J.Crowley,Menace Publishing

Good Father, Bad Father

Now if the Bible spoke about the French Revolution, is it possible that they would also speak of America as well? The answer is yes, John in Revelation did take into account America. In John Revelation 13:11, he states "And I beheld another beast coming up out of the earth; and he had two horns like a lamb, and he spake as a dragon."

Before explaining verse 11, you must understand Revelation 13:verses 9-10 in order to gain a sense of where in history is John referring is to in this part of the Bible. John here is describing the time period towards the end of Papal authority of 1260 years which ended in 1798. John describes the mortal wound of the Papacy in Revelation 13:9-10, "If any man have an ear, let him hear. He that leadeth into captivity shall go into captivity; he that killeth with the sword must be killed with the sword. Here is the patience and the faith of the Saints." John here like Christ parables cover multiple layers of truth within a span of a few words. In the literal sense, John was giving advice to future generations of God's people of what to do in captivity, if you are to be taken captive then into captivity you shall go without resistance. In doing so, you show that you trust God and His promises. If you are to die for Christ's namesake, then you will die for Christ's namesake and then you will be resurrected to eternal life as Christ was when He died. If you decide to kill anyone, you eventually have to die in a like manner. In the historical sense, John was also describing in a detailed way in which Napoleon, through his General Berthier, would capture the Pope and the Pope remained in captivity, and thus the 1260 years of prophecy ended. Napoleon, who gave the order for Pope Pius VI to be captured, was himself in captivity in the last days of his life[193]. Both interpretations also tie into the following

---

[193] "Napoleon," American Peoples Encyclopedia, Volume 13,

expression in verse 10 of "the patience and faith of the saints." John in describing the rise of another beast after the mortal wound and the end of the 1260 years of papal supremacy is describing how another type of beast government will grow after 1798. Instead of growing out of many waters, or many multitudes of people in Europe, this beast will grow from an area that was sparsely populated region of the earth. Which government after the mortal wound of the Roman Catholic Church rose to world supremacy starting from an area not heavily populated as in Europe? The United States of course fits the description because it was a country formed primarily of Protestants that fled oppression in Europe. The United States was also a country formed by other European merchants who entered into business ventures in the Colonies, and the native indigenous population, as well as the many African slaves all would eventually call America home. This identity is further corroborated by the following phrase in verse 11, "he had two horns like a lamb, and he spoke as dragon." In other words, the Bible is stating that the United States throughout its history has been under the influence of the Good Father God, and the bad father, Satan.

The way in which a beast speaks is through its laws. Early on in America's history, despite passing laws that reflected Protestant Christian values such as the U.S. Constitution and Bill of Rights, the same lawmakers would make laws that would reflect the principles of Satan, which was evident in laws that further enhanced slavery. An example of such a law early in America's history that received, approval was "The Three/Fifths Compromise." If you are not familiar with the Three/Fifths Compromise, it was a passed resolution to count

---

Pg. 254, Grolier incorporated, New York, NY, 1967

Good Father, Bad Father

a slave, usually of African descent, as three/fifths of a person. This was done in early days of the U.S. Government in figuring out a fair way to count and compare the populations of the North, where slavery was rarely seen, from the populations of the South, which was an early major agricultural center that commonly used slaves or indentured servants. It would take about 100 years, up until in 1863 to emancipate or free the slaves, and it would take another 100 years for them many to have equal learning opportunities.

America's ultimate purpose and destiny according to the Bible would be in reviving the Roman Catholic Church and its powers of the Middle-Ages. If John with the Holy Spirit was accurate with the French Revolution, John would also be accurate concerning the America and its future. John states in Revelation 13:12, "And he exerciseth all the power of the first beast before him, and causeth the earth and them which dwell therein to worship the first beast, whose deadly wound was healed." This description by John is significant if you take into account what is said in Revelation 13: 2, when referring to the 1st beast "the dragon gave him his power, and his seat, and great authority." Therefore, if the 2nd beast exerciseth all the power of the 1st beast, and if the dragon gave the 1st beast His power then, then the 2nd beast exerciseth the power of the dragon. In laymen's terms, that concludes Satan gave his power to the Papacy and the Roman Catholic Church, and the 2nd beast the United States exerciseth all the power of Papacy, which was given by Satan. Thus, when John describes the United States as "having two horns like a lamb and he spake as a dragon," John is describing what will America will ultimately become, it would become a government that began with Christ-like Protestant principles and then it will end up becoming a government that speaks "or creates" laws which are Satanic in nature. Throughout history of the 2nd Beast, Satan has been secretly working and influencing America, to gain control of America, and then use America as the vehicle to bring back his church, the Roman Catholic Papacy back into power. Signs of Satan gaining control over America and its laws have been evident in two statues dedicated to Satan in Oklahoma, and the other in Detroit. Keep in mind, that statues of the Ten Commandments were taken down, and instead of seeking God, people seem to be seeking Satan.

John explains how this will be done in Revelation 13:13-15, when he states,

> *And he doeth great wonders, so that he maketh fire come down from heaven on the earth in the sight of men. And deceiveth them that dwell on the earth by means of those miracles, which he had power to do in sight of the beast; saying to them that dwell on the earth, that they should make an image to the beast, which had the wound by a sword, and did live. And he had power to give life unto the image of the beast, that the image of the beast should both speak, and cause that as many as would not worship the image of the beast should be killed.*

Apostate Protestantism is the image of the beast that will be formed in America. The image of the beast, is an expression that symbolizes something that is done to show honor to the beast. Apostate Protestantism primarily grew in the United States and it will gain a greater influence on the government until their influence will be as such that they will come to resemble the 1st beast. A sign that this will occur in America, is in verse 14, "And deceiveith them that dwell on the earth by means of those miracles which he had power to do in the sight of the beast; saying to them that dwell on the earth, that they should make an image to the beast, which had the wound of the sword and yet lived." This means that the form of government of the 2nd beast is a form of government where the people have a say in the laws of the land, and thus, this is why the 2nd beast must convince the people to make an image to the beast. Notice that this different from Daniel 3, where the King Nebuchadnezzar was able to call for a statue or image without convincing the people of it. The 2nd beast will convince the people by working great signs and wonders in order to deceive the people into believing that they should make an image of the beast, when in fact it is prohibited in the Bible because it is idolatry. Revelation 13 verse 15 states that it was the 2nd beast, "And he had power to give life unto the image of the beast, that the image of the beast should both speak, and cause that as many as would not worship the image of the beast should be killed." Here John is explaining that in America, the image of the beast of Apostate Protestantism, or in other words, a Protestantism that follows the Roman Church rather than God and His Biblical words, will gain influence over the government so that "the image of the beast, would be worshipped by everyone or else they will be killed. In Revelation 13:16-17, describes a law that would be made at the request of the image of the Beast (Apostate Protestantism), "And he causeth all, both, small and great, rich and poor, free and bond, to receive a mark in their right hand, or in their foreheads. And that no man might buy or sell, save he that had the mark, or the name of the beast, or the number of his name." Therefore, the mark of the beast is a law that will be passed in America at the request of Apostate Protestantism, for the purpose of implementing a nationwide enforced Sunday law. This law will require that every single man, woman, and child to go to church on Sunday. If you don't then you lose access to your bank account. Why is the mark of the beast a Nationwide Sunday law? First, keep in mind that a beast is a king on earth who seeks to become like a god. Therefore, a mark of the beast is a sign of his authority of convincing the people that he is someone like a god. Second, John uses language that is similarly used in the Old Testament when describing God's Ten Commandments in Deuteronomy 6: 8, states, "And thou shalt bind them for a sign upon thine hand, and they shall be as frontlets between thy eyes." The Mark of the beast will seek to counter God's law and His 4th Commandment concerning remembering the worship of the 7th Day Sabbath. God's 4th commandment reads,

> *Remember thy Sabbath day, to keep it holy. Six days shalt thou labor, and do all thy work. But the seventh day is the Sabbath of the Lord thy God: in it thou shalt not do any work, thou, nor thy son, nor thy daughter, thy manservant, nor thy maidservant, nor thy cattle, nor thy stranger that is within thy gates. For in six days the Lord made the heaven and earth, the sea, and all that in them is, and rested the seventh-day: wherefore the Lord blessed the Sabbath day, and hallowed it. – Exodus 20:8-11*

Therefore, because God created us, and the heavens, and the earth, and filled it with natural mechanisms to ensure life on the planet continues, God rested on the 7th Day Sabbath, as memorial of His creation and to spend time with humanity and His creation. Therefore, in keeping the 7th Day Sabbath, you not only recognize God as the Creator, but also recognize that He is in control of the universe. It is by keeping the 7th-Day Sabbath of God, that an individual shows His love and devotion toward God. By believing in the 7th-Day Sabbath, you also recognize that 2nd Coming of Christ and His words that He was in fact the Son of God, who was also present during the Creation of the earth.

In order to undermine the Ten Commandments, of God and the laws of the nation, there have been many secret societies, who all strive for building and ushering in the world system that will lead to the downfall of humanity rather than its rise.

Chapter 24: Subversive Secret Societies in America

John in the Book of Revelation 13:12 states concerning America's future "And he exerciseth all the power of the first beast before him, and causeth the earth and them which dwell therein to worship the first beast, whose deadly wound was healed." Therefore, given the symbolic language employed thus far, John foretells how America would help the first beast regain control and until the mortal wound of the Roman Catholic Church is fully healed. In the early days of framing the U.S. government and constitution, Benjamin Franklin and the other founding fathers were debating the design of the U.S. Flag and also which animal would best reflect the principles of the young Nation. The American Encyclopedia states:

> *"Prior to 1782 Benjamin Franklin pointed out to Congress that the bald eagle, because a great deal of its food is secured by robbery, and because it is sometimes bullied out of its nest by the much smaller great horned owl, it was not a sufficiently noble bird to be chosen as the nation's emblem. He proposed the wild turkey more suitable."*[194]

---

[194] pg.3, Eagle, American People's Encyclopedia, Vol. 7, Grolier Incorporated, 1967, Library of Congress Catalog Card Number: 67-10584

Eliseo Santos

Here Benjamin Franklin is in essence symbolically restating what John foresaw in America more than 1700 years earlier in his prophetic vision. John saw the beast that had "two horns like a lamb and he spake as a dragon," (Revelation 13:11). Like the Bible stated how America would appear to be a nation that values the principles of Protestantism, such as God, civic, and religious freedom, it would secretly become a government that would value Papal despotism, Satan, indoctrination, and oppression. John even foretells that America would one day turn its back on the foundational principles of Protestantism and would try to replace them with subversive human principles. Like Benjamin Franklin fittingly said how "the bald eagle is bullied out of its nest by the much smaller owl" these subversive human principles would gain ground in America because many Americans would allow for secret societies to gain power in society by keeping secrets and by lying to the American public. John foretells how the United States would one day seek to help the 1st beast of the Papacy regain its power and control. This work has been done in secret through the various networks of secret societies that exist in America and throughout the world.

In order to allow the Roman Catholic Church to control the United States, it would require the Jesuit order to be back in power and reinstated. This occurred in 1814 when the Jesuits order were suddenly and out of the blue reinstated by the very Roman Church that condemned them 41 years earlier in 1773. Do you really believe that the Jesuits would just sit back and wait for the church to reinstate them? No, the Jesuits were very much covertly active throughout Europe, working through several different front groups. Keep in mind that the Jesuits were banned in 1773 and thus, needed a new cover for their operations. In 1776, a Jesuit Professor of theology from

Good Father, Bad Father

Ingolstadt University, which at that time was a major Jesuit college in Bavaria would initiate the dreaded Illuminati of Bavaria. The Illuminati using the cover of a freemasonic secret society would be a cover for the Jesuits to infiltrate governments, businesses, and other areas of societies throughout the world for the purpose of gaining control over all the major leaders of the world, and the Jesuits would eventually be in control of them. Remember, one of the important classes within the Jesuit organization are coadjutors, thus when a mason within freemasonry reaches a high enough level, he then becomes aware that they are actually working for the reestablishment of the Pope and his political power and authority worldwide. Thus, freemasonry is the training ground for many of the coadjutors of the Jesuit order that will infiltrate and follow the directions of the order. Similar to the Knight Templars, who were created by the Roman Church and were then abolished were by the church when they saw how powerful they had become, the Jesuits also gained much power and influence in not only society but in the Roman Church. The Jesuits had acquired so much power and influence that they were able to reinstate the Jesuit Order even after Pope Clement XIV had suppressed and abolished the Jesuit Order. This means that from 1814 and onwards the Jesuits would carry great power and influence within the Roman Catholic Church. Usually, a pope does not undo a legal order, because then their infallibility would be put into limbo. The Jesuits were able to regain the power and influence in society by creating the Illuminati as a front group for their operations.

How do we know this is the case? First, let's look at the founder of the Jesuit Order who was Loyola. Loyola was involved in the order of The Alumbrados (or the enlightened ones in Spanish), which began in 1520[195]. This secret order much like the Rosicrucian of the Dark and Middle Ages, practiced occult arts such speaking with spirits or demons, and also practiced the things which are an abomination to the Lord, mainly, "witch craft, wizardry, divination, and other practices that involve contact with demons," (Deuteronomy 18:9-12). Ingolstadt University was one of the many universities that were under the control of the Jesuit's from the 16th to 18th century. After the order of suppression was given to the Jesuits, they headed toward Prussia, Bavaria, and Russia whose monarchs felt they were obliged to give the Jesuits asylum at that time. However, the monarchs in Prussia and Russia would eventually remove the Jesuits from their kingdoms as well. The monarch Frederik of Prussia realized that they were up to the same schemes of seeking power and control this time for the suppressed order. He through extraordinary circumstances found documents belonging to the Bavarian Illuminati. After finding these documents, Frederik of Prussia banned and dissolved the order of Illuminati from Bavaria in 1785[196]. In the following year in 1786, Frederik of Prussia decided to expel the Jesuits out of Prussia and no longer afford them asylum[197]. Eventually, the Jesuits were also removed from Russia after being granted asylum by Empress Catherine. In 1820, the Jesuits were removed from Russia by Tsar Alexander I. Frederik of Prussia's expulsion of the Bavarian Illuminati and the Jesuits in consecutive years from Bavaria is a sign that the Jesuits are linked to the Illuminati. Given the fact that at the time, they were suppressed and expelled from the Roman Church then it would make sense for the Jesuits to continue their operations under

---

[195] Illuminati, Pg. 10-932, Illuminati, A.P.E., vol.10, 1958, Chicago, Spencer Press Inc.
[196] Pg.10-932, Illuminati, Ibid.
[197] pg. 102, Secret History of the Jesuits, Edmond Paris

Good Father, Bad Father

the cover of their creation of the Bavarian Illuminati. Therefore, this is a sign that the Jesuits are linked with the Illuminati, and thus the most logical explanation is for the Jesuits to have created the Illuminati in 1776, after the Jesuits were suppressed in 1773.

Now the first signs of the Illuminati was during the French Revolution. Napoleon's older brother during the French Revolution was the head of the Illuminati in Europe. Thus, the Jesuits used Napoleon to overthrow and kill off the French monarchy for their role in the demise of the Jesuits, and the demise of the Knight's Templars in the 14th century. Once they overthrew the government they substituted it with an atheist government that was based on civil rights instead of the self-evident rights that proceed from the Ten Commandments of God. As a result of being based on civil rights instead of the Commandments of God, France plunged itself into widespread lust and savagery. In 1797, after three and a half years, the French government reinstated religion for the people allowing the practice of religion because they saw the catastrophic results without God, in the lives of French citizens.

After the death of Pope Pius VI in French captivity, Pope Pius VII was elected to the Papal throne in 1799. During this time Napoleon, under the direction of the Jesuits, would seek to conquer Europe and unite all of Europe under one ruler, who would then be controlled by the Jesuits. The Jesuits were controlling Napoleon Bonaparte and his attack on the nations of Europe during the Napoleonic wars. Napoleon's motive for waging such wars on other European nations has never been questioned and always explained as the result of one man's ambition and greed for power. However, given the historical facts from the time period, the most likely explanation for the Napoleonic Wars is that it was a form of revenge on the part of the

Eliseo Santos

Jesuits against the countries that supported the suppression and abolishment of the Jesuits. The Vatican and the monarchs of Europe roles' in the suppression and abolishment of the Jesuit order led to their removal from power through Napoleon under the direction of the Jesuit Order. Napoleon had these words to say about the Jesuits:

> *The Jesuits are a military organization, not a religious order. Their chief is a general of an army, not the mere father abbot of a monastery. And the aim of this organization is: POWER. Power in its most despotic exercise. Absolute power, universal power, power to control the world by the volition of a single man. Jesuitism is the most absolute of despotisms; and at the same the greatest and enormous of abuses... The general of the Jesuits insists on being master, sovereign, over the sovereign. Wherever the Jesuits are admitted they will be masters, cost what it may. Their society is by nature dictatorial, and therefore it is the irreconcilable enemy of all constituted authority. Every act, every crime, however atrocious, is a meritorious work, if committed for the interest of the Society of Jesuits, or by the order of the general.* $-^{198}$

The Jesuits are at odds with the principles and teachings of Jesus Christ. Christ says in Mark 8:36, "For what shall it profit a man, if he shall gain the whole world, lose his own soul?" This point also reiterated in Matthew 16:26, and Luke 9:25. Christ is saying essentially that selfishness and greed eventually led to death. Selfishness and greed were the primary motivation behind the Jesuits who sought to create a New World Order under the authority of one man, the Pope. It is better for an individual to renounce the whole world, and sell or give away everything he owns and follow in the

---

[198] General Montholon, Memorial of the Captivity of Napoleon at St. Helena pp. 62, 174- as quoted in pg.13 of the Secret Terrorists By Bill Hughes

footsteps of Christ because then not only do you get to obtain eternal life, but also as Christ states in Revelation 3:21, "To him that overcometh will I grant to sit with me in my throne, even as I also overcame, and am set with my Father in his throne." In other words, Christ is so unselfish and selfless that he even offers us the opportunity to rule the universe alongside Him and His Father. Take a moment for that to sink in and think about how large and expansive is the known universe. Not only does Christ offer us, eternal life but also offers us the ability to rule with Him. This shows how human words fail to describe how infinitely abundant is His love for us. This shows how the Jesuits are far from the principles of Jesus Christ of the Bible and closer to the principles of Satan, whose highest aim is to impersonate Jesus Christ as the anti-Christ.

Despite this Jesuits will set the framework for acquiring control of the whole world through the use of the illuminati and other Freemasonic organizations, for the purpose of infiltrating every government, religion, and major industry to secure global control for the Pope and Jesuit order. The Jesuits first used the Napoleonic wars in an early bid to unify all of Europe. The Jesuits failed to achieve their goal. Through Napoleon, the Jesuits did get some revenge on the monarchs and countries that implored Pope Clement XIV to sign the order of suppression. The Jesuits knowing that their plan to conquer Europe failed, asked Napoleon to reinstate the Papacy and Pope Pius VII. By reinstating Pius VII, the mortal wound began to heal, although very slowly. The Papacy at the time was still heavily influenced by Napoleon and the Jesuits, who were still operating against the orders of the Papacy. In 1800, Pope Pius VII returned to the Vatican and Napoleon and the Pope drew up articles for the Concordat of 1801. However in 1802 Napoleon issued the organic articles which greatly diminished the abilities of the Vatican from the previous Concordat[199]. Pius VII then agreed to crown Napoleon the emperor of France to regain the concessions.[200] Napoleon refused to lose power and thus he crowned himself as emperor on Dec. 2, 1804 in Notre Dame Cathedral in the presence of Pope Pius VII as a sign of approval[201]. Then, Napoleon would once again run into trouble with the Vatican. In 1808-1809, self-proclaimed Emperor Napoleon decided to annex Rome and the Papal states. Pope Pius VII retaliated by threatening to excommunicate Napoleon. In response, Napoleon once again arrested the Pope and transferred him to Florence, Grenoble, and Savona. Eventually, once the Jesuits saw again Napoleon was on the losing side of the war then in 1814 the Jesuits approached Pope Pius VII and reinstated the Jesuit Order.

Therefore in terms of the Bible and Bible prophecy, the Papacy has still suffered its mortal wound, and still has limited power. John writes in Revelation 13:3, "And I saw one of his heads as it were wounded to death; and his deadly wound was healed." At the turn of the 19th century, the Papacy was still in critical condition after receiving a deadly wound. However, John sees that from his perspective the mortal would be healed, meaning the Bible foretold how the Papacy would regain the overt power, strength, and influence it lost when Pope Pius VI was arrested in 1798. Overall, the events from the mortal wound and loss of papal political power in 1798, to their slight healing during 1800-1814 would be a sign that it would be a long time before the Papacy wields the same papal political power

---

[199] pg. 71, Pius VII, American Peoples Encyclopedia, Vol.15, 1967, Grolier incorporated

[200] pg. 71, ibid

[201] pg. 253, Napoleon Bonaparte APE, , Vol. 13, 1967, Grolier,

Good Father, Bad Father

that it wielded during the Dark and Middle Ages. It would take a long time for example for the Papacy to regain the overt political power it once enjoyed to publicly call for the deaths of Bible-believing Christians as it once was able to do openly during the Dark and Middle Ages. The Papacy would be forced into the "wilderness" as John describes the Papacy in Rev. 17:3, "So he carried me away in the spirit into the wilderness: and I saw a woman sit upon a scarlet colored beast, full of names of blasphemy, having seven heads and ten horns." Here this woman is a symbol of the Roman Catholic Church, who is in the wilderness sitting upon a scarlet colored beast, full of names of blasphemy with seven heads and ten horns. Therefore, if we compare this scarlet colored beast with the leopard beast of Rev. 13 they have the same description of 7 heads and ten horns, as well as the blasphemous names on its heads. The only difference between the scarlet beast of Rev. 17 and the first beast of Rev. 13 is that the leopard beast rose out of the sea, and the scarlet beast in Rev. 17 is currently standing in the desert. Keep in mind that in the Bible, "wilderness" is another word that describes a desert, or a period of time of restraint. Israel spent forty years in the wilderness according to Deuteronomy 1:1. When wilderness is mentioned, it is referring to Israel's time in the desert. During this time in the desert, Israel was in restraint. Likewise after 1798, the Papacy would symbolically be in the desert and would lose the overt political power and influence that it previously had in the world. This caused the papacy to enter a period of political and temporal restraint. The desert is another fitting symbol to describe the lack of "waters" or people, multitudes, nations, and tongues that would be under the control of the Papacy. However, when John first sees the woman in Rev. 17:1, John describes her in the following manner, "And there came out one of the seven angels which had the seven vials, and talked with me, saying unto me, Come hither; 'I will show unto thee the judgment of the great whore that sitteth upon many waters.'" Here John is referring to a future time when God will have judgment upon the woman. Thus, from verse 3 and onwards John is describing the woman in the past tense. This signifies that John is describing the woman, or the Roman Catholic Church after its mortal wound in 1798. Therefore, the scarlet colored beast in this case is a symbol of all the cardinals that have become Pope and have led the great whore the Roman Catholic Church after 1798. This interpretation is validated by the following verse that states, "And the woman was arrayed in purple and scarlet colour, and decked with gold and precious stones and pearls, having a golden cup in her hand full of abominations and filthiness of her fornication." The scarlet colored beast, in other words, is a kingdom that seeks to become like God that carries its own church. The Great Whore or the Roman Catholic Church is dressed in purple and scarlet, or by the archbishops and cardinals that control the many diocese and archdiocese of the Roman Church. Just so that the reader can be very clear and not confused on the identity of this woman, John states, "that the woman has a golden cup in her hand full of abominations and filthiness of her fornication,"(Revelation 17:4). The golden cup in the hand of the woman represents the chalice that at times holds the communion wafer, and is a sign of the doctrine of the Eucharist and mass.

In the Roman Catholic mass Christ is once again transubstantiated and sacrificed before the altar to the attendees of a Roman Catholic Mass. This is blasphemy and an abomination because according to Roman Catholic theology, the priest has the ability to once again sacrifice the same Jesus Christ that died on the Cross. Apparently

Good Father, Bad Father

Roman Catholic theologians, and through the ecumenical movement theologians from other churches, do not recognize Hebrews 10:10-12, when referring to the New Covenant where in Jesus is the only High-Priest who forgives sins:

> *"By the which will we are sanctified through the offering of the body of Jesus Christ once for all. And every priest standeth daily ministering and offering sometimes the same sacrifices, which can never take away sins. But this man, after he had offered one sacrifice for sins forever, sat down on the right hand of God."*

Therefore this quote explains why it is an abomination for a Roman Catholic Priest to claim to have the ability to turn ordinary bread into the actual body and blood of Christ, and then in breaking that bread he once again sacrifices the body of Christ. Christ sacrificed Himself for the sins of humanity once for all, therefore no more priesthood is needed nor any other sacrifice. Paul states in 1 Timothy 2:5, "For there is one God, and one mediator between God and men, the man Christ Jesus." To continue a priesthood and daily service of sacrifice is to continually belittle the infinite redemptive power of Christ to save humanity. How can the body of Christ be broken by the priest if there was no broken bones found in Him? John 19:36 states "For these things were done, that the scripture should be fulfilled, A bone of him shall not be broken." When the Bible mentions the "golden cup full of abominations and the filthiness of her fornication" it refers to the Eucharist and mass are services in which have a human pagan origin that is not pleasing to God because it does not come from the Bible. Therefore, when the Bible calls this mass service an abomination, it does so because it is a service based on the confusion of the real Jesus Christ of the Bible, with the pagan esoteric Jesus Christ, who was created as Satan's future role as a literal anti-Christ.

The restoration of the Jesuit order was a significant step for the Vatican to take especially after officially banning them in 1773. Usually a Pope does not undo a decision, to do so would admit that the first decision was a mistake and thus the Pope comes to obvious reality that he is fallible like other humans. However, the reasoning behind Pius VII decision was that the Papacy is a lot stronger in terms of political power with them than without them. In reinstating the Jesuits, the Pope and the papal chair would forever fall under control of the Black pope or the Superior General of the Jesuit order. In the Papal bull that re-established the Jesuits Pope Pius VII stated the following:

> *After having by fervent prayers implored the Divine assistance, after having taken the advice and counsel of a great number of our venerable brothers, the cardinals of the Holy Roman Church, we have decreed, with full knowledge, in virtue of the plenitude of apostolic power, and with perpetual validity, that all the concessions and powers granted by us solely to the Russian empire and the kingdom of the Two Sicilies, shall henceforth extend to all our ecclesiastical states, and also to other states.* [202]

Here Pope Pius VII, gives notice in an implicit way, that the United States would be targeted by the Jesuits. At that time, the United States were the only group of States in the whole world that never recognized the Roman Catholic Church and the Pope as a

---

[202] pg.445,History of the Jesuits,G.B.Nicolini,1854

political authority. It was a government based on Protestant values based on the early settlers of the nation. Now it would be the subversive secret society of the Jesuits, with the help of its front organizations of the Illuminati and Freemasonry that would gain control of America. Once it gained control of America, the Jesuits would work through their networks of secret societies as a vehicle to revive the overt political power of the papacy. This became evident in the latter half of the 20th century, when the Pope started to become a popular political/religious figure. The words of John in Rev. 13:12 will become even more evident in the future. "And he exerciseth all the power of the first beast before him, and causeth the earth, and them which dwell therein to worship the first beast, whose deadly wound was healed."

Chapter 25: Revelation 17 and 666

Out of the many amazing prophecies that have been fulfilled according to God's words, the most unknown and misunderstood is Revelation 17: 9-11,

> *"And here is the mind which hath wisdom. The seven heads are seven mountains, on which the woman sitteth. And there are seven kings: five are fallen, and one is, and the other is not yet come; and when he cometh, he must continue a short space. And the beast, that was, is not, even he is the eighth, and is of the seven, and goeth into perdition."*

These three verses have confused many Bible scholars for centuries. Many have related the seven mountains to the hills of Rome, which was a valid interpretation for the past generations who were not living in the End Times. However, these End-Time verses are actually linked with the End-Time verse of Revelation 13:18, "Here is wisdom. Let him that hath understanding count the number of the Beast: for it is the number of a man; and the number is six hundred threescore and six." The previous verse is linked to the previous passage from Revelation 17:9-11 because both require wisdom. What wisdom is God referring to in these two passages?

First, it is important to take note of Babylonian history. Ancient Babylon was a civilization that was proficient in arithmetic. The

Eliseo Santos

Babylonian priests would create amulets that had a six by six square. In the squares of the amulet, the numbers 1-36 would be arranged in such a way so that if you add each row, or column you would get the number 111. Then 111 for 6 rows or columns would equal six hundred sixty six. When the Bible labels the Roman Catholic Church as "Mystery Babylon," in Revelation 14:8; 17:5; 18:2, the Bible is telling the reader that the Roman Catholic Church system possesses similar spiritual qualities and attributes with Babylon. Thus, the eighth from Rev. 17 and the number of a man six hundred sixty six have to be related to the practices that were done in Babylon. Also, in using the eighth in Rev. 17 and using the information from Rev. 13:18, it tells you to count or add to arrive at the number of a man six hundred sixty six. In order to understand, it is important to review important mathematical identities via arithmetic sums that were also prominent in Babylon. In order to fully understand, you must be aware of the following arithmetic sums of 8 and 36. In other words, when you add $1+2+3+4....+8 = 36$ and when you add from 1 to 36 you arrive at the following number $1+2+3+4+5+6+7...+36 = 666$. Therefore, when you add 1-8, then it will eventually lead you to the sum of 666.

Now how do these numbers relate to the Bible? In the Book of Daniel there are several important ideas that will be important to remember. The first, in Dan 2:37-38,

> *"Thou O king, art a king of kings; for the God of heaven have given thee a kingdom, power, and strength, and glory. And wheresoever, the children of men dwell, the beasts of the field and the fowls of the heaven hath he given thee unto thine hand, and made thee ruler over them all. Thou art this head of gold."*

Good Father, Bad Father

In Babylon, there was a king who was also compared to a head of the statue of Daniel's dream. Remember, Daniel had Nebuchadnezzar's dream and saw a statue built with the head of Gold, chest and arms of Silver, thighs of bronze, and legs of Iron, and feet of Iron and Clay. Many fail to notice that this head, not only referred to Nebuchadnezzar, but all the kings who ruled over Babylon. The head of gold represented first Nebuchadnezzar and ended with the last king of Babylon, when it fell to the Medes and Persians as foretold by Daniel 2. This is evident in Daniel Ch. 5 when Belshazzar who was the last King of Babylon before it was destroyed. [203]Also, keep in mind, in Daniel 3, Nebuchadnezzar after receiving Daniel's interpretation in Daniel 2 sought to become like a god by creating a statue of pure gold, and have everyone worship it. This was a statement that the Kingdom of Babylon would last forever. However, there were three Hebrew youths who did not abide by Nebuchadnezzar's law of enforced idolatry, which went against the Ten Commandments of God. Thus, the three Hebrew youths (Hananiah, Mishael, Azariah – known as Shadrach, Meshach, Abednego) were thrown in a furnace oven for disobeying the command of Nebuchadnezzar because it directly opposed the greater Ten Commandments of God. Because they chose to listen to God rather the human king who sought to become like a god, the Three Hebrew Youths were unharmed by the intense flames because they were with the Son of God, who in the New Testament is Jesus Christ (Daniel 3:25). Also remember in Daniel 4, that also the King of

---

[203] Belshazzar, Funk & Wagnalls New Encyclopedia, Vol.3, New York, Funk & Wagnalls, Inc., 1971, Library Congress Catalog Card Number 72-170933).

Babylon was equated with a beast, thus establishing the definition of the beast being a king who sought to become like a god.

Therefore as it states in Rev. 17:9 "And here the mind with wisdom, the seven heads are seven mountains, on which the woman sitteth." The woman is the symbol of the Roman Catholic Church and she sitteth on a scarlet colored beast with blasphemous names, which is a symbol of all the cardinals that have become Pope. Remember, the woman spoken of is dressed in purple and scarlet. Therefore, the seven heads of the beast are the different Popes throughout a specific time in history that led the Roman Church and her daughter churches. The mountain in the Bible is a symbol of a gathering of people, such as Mount Zion is a gathering of God's people, (Revelation 14:1). Thus, the seven mountains are the seven groups of popes according to their Papal names that have led the Roman Catholic Church. The seven different lines of Popes are the seven different papal families or names that are taken by the popes. Now this is where all the previous information comes into play. By adding the number of the name of each individual Pope, for all of the 7 different lines of popes plus the eighth line then this will give you 666.

Now all that is needed is to know the time period you should start from to reach 666. Given the eighth dies at the return of Jesus Christ, and given that the Woman in Revelation 17 is in the wilderness, instead of being on water as it was in Rev. 13, then this means you should begin in the year in which she went into the wilderness setting. Remember, the symbol of waters means "peoples, multitudes, nations, and tongues, (Rev. 17:15). Thus, when the leopard , beast in Rev. 13 is on the water it is during a time in history where the Roman Church had power and influence over many people. This occurred during the height of papal dominion of 1260 years from 538-1798

Good Father, Bad Father

A.D. Therefore in 1798 A.D., when Pope Pius VI was arrested by Napoleon's General Berthier, then the Papacy lost its political and temporal power and with it lost its influence over many peoples.

If you look at the list of Popes from 1798 and onward after Pope Pius VI received the mortal wound of losing the political and temporal power, then you will see that from 1798 to today there have been seven papal names plus Francis's name that have been used. This is not to say that Francis is the Eighth, later on I will explain where he stands in Bible Prophecy. But I must first explain, the 1st seven papal names used from 1798 and onward. Those names are below

Pius
Leo
Gregory
Benedict
John
Paul
John Paul

The eighth is not Pope Francis, but his predecessor Benedict XVI. Why you may ask? First in Revelation 17: 10 it states, "And there are seven kings: five are fallen, and one is and the other is not yet come; and when he cometh, he must continue a short space."

When John is viewing the prophecy of Rev.17 he is seeing it from the point of view of living during the times of Pope Paul VI. Why do I say this? The Bible tells us clearly "five are fallen" referring to its heads. In order for a head to fall there will no longer be a man who will die with the given papal name before the 2nd Coming of Christ. So therefore according to this rule you will see all the heads start to fall after 1846, two years after the beginning of the last Church of

Eliseo Santos

Laodecia and two years after Jesus Christ enters into the Holies of Holy in the Temple Sanctuary of God.

1st head fell: Gregory in 1846

2nd head fell: Leo in 1903

3rd head fell: Benedict in 1922

4th head fell: Pius in 1958

5th head fell: John in 1963

The "One Is": Paul VI - 6th head to collapse: Paul in 1978

The 7th head to fall that "did not yet come but when he cometh, he must continue a short space," was the Papal family name of John Paul which fell in 2005. It continued a short space because it only lasted from 1978-2005 or 27 years. When compared with the other heads such as Leo that have been in existence for 1463 years before they fell. [204]

Now therefore, the eighth is Pope Benedict because verse 11 states "And the beast that was, and is not, even he is the eighth, and is of the seven, and goeth into perdition." So far the man, Cardinal Ratzinger, went through a period where he was Pope Benedict XVI, 2005-2013. Cardinal Ratzinger is now in the "Is not" period – 2013-Present, where Francis covers his place. In the near future, Cardinal Ratzinger returns with a new papal name. Currently it's Pope Emeritus, but it may change. When Cardinal Ratzinger returns as the eighth, with a new name, he will revive the beast from 1260 years, which overtly called for the deaths of bible-believing Christians and the Pope will once again seek to control the entire political and religious world. Pope Benedict's name is of the seven Papal names as John mentions

---

[204] Pope Leo I – 440- 461 A.D. pg. 174-175, The Popes and Their Pontificates, American Peoples Encyclopedia, Vol.15, Grolier, 1967

Good Father, Bad Father

in Rev. 17:11, but Pope Benedict XVI will change His name when he returns to a name never before used. At this moment in time, he refers to himself as Pope Emeritus and can possibly change this name later on.

To see if this interpretation works you have to check out Revelation 13:verse 3 says, "And I saw one of his heads as it were wounded to death; and his deadly wound was healed: and all the world wondered after the beast." Therefore this is describing in modern-times when the overt temporal and political influence of the Papacy has returned. All that is needed for the wound to be completely healed is for the Papacy to publicly call for the persecution and death of the Christians.

If in 1798 one of the seven heads was wounded, then would the same head that was injured be healed? The answer is yes. Pope Pius VI was the Pope in 1798 when he was arrested it caused the lost of temporal and political power which the Bible speaks of as the "deadly mortal wound." Under Pope Pius VII and Pope Pius XI, the papacy would make major strides toward healing that wound. After Pope Pius VII, reinstated the Jesuits he would arrange concordats with the previously Pro- Jesuit countries, Sardinia, Bavaria, Naples, Russia, and Prussia, (1817-1821) and established a new diocese in America.[205] Under Pope Pius XI, the Papacy would sign the Lateran Pact with Italy and later a pact with Nazi Germany in 1933.

Now how does the seven heads and eighth relate to the number 666? If you read in Revelation 13:18, "Here is wisdom: let him that hath understanding count the number of the beast: for it is the number of a man; and his number is six hundred threescore and six." The key

---

[205] pg. 71, Pius VII, A.P.E, Vol. 15, Grolier,1967

Eliseo Santos

phrase here is that it is a number of a man, and this man is also a beast, which means according to Daniel 3 and Daniel 4 that this man is a king who seeks to become like a god. Thus, all Popes by the blasphemous and unauthorized title of "Vice Regent of Christ on earth" elevate themselves to a place only Christ should be. Why? Because Christ died for us on the Cross and resurrected, thus Christ has no equals. The words of God found in Acts 4:11-13 state clearly and plainly, "Neither is there salvation in any other, for there is none other name under heaven given among men, whereby we must be saved." Jesus Christ should always be the name you seek and not the man of sin sitting on the papal chair.

Therefore, if you count the individual men with the number associated with the individual popes in each of the 7 papal families from 1798 onwards, including the eighth then you will arrive at 666.

The Seven Mountains, Heads, and Kings of Rev. 17:9-11 and Rev. 13:18

Pius	Leo	Gregory	Benedict	John	Paul	John Paul	The Eighth
				1			
				2			
				3			
				4			
		1		5			
		2		6			
		3	1	7			
	1	4	2	8			
1	2	5	3	9			
2	3	6	4	10			
3	4	7	5	11			
4	5	8	6	12			
5	6	9	7	13			
6	7	10	8	14			
7	8	11	9	15	1		
8	9	12	10	16	2		
9	10	13	11	17	3		
10	11	14	12	18	4		
11	12	15	13	19	5	1	
+12	+13	+16	+14	+21	+6	+2	
78 +	91 +	136 +	105 +	231 +	21 +	3	=665 + 1 = 666

Rev. 13:18 – "Here is wisdom. Let him that hath understanding count the number of the beast: for it is the number of a man; and his number is Six hundred threescore and six."

The 8th, that goes to perdition – Pope Benedict XVI will return to Papal throne with a new name and authority to kill Christians. This man will die the day when the real Jesus Christ returns See 2 Thessalonians (2:3-9)

There are some things I need to explain with the following calculation. If you look at the Benedict column there you will see an

Good Father, Bad Father

arithmetic sum of 14 instead of 16. The Eighth took the name Benedict XVI, shouldn't you add 16 instead? The answer to that question is if you look at an official list of the Vatican Papal list, you will notice there was never an official Pope called Benedict X because he was an anti-pope or illegitimate pope. In the official Papal list you will see that from Benedict IX it goes to Benedict XI. Also, keep in mind Benedict IX was pope three times (1032-1044, 1045, 1047-1048) and removed from office twice and once resigned. Therefore, Benedict XI was really Benedict X because he was actually the tenth man to officially take the Papal throne with that name and die with that same name. Keep in mind, the Bible in Revelation 13:18 says it is the number of a man and the number of a beast. The same problem occurs in the John column where there was never an official John XVI and John XX. Thus, there were only twenty-one men who took the papal throne with the name John and died with that name. Benedict XVI is not counted as Benedict because he resigned and will change his name. When he returns, he will gain the beast powers to persecute and kill Christians like the popes did during the Middle-Ages. Francis is not listed because he is a placeholder for the last return of Pope Benedict XVI, while Benedict is out of office. Francis will be deposed from office and the current Pope Emeritus will return to persecute Christians.

As for Pope Francis his name is not of the seven papal family names, and thus his name is not applied to the count. Also keep in mind, that not only is Francis' name is not of the seven, but also he is unlike the previous popes. Francis is the first pope from South America and from Argentina. Francis also has a public persona and demeanor that separates him from the other Popes from the seven Papal families. But, the most important characteristic that separates him from all the popes in the seven papal family names is that Pope Francis is a Jesuit. Before ascending to Papal chair in March 2013, Cardinal Bergoglio was at one time the Jesuit Provincial Superior of the Jesuit Order of Argentina. Francis being a Jesuit means that he is totally obedient to not only Pope Benedict XVI, but also his Superior General of the Jesuit Order Adolfo Nicholas Pachon.

Therefore today, we are living in the "is not" phase of the eighth and last pope. During this phase, Francis, who will later step down or be removed from the papal throne, when it comes time for Pope Benedict XVI to return to the throne under a new name. It seems that this prophecy of the last pope and the penultimate pope were sealed and classified information that God revealed to His people in the End Times. In the Book of 2 Thessalonians Ch. 2, Paul not only explained the larger phase of the arrival of the Roman Catholic Church and the Little Horn, but also it seems that the literal reading is concerning these End Times. Starting from 2 Thessalonians verse 3,

> *"Let no man deceive you by any means: for that day shall not come, except there come a falling away first, and that man of sin be revealed, the son of perdition; Who opposeth and exalteth himself above all that is called God, or that is worshipped so that he as God sitteth in the temple of God, showing himself that he is God. Remember ye not, that, when I was yet with you, I told you these things? And now ye know what withholdeth that he might be revealed in his time. For the mystery of iniquity doth already work: only he who now letteth will let, until he be taken out of the way. And then shall that Wicked be revealed, whom the Lord shall consume with the spirit of his mouth, and shall destroy with the brightness of his coming: Even him, whose coming is after the working of Satan with all power and signs and lying wonders, - (2 Thessalonians 2:3-9, KJV)*

Therefore, the man of sin and the son of perdition are described with similar language when compared to the eighth from Revelation 17:11 when it states, "And the beast that was, and is not, even he is the eighth, and is of the seven, and goeth into perdition." Thus, the eighth from Rev.17 and the Son of perdition and man of sin from 2 Thessalonians are both describing the Last Pope, who will go through a time when he steps down and then returns with a new name and power to persecute Christians and kill "heretics," or anyone who decides for himself how to worship and follow God. According to the Bible Prophecy, Cardinal Ratzinger who was Pope Benedict XVI, and is currently named Pope Emeritus will die the day of the 2nd Coming of Christ with all the glory and all the angels of heaven. Therefore, the number 666 not only represents the number of a man or of the beast, but it is also a count, whose number indicates how close we are towards the 2nd Coming of Jesus Christ. It is when Pope Benedict XVI returns with a new name and dies with that name during the 2nd Coming of Christ, only then will the number 666 will be complete.

This is why it is your upmost duty to not only prepare spiritually, physically, and mentally for the 2nd Coming of Christ, but also to alert and wake up those who are sleep walking and are not yet aware of the coming persecution of Bible-believing Christians. At the end of time, much to the surprise of the inhabitants of the world, the false good and false evil will suddenly disappear giving a much brighter glimpse of the true good and true evil in this world. Let us do all we can today, to give our hearts and burdens to Christ and seek Eternal life.

Chapter 26: End of 2300-Day Prophecy and the Investigative Judgment

During the Church of Philadelphia, there was a great revival in the study of Bible prophecy. Many Protestants were now able to read and study their Bibles. Protestants were during this time unfettered from the Roman Church and other authoritative Protestant religions. After many Christians in America witnessed the signs spoken of by Christ in the sixth seal many began to wonder about the fulfillment of Bible Prophecy and how close we are to the Second Coming of Christ. One of these individuals was William Miller, who formed the Millerite movement in the 1830's and 1840s.

William Miller was at one time in the early part of his life a deist. He remained a deist until one day, he felt that he needed help with the problems of life. He felt convicted and guilty of his sins. For Miller, he found the peace that the Gospels bring to those who accept Christ as their savior. Miller found in the Bible a new life as he studied upon the many promises that Christ Our Savior brings to those who give themselves, and their lives with its problems to Him. But the greatest of Christ's promises concerning His 2nd Coming, entered first and foremost in Miller's mind. Miller would begin to study his Bible and would begin to prove the divine authority of the Bible, by beginning to studying the many prophecies that the Bible foretells. One of these prophecies was the 2300 days prophecy from Daniel 8 and 9. The verse that stood out to Miller was the verse from Daniel 8:14, which states, "And he said unto me, Unto two thousand and three hundred days then shall the sanctuary be cleansed." This quote along with Daniel 9:24-27,

> *"Seventy weeks are determined upon thy people and upon the holy city, to finish the transgression, and to make an end of sins, and to make reconciliation for iniquity, and to bring in everlasting righteousness, and to seal up the vision and prophecy, and to anoint the most Holy. Know therefore and understand, that from the going forth of the commandment to restore and to build Jerusalem unto the Messiah the Prince shall be seven weeks and threescore and two weeks: the street shall be built again, and the wall, even in troublous times. And after threescore and two weeks shall Messiah be cut off, but not for himself: and the sanctuary; and the people of the prince that shall come shall destroy the city and the sanctuary; and the end thereof shall be with a flood, and unto the end of the war of desolations are determined. And he shall confirm the covenant with many for one week and in the midst of the week he shall cause the sacrifice and the oblation to cease, and for the overspreading of abominations he shall make it desolate, even until the consummation, and that determined shall be poured upon the desolate."*

Remember in Ch. 13 of this book, we reviewed the Prophecy explaining what Christ did when he resurrected into heaven. If you remember, the Earthly sanctuary and the Temple of Solomon were but models of the temple in heaven. The temple contained three major parts. The first part was the courtyard where on earth the sacrifice was made. The second part was the Holy Place of the temple where there would be the 7 lamps, the table of 12 shewbread, and incense. Then the last part was the Most Holy or "Holies of Holy" Place of the

Good Father, Bad Father

Temple, where on earth was found the Ark of the Covenant and above which the Spirit of God would appear as a symbol of what occurs in heaven. The 2300-Day prophecy connects the earthly model of the sanctuary with the heavenly model of the sanctuary. The 2300 years of this prophecy begins in the Autumn of 457 B.C. when the Media-Persian King Artaxerxes gives the order to reestablish Jerusalem and the Temple, (Ezra Ch.7). Remember, the 70 weeks prophecy is a portion that is cut off from the overall 2300-day prophecy. The 70 weeks, which translate to 490 actual years(a prophetic day = 1 actual year; 1 prophetic week = 7 actual years), foretold from the order given by King Artaxerxes to rebuild the temple of Jerusalem it would be 49 years (7 weeks) until the Temple of Solomon was rebuilt. From the rebuilt temple, to the Messiah would be 434 years (62 weeks), and then in the final week in the middle of the week, (3 ½ years) Christ would die once and become the infinite sacrifice for humanity, at the end of the 70 weeks in 34 A.D., Stephen would be stoned to death and the early Christians would be persecuted out of their homes in Jerusalem. This was all part of only the 70 weeks (490 years) out of the 2300 days of prophecy.

William Miller then became aware that humanity was entering the End Times and the Last Days of humanity. He realized that the 2300-day prophecy would end in his generation. If you subtract 490 years from 2300 years, it equals 1810 years. If you add the remaining 1810 years to 34 A.D., then you arrive at 1844 A.D. The date in which he arrived at after trial and error was correct, but the significance of the event William Miller still did not understand. Keep in mind, the world had only spent 46 years living without Papal supremacy over the land, and the people began studying the Bible prophecy on their own, being led by the Holy Spirit. This especially occurred after the many

Americans witnessed the signs of the End Times of the day the sun was covered in darkness in 1780, and the stars falling from the sky in 1833. These things left a deep impression on their minds to study the Bible.

So what occurred during the last 1810 years of the 2300 years of prophecy? Remember the 2300-year prophecy connects the earthly Temple of God with the Heavenly Temple of God. For the remaining 1810 years of the prophecy, Jesus Christ was in the Temple hearing the prayers of humanity and forgiving them instantly of their sins because now no further sacrifice was needed to atone for the sins of mankind. The office of the High Priest and the role of the sacrificial lamb became intertwined in the Lord and Savior Jesus Christ. Now the process of salvation became infinitely efficient in the hands of Jesus Christ. At the end of the 1810 years of Bible Prophecy, Jesus would leave the Holy Place of the Temple of Heaven, and enter the Most Holy Place in the Temple of heaven, which is the throne room of majesty of God, the Good Father.

The Angel Gabriel who was sent to explain to Daniel the prophecy gives us the hint in the beginning of his speech to Daniel explaining the significance of the 2300-year prophecy. In Daniel 8:14, Daniel writes, "And he said unto me, Unto two thousand and three hundred and days then shall the sanctuary be cleansed." However after witnessing the stars falling from heaven in November of 1833, then Miller became convinced that we were approaching in the End Times. Miller was right, in the fact that it was only the beginning of the End Times not the final end when Jesus Christ would make His 2nd Coming. When Miller read the words of Christ in Matthew 24: 29, 30, which give a general recap of the history of the world before His 2nd coming, to the Apostles and future generations,

Good Father, Bad Father

> *"Immediately after the tribulation of those days shall the sun be darkened, and the moon shall not give her light, and the stars shall fall from heaven, and the powers of the heavens shall be shaken: And then shall appear the sign of the Son of Man in heaven: and then shall all the tribes of the earth mourn, and they shall see the Son of man coming in the clouds of heaven with power and great glory."*

Miller had after witnessing the stars falling from the sky believed that when the 2300-day prophecy ended in 1844 that Jesus Christ would also return to earth. When October 22, 1844 came and went , and nothing happened on earth there was a great disappointment amongst Miller and many of the followers who had believed in the 2nd Coming of Christ. However, on that same date in heaven, something significant did indeed occur. Christ entered the Holy of the Holies Place in heaven where is found the throne of God. In the earthly sanctuary, this was represented by the Ark of the Covenant.

When Christ moved from the Holy place to the Holiest of Holies place in the temple, then the investigative judgment began. It is a judgment of those all those who proclaimed the name of God and Christ during their lives and died with the hope of God and Christ. The records of the all these people will come up for review before God in heaven. The dead will first be judged and eventually those living on earth will be judged by the Good Father God if they will be admitted into heaven with eternal life. Those who have not fully lived their lives according the Word of Christ and have not repented or confessed their sins before Christ will have to bear an account for these sins in the Day of Judgment. Therefore, if you wish you to attain eternal life, you must confess any and all sins before God, whether they be done openly or in secret, and repent of them or stop doing them. Aside from confessing and repenting of sins, all who would confess Christ as their savior will have to give an account for their works they have done for Christ on earth. Every person who you have helped or denied help, every opportunity cherished or wasted for sharing the Good news gospel of the 2nd Coming of Christ, and will be accounted for eternal life in heaven. The Lord will blot out the sins of those who accomplish all three things confession, and repentance of sins, and accomplish the will of God on earth in sharing the message of salvation and also doing the things in which they have promised for God.

In Matthew 24:37-51, Christ gives us an account of these End Times,

> *"But as the days of Noah were, so shall also the Coming the Son of man be. For as in days, that were before the flood, they were eating and drinking, marrying, and giving in marriage, until the day that Noah entered into the ark, And knew not until the flood came, and took them all away; so shall also the coming of the Son of man be. Then shall two be in the field; the one shall be taken, the other left. Two women shall be grinding at the mill; the one shall be taken, and the other left. Watch therefore: for ye know not what hour your Lord doth come. But know this, that if the Goodman of the house had known in what watch the thief would come, he would have watched, and would not have suffered his house to be broken up. Therefore, be also ready for in such an hour as ye think not the Son of man cometh. Who then is a faithful and wise servant, whom his lord hath ruler over his household, to give them meat in due season? Blessed is that servant, whom his lord when he cometh shall find so doing. Verily, I say unto you, That he shall make him ruler over all his goods. But if that evil servant shall say in his heart, My lord delayeth his coming; And shall begin to smite his fellow servants, and to eat and drink with*

Good Father, Bad Father

the drunken; The lord of that servant shall come in a day when he looketh not for him, and in an hour that he is not aware of. And shall cut him asunder, and appoint him his portion with the hypocrites: there shall be weeping and gnashing of teeth.

Like the civilization at the time of Noah, our civilization today is living their life as if they will grow old, and live like their grandparents did. It is within our generation in which humanity will witness the catastrophic consequences of sin and rejection of God's love made evident in His Law or Ten Commandments. Jesus Christ states in John 14:15, "If ye love me, keep my commandments." It is by rejecting the Ten Commandments of God in which you reject the Love of God, and thus, humanity will go through the seven last plagues of God. Christians living in the Last Days have a solemn testimony, to tell the world concerning the 2nd Coming of God and the destruction of the world as we know it today. Christians before God will be divided into faithful servants and unfaithful servants. Those Christians who are faithful servants are actively working toward the salvation of souls and calling out of the world those who are living in their sins, to repent and confess their sins before Christ. These Christians will be rewarded according their works and faithfulness. However, Christians who have yet to confess, or repent of their sins, and who are not actively doing their part to spread the salvation of God to others will be found wanting before God, as in the story of Belshazzar of Babylon in Daniel 5.

Much like the night when Babylon fell in destruction at the hands of the Medes and Persians, many within the world today are living their lives in much the same manner. Many are blaspheming god by seeking to become like gods as Belshazzar was who decided to use the sacred vessels to drink alcohol, party, and fornicate. As Daniel 5:1-4,

> *Belshazzar the king made a great feast to a thousand of his lords, and drank wine before the thousand. Belshazzar, whiles he tasted the wine, commanded to bring the golden and silver vessels which his father Nebuchadnezzar had taken out of the temple which was in Jerusalem; that the king, and his princes, his wives, and his concubines, might drink therein. They drank wine, and praised the gods of gold, and of silver, of brass, of iron, of wood, and stone.*

Much like Belshazzar many leaders today are losing respect for the things that are of God and Holy. Leaders both in the political and religious world, have sought to use the sacred vessels of God, as if they were God. This will culminate when the mark of the beast is proclaimed as the mark of allegiance to those who set themselves as a god instead of allegiance to the God of the universe.

The 2nd beast represented by the America mixed with Apostate Protestantism, which is a Protestantism that still follows in the Worship of Sunday that originated when paganism entered into the Early Church of Pergamos. During that time, Constantine enacted the first Sunday law throughout the Roman Empire in 321 AD. In these modern times, you and I will witness the Mark of the beast be enforced, which is a symbol of a National Sunday law.

Chapter 27: The Mark of the Beast

In Revelation 13:11-18, when speaking about the 2nd beast, The Bible says

> *"And I beheld another beast coming up out of the earth; and he had two horns like a lamb, and he spake as a dragon. And he exceriseth all the power of the first beast before him, and causeth the earth and them which dwell therein to worship the first beast, whose deadly wound was healed. And he doeth great wonders, so that he maketh fire come down from heaven on the earth in the sight of men, And he deceiveth them that dwell on the earth by the means of those miracles which he had, power to do in the sight of the beast; saying to them that dwell on the earth, that they should make an image to the beast, which had the wound by a sword, and did live. And he had power to give life unto the image of the beast, that the image of the beast should both speak, and cause that as many as would not worship the image of the beast should be killed. And he causeth all, both small and great, rich and poor, free and bond, to receive a mark in their right hand, or in their foreheads: And that no man might buy or sell, save he that had the mark, or the name of the beast, or the number of his name. Here is wisdom. Let him that hath understanding count the number of the beast: for it is the number of a man; and his number is Six hundred threescore and Six."*

The 2nd beast is the United States and the Apostate Protestantism is the image of the beast that grew on these shores and will once again manifest itself to the current inhabitants of the earth[206]. Apostate

Eliseo Santos

Protestantism means a Protestantism that pays homage and honor to the first beast of Revelation 13:1-10, which was stated earlier to be the Roman Catholic Church. How can Protestantism pay honor to the first beast? By engaging in the same actions in which the first beast did for 1260 days. Some of those actions included as the Bible states in Revelation 13:6-7 "And he opened his mouth in blasphemy against God, to blaspheme his name, and his tabernacle, and them that dwell in heaven. And it was given unto him to make war with the saints, and to overcome them: and power was given him over all kindreds, and tongues, and nations." Much like the Roman Catholic Church, within the Protestant world unbiblical doctrines have entered and have gained sway over many people. Some of these unbiblical doctrines that are present in many Protestant churches today include the doctrine which does away with the Law of God, and says that after the death and resurrection of Jesus Christ that the Ten Commandments of the Old Testament are not important. This couldn't be any further from the truth. Christ died and resurrected in order to bear account for the Law of God, which is the Character of the Good Father in heaven. Paul writes in Romans 3:31 on the continued validity of the law, "Do we then make void the law through faith? God forbid: yea, we establish the law." John writes in 1 John 2:3-4, "And hereby we do know that we know him, if we keep his commandments. He that saith, I know him, and keepeth not his commandments, is a liar, and the truth is not in him." If as Peter states in 1 Peter 1:25,"But the word of the Lord endureth for ever. And this is the word which by the gospel is preached unto you" then Christ words in Matthew 5:17-19 stand forever as well. Christ states in Matthew 5:17-19,

---

[206] pg. 51, National Sunday Law, By A. Jan Marcussen

> *"Think not that I am come to destroy the law, or the prophets: I am not come to destroy, but to fulfil. For verily, I say unto you. Till heaven and earth pass, one jot or one tittle shall in no wise pass from the law, till all be fulfilled. Whosoever therefore shall break one of these least commandments, and shall teach men so, he shall be called the least in the kingdom of heaven: but whosoever shall do and teach them, the same shall be called great in the kingdom of heaven."*

Other unbiblical doctrines that are taught in many Protestant Churches include the theory of "secret rapture," considering that speaking in tongues is speaking in strange and indiscernible language that has become a hallmark of the Charismatic movement. But the greatest unbiblical doctrine that is still in the minds of many Protestants and considered to be true is the doctrine of Sunday observance.

So then what is the mark of the beast? The Mark of the beast is the opposite of the Sign of God, which is keeping his Commandments most especially the Fourth Commandment Sabbath-day. Some of the early Protestant settlers of America followed in the footsteps of the oppressive and authoritative regime of Church and State promulgated by the Papacy. The first Sunday law in America occurred in 1610, in Virginia, and it stated:

> *"Every man and woman shall repair in the morning to the divine service, and sermons preached upon the Sabbath [Sunday], an in the afternoon to the divine service, and catechizing, upon pain for the first fault to their provision and the allowance for the whole week following; for the second, to lose the said allowance and also be whipped; and for the third to suffer death," [207].*

---

[207] Laws and Orders: Divine, Politique, and Martial, for the colony in Virginia: first established by Sir Thomas Gates,

Eliseo Santos

The Mark of the Beast is therefore a National Sunday Law. This nationally enforced Sunday Law would be called by Protestants in the future to force everyone to go to Church on Sunday or else face the penalties as described above, but with more modern systems and technology for implementation. John mentions that the 2nd beast of the United States and the Apostate Protestantism unites with the Roman Catholic Church and will like Satan, seek to deceive the inhabitants of the world. Those already trained to believe with their eyes will seek to break the law of God, and thus, the words of Christ in John 20:29 have greater significance today, "Blessed are they that have not seen, and yet have believed."

Another important part of Revelation is ch.13:16-18, "And he causeth all, both small and great, rich and poor, free and bond, to receive a mark in their right hand, or in the their foreheads, And that no man might buy or sell, save he that had the mark, or the name of the beast: "Here John uses the similar language that was used in the Old Testament when referring to The Ten Commandments. In Deuteronomy 6:1-8, the Ten Commandments of God are described as a mark or sign between Him and His people:

> *"Now these are the commandments, the statues, and the judgments, which the Lord your God commanded to teach you, that ye might do them in the land whither ye go to possess it: That thou mightest fear the Lord thy God, to keep all his statutes and his commandments, which I command thee, thou, and thy son and thy son's son, all the days of thy life; that thy days may be prolonged. Hear therefore, O Israel, and observe it to do it; that it may be well with thee, and that ye may increase mightily; as the Lord of thy fathers hath promised thee, in the land that floweth with milk and honey. Hear, O*

Knight, Lieutenant –, the 24th of May, 1610

Good Father, Bad Father

Israel: The Lord our God is one Lord: And thou shalt love the Lord thy God with thine heart, and with thy soul, and with all thy might, And these words, which I command thee this day, shall be in thine heart: And teach thy children, and shalt talk of them when thou sittest in thine house, and when thou liest down, when thou risest up. And thou shalt bind them for a sign upon thine hand, and they shall be as frontlets between their eyes."

The Ten Commandments being a sign or mark of God, is also seen in the Book of Ezekiel, "I am the Lord; walk within my statutes, and keep my judgments, and do them; And hallow my Sabbaths; and they shall be a sign between me and you, that ye may know that I am the Lord your God." (Ezekiel 20:19-20).

Like the words of John, led by the Holy Spirit, John uses similar language to describe the Mark of the beast, or the mark of allegiance to a man who proclaims himself to be a god. Therefore Protestants who don't recognize the Law of God including the 7th- Day Sabbath Saturday will suffer from judgment and will not be saved from the wrath of God poured out in the plagues.

Chapter 28: The Three Angels Messages

This leads us to the three angels messages, which encapsulates in a brief manner the totality of responsibility for all Christians living today on the planet. In Revelation 14:6-7 is found the first message, which states,

> *"And I saw another angel fly in the midst of heaven, having the everlasting gospel to preach unto them that dwell on the earth, and to every nation, and kindred, and tongue, and people. Saying with a loud voice, Fear God, and give glory to him; for the hour of his judgment is come: and worship him that made heaven, and earth, and the sea, and the fountains of waters."*

The first message deals with God's first act of love on this planet, which was the act of creation. God did so much for the living beings on this planet. In order to believe God and follow His Fourth Commandment, then you must recognize the creation of the planet, if not then you will not keep the Commandments of God, most especially the 4th commandment concerning Saturday or the 7th Day Sabbath.

Two signs of God's work of creation is that the week that is part of our current calendar originates since from the 1st week of creation.

Eliseo Santos

It is a sign of creation because the days of the week have continued to be uninterrupted. One revolution of the earth around the sun corresponds with the year, and the one rotation of the earth on its axis constitutes a day. The week is not tied to the moon or any other celestial body, yet it is recognized in all cultures the concept of a week with 7 days. From reading the Bible it shows that we are created in the image of God and through sin, we fell from the pristine image of God, to a sinful state where death, fear, and evil abound. Thus, because we are created we listen to God, the Creator and His Ten Commandments. God can give us eternal life, but you must continue to believe in Him and His Son Jesus Christ and their words of truth and hope found in the Bible. Another sign of the creation of the earth, is found in the simple and yet profound example of the phenomena of the solar eclipse. When the sun and moon appear to be the same size in the sky and yet the sun is hundreds of times larger than the moon, then it shows the work of God the Creator. It is impossible for the solar eclipse to be the result of chance. It is more than a coincidence. The sun and moon appear the same size in the sky, and yet there is a vast difference in actual size between one another. Not only this but keep in mind, that the Sun and the planets of this solar system are moving rapidly through the universe, so for solar eclipse to occur regularly and for the Sun and moon to appear the same size in the sky from the only planet in the solar system that contains life, speaks volumes to the intelligent design of the All-mighty God. The Bible is not lying when it says "For thus saith the Lord that created the heavens; God himself that formed the earth and made it; he established it, he created it not in vain, he formed it to be inhabited: I am the Lord; and there is none else," (Isaiah 45:18). Therefore, let us be grateful for God for creating and sustaining the beautiful planet we

Good Father, Bad Father

call home, and filling this planet with all forms of vibrant life. Take not only better care of yourselves, but His creation, most especially your other human brothers and sisters.

The 2nd message of the three angels, states in Revelation 14:4, "And there followed another angel, saying 'Babylon, is fallen, is fallen, that great city, because she made all nations drink the wine of the wrath of her fornication." The 2nd message of the 2nd angel involves knowing the truth about the 1st beast or the Roman Catholic Church . The 2nd angels message announces the quickly approaching destruction of all false religious systems that mix the name of God with pagan doctrines such as the Eucharist and Sunday worship and others. As Protestant Churches continue to unite with Rome through the ecumenical movement, many of God's people in these churches will be called out and will be led by the Holy Spirit to realize the errors of their churches and how the Roman Catholic Church and other Protestant Churches continue to believe in unbiblical doctrines. John uses a similar expression in Revelation 18 to describe the fall of Babylon. He states in Revelation 18:1-5,

> *And after these things I saw another angel come down from heaven, having great power; and the earth was lightened with his glory. And he cried mightily with a strong voice, saying, "Babylon the great is fallen, is fallen, and is become the habitation of devils, and the hold of every foul spirit, and a cage of every unclean and hateful bird." For all nations have drunk of the wine of the wrath of her fornication, and the Kings of the earth have committed fornication with her and the merchants of the earth are waxed rich through the abundance of her delicacies. And I heard another voice from heaven, saying "Come out of her, my people, that ye be not partakers of her sins, and that ye receive not of her plagues."*

Eliseo Santos

Much like the night of the fall of Babylon, where Belshazzar drank from the sacred vessels, the spiritual Babylon has used sacred vessels for also congregating and uniting with world in giving people of the wine of the wrath of her fornication or the non-biblical doctrines in which she uses human authority rather than the divine authority of the Bible to defend. There are still many of God's people who are still in these Churches, but when they hear the message to leave of the Roman Church and Apostate Protestantism and will work with the Holy Spirit to lead them out of whatever Church they are currently attending to develop a closer relationship with God through the study of His words in the Bible.

The final message of the Three angels messages states,

And the third angel followed them, saying with a loud voice, If any man worship the beast and his image, and receive his mark, in his forehead, or in his hand. The same shall drink out of the wine of the wrath of God, which is poured out without mixture into the cup of his indignation; and he shall be tormented with fire and brimstone of holy angels, and in the presence of the holy angels, and in the presence of the Lamb; And the smoke of their torment ascendeth up forever and ever; and they have no rest day nor night, who worship the beast and his image, and whosoever receiveth the mark of his name. Here is the patience of the saints: here are they that keep the commandments of God, and the faith of Jesus. – Revelation 14:9-12

Here the message of the Third Angel applies to these same End Times. Those who worship the beast (The Pope and Roman Catholicism) and His image (Apostate Protestantism), and receive his mark (Sunday law), by either believing in it (forehead) or not working on Sunday and working on Saturday(hand), will suffer for listening to human laws that transgress God's law. It is by remembering the 4th Commandment as stated in Exodus 20 that will please God over man:

> *Remember the Sabbath day, to keep it holy. Six days shalt thou labour, and do all thy work: But the seventh day is the Sabbath of the Lord thy God: in it thou shalt not do any work, thou, nor thy son, nor thy daughter, thy manservant, nor thy maidservant, nor thy cattle, nor thy stranger that is within thy gates: For in six days the Lord made heaven and earth, the sea, and all that in them is, and rested the seventh day: wherefore the Lord blessed the Sabbath day, and hallowed it. – Exodus 20:8-11*

Jesus explains in Matthew 15:9, the major problem today in many Christian churches, where Christ says, "But in vain they do worship me, teaching for doctrines the commandments of men." Thus, in the End Times, many will allow themselves to be used by the enemy Satan just by taking the Mark of the beast (Sunday) thinking it is good when in fact the reunification of the Church and state authority will force you to break the Commandments of God concerning the Seventh-Day Sabbath (Saturday). If you would like for God to remember you, then it will be a good idea to remember the 4th Commandment. It is by adhering to all three angels messages that any individual can prepare to meet their Creator in heaven. But to do so it requires the aid of Jesus Christ. He is in the Sanctuary willing to help those who come to Him believing He is the Son of God, and seeking eternal life. Only Christ and Christ alone should be the person who all Christians seek to follow. Jesus said very clearly "I am the way, the truth, and the life, and no man cometh unto the Father but by me," (John 14:6). Which means if we desire to have eternal life with the Good Father, God, then we must seek His Son Jesus Christ and pray to Him and Him alone. It's most important to develop a firm belief in Christ and that He is the Son of God, who died for the sins of humanity. Christ resurrected to hear the prayers and forgive the sins of anyone who comes to Him seeking forgiveness for their sins, and recognize the value and truth of eternal life.

Chapter 29: The Church of Laodecia and the 7th Seal

Out of the seven Churches, the Church that has had much trouble seeing and laboring is the Church of Laodecia or the Church in the Modern-Era. Laodecia means Nation in judgment in ancient Greek. It is the Church that starts from the End of 2300 year- prophecy in 1844 and ends with the 2nd Coming of Christ. It is a church that has lived in most cases in overwhelming wealth and prosperity compared to the Church of Ephesus or Smyrna, who at times were forced to live solitary lives in caves and underground caverns due to the intense persecution of the times. Jesus Christ states concerning the Church of Laodecia and the 7th Seal:

> *"And unto angel of the Church of the Laodiceans write; These things saith the Amen, the faithful and true witness, the beginning of the creation of God; I know thy works, that thou art neither cold nor hot, I would thou wert cold or hot. So then because thou art lukewarm, and neither cold nor hot, I will spue thee out of my mouth. Because thou sayest, I am rich, and increased with goods, and have need of nothing; and knowest not that thou art wretched, and miserable, and poor, and blind, and naked: I counsel thee to buy of me gold tried in the fire, that thou mayest be rich; and white raiment, that thou mayest be clothed, and that the shame of thy nakedness do not appear; and anoint thine eyes with eyesalve, that thou mayest see. As*

Eliseo Santos

many as I love, I rebuke and chasten: be zealous therefore, and repent. Behold, I stand at the door, and knock: if any man hear my voice, and open the door, I will come in to him, and will sup with him; and he with me. To him that overcometh will I grant to sit with me in my throne, even as I also overcame, and set down with my Father in his throne. He that hath an ear, let him hear what the Spirit saith unto the churches. – Revelation 3:14-22

And when he had opened the seventh seal, there was silence in heaven about the space of half an hour. Rev. 8:1

The Church of Laodecia is the church living in the modern world with all of its comforts, technology, and amenities. This convenience can be a distraction as well as an inhibiter of spiritual growth. The modern way of life creates the conditions for people, especially Bible-believing Christians to become lazy and complacent with exercising their faith in Jesus Christ. Many Christians today will face the investigative judgment and it will test us and our characters to see if we are worthy or warm enough to actually be taken to the Heaven. Those Christians found to be lukewarm will be spued out as a result of the final Investigate judgment. However, if you allow Christ to symbolically apply the fire and pressure of trials and persecution necessary to attain the purity in Christ, then by relying on Christ alone you can reach eternal life, and receive your white raiment. All Christians at one point or another will need the help of God, Jesus Christ, and the Holy Spirit to become prepared for the heavenly kingdom. Christ has prepared for His redeemed, since the Foundation of the World, the Heavenly Kingdom and filled it with mansions and

Good Father, Bad Father

vineyards for those who became redeemed in the name of Christ. Jesus Christ will say to the redeemed once they arrive in Heaven, "Come, ye, blessed of my Father, inherit the kingdom prepared for you from the foundation of the world," (Matthew 25:34).

The Good Father, God, is calling now on all who may hear and listen to His words to "Come out, of Babylon," and come out of the anti-Christian system of worship. If you sincerely seek eternal life, believe and act upon Jesus Christ of the Holy Bible and study His words and principles, then confess and repent of your sins before Christ in prayer. In doing so, you exercise and demonstrate your belief in the power of Salvation of Christ, evident in His death, resurrection, and current role as the High-Priest in heaven. Some within the Church Laodecia are still not able to discern and see the effects of sin, in their lives and therefore, Christ will at times need to rebuke and chasten to correct sinful behaviors for the purpose of preparing them for the eternal heaven. In God allowing evil to be fully demonstrated and expressed on earth, it will ensure that evil will never ever again surface. God has been patient with evil for the sake of those who Christ redeemed on the Cross. Christ already knew them and knew their trials and tribulations in these End Times. Christ has already known how in the End Times they will experience times of tribulation that earth has never before witnessed as some men would sit in the Temple of God pretending to be God, (2 Thessalonians 2:4, John 2:20, 21). If Christ compared the Temple of God, as a human body then sitting on the temple of God would mean how mankind will eventual seek to become like God by seeking to place themselves in the minds of others. The way to overcome this is by having a fierce and continued reliance on the Holy Spirit and the Holy Bible as the only way anyone can overcome the unwarranted access to a person's mind. For because Christ is infinite, then the odds will always be in your favor if you believe in Christ and continue to work in teaching others, the many promises and truths of the Bible.

Chapter 30: The Seven Last Plagues

In Revelation 16, John writes down the most frightening events that will occur before the 2nd coming of Christ. Imagine witnessing these plagues consecutively, as the people of the earth begin to face punishment for their incredulity and for their rejection of the God of life, love, and truth. These plagues will fall on those who enjoyed death, lies, hatred, and apathy. God's anger is not only for the Sunday worship involved with the Mark of the beast, but it is more so on the fact that people will allow another human being to govern over their freewill to worship God.

The seven plagues start in Revelation 16:1-2 when John writes,

> *"And I heard a great voice out of the temple saying to the seven angels, Go your ways, and pour out the vials of the wrath of God upon the earth. And the first went, and poured out his vial upon the earth, and there fell a noisome and grievous sore upon the men which had the mark of the beast, and upon them which worshipped his image."*

The first plague will target those who accepted the National Sunday law, and worshipped the leaders of Apostate Protestantism and Roman Catholicism. The plagues will fall on those who rejected God and His eternal divine laws for transient human laws. The plagues will not fall on those who followed the laws that prepared an individual for a heavenly home(The Ten Commandments), but on those who followed the law of destruction (National Sunday law). In order to be able to withstand persecution as a result of not submitting to the enforced Sunday worship, you will have to rely upon, and have faith and trust in Jesus Christ. Only Christ alone will able to take care of all of your needs and your problems.

In Psalms 91, you get an idea of how the Good Father's children of grace will be alive and live through these plagues. Psalm 91:7-8 states, "A thousand shall fall at thy side, and ten thousand at thy right hand; but it shall not come nigh thee. Only with thine eyes shalt thou behold and see the reward of the wicked." Meaning some of the people of God will escape terrible destruction of the plagues and the final conflicts that will occur in the final days. This destroys the false theory of a secret rapture, which suggests the people of God will not be on earth during the time of great tribulation and plagues. God in Psalm 91:9-10 states, "Because thou hast made the Lord, which is my refuge, even the Most High, thy habitation; there shall no evil befall thee, neither shall any plague come nigh thy dwelling." The Lord will protect those who fully will trust Him when the plagues come on the earth. Because Jesus Christ will cease to intercede for humanity during the time of the plagues, God will directly send angels to protect those who will be alive during the final plagues of the earth.

There will come a time when Christ's work in the sanctuary will conclude and then He will pronounce the words, "He that is unjust, let him be unjust still: and he which is filthy, let him be filthy still; and he that is righteous, let him be righteous still: and he that is holy, let him be holy still," (Revelation 22:11). Therefore it is best to seek Christ now while Christ is still hearing and forgiving the prayers of humanity, because there will come a time when heaven will be silent in preparation for the 2nd Coming of Christ. Christ's words in

Good Father, Bad Father

Revelation 22:7 have even greater significance today referring to the Book of Revelation, "Behold, I come quickly: blessed is he that keepeth the sayings of the prophecy of this book."

The 2nd and 3rd plagues both involve the plagues of blood in which a major ocean turns into dead human blood. The third plague will be also a plague of blood but going from an ocean into a river. Revelation 16 verses 3-6 state,

> *"And the second angel poured out his plagues, his vial upon the earth; and it became the blood of a dead man: every living soul died in the sea. And the third angel poured out his vial upon the rivers and fountain of waters; and they became blood. And I heard the angels of the waters say, "Thou art righteous, O Lord, which art, and wast, and shalt be because thou hast judged thus. For they have shed the blood of saints and prophets, and thou hast given them blood to drink; for they are worthy."*

The plagues of water into blood are punishments for all the innocent deaths that have occurred on this planet. God remembers the bloodshed of each individual life that was murdered without cause, every child's life ended short before it can experience the joys of life. Revelation 16:7 states "And I heard another out of the altar say, "Even so, Lord God Almighty, true and righteous are thy judgments." Like the blood of Abel that cried out after his brother murdered him without a cause, so does the blood of the martyrs who die in the name of Christ and for not taking the Mark of the beast will cry out to God.

The 4th plague will be the sun heating the surface of the earth. The 4th plague in Revelation 16:8,9 states "And the fourth angel poured out his vial upon the sun; and power was given unto him to scorch men with fire. And men were scorched with the great heat, and blasphemed the name of God, which have power over these plagues: and they repented not to give Him glory."

The enemy is preparing to lie to humanity and say that this plague would be the result of man-made global warming, and the inhabitants of the earth will see for themselves what that really means. The intense heat of this plague will potentially cause the ice in the polar ice caps to melt. In viewing the future right before the 2nd Coming of Christ, Peter saw what John described in Revelation. He wrote in 2 Peter 3:10, "But the day of the Lord will come as a thief in the night; in the which the heavens shall pass away with a great noise, and the elements shall melt with fervent heat, the earth also and the works that are there in shall be burned up." Peter here describes the 4th plague right before the 2nd Coming of Christ. Isaiah also caught a glimpse of this plague by God and had this to say concerning this plague, "As when the melting fire burneth, the fire causeth the waters to boil, to make thy name known to thine adversaries, that the nations may tremble at thy presence!,"(Isaiah 64:2). Peter adds advice for those who find this information and are living during these End times,

> *"Seeing then that all these things shall be dissolved, what manner of persons ought ye to be in all holy conversation and godliness. Looking for and hasting unto the coming of the day of God, wherein the heavens being on fire shall be dissolved, and the elements shall melt with fervent heat? Nevertheless we, according to his promise, look for new heavens and a new earth, wherein dwelleth righteousness. Wherefore, beloved, seeing that ye look for such things, be diligent that ye may be found of him in peace, without spot, and blameless."- 2 Peter 3:11-14*

Good Father, Bad Father

Peter is saying to not take these plagues lightly and that we should all seek God now while He is still listening to the prayers of humanity.

The fifth angel in verse Revelation 16: 10, 11 brings darkness upon the seat of the beast or Rome and Europe, "And the fifth angel poured out his vial, upon the seat of the beast; and his kingdom was full of darkness; and they gnawed their tongues for pain, And they blasphemed the God of heaven because of their pains and their sores, and repented not of their deeds." For those responsible for the pagan sun worship and the spiritual darkness of the earth, God will send them what they loved to worship on earth. If you understand that everything God has said in the Bible He will do, then you should realize that God is offering you the solution, which is praying to the savior and mediator Jesus Christ before it's too late.

For the Sixth plague John states, in Revelation 16:12-16,

> *"The sixth angel poured his vial upon the great river Euphrates, and the water thereof dried up that the way of the kings of the east might be prepared. And I saw three unclean spirits like frogs come out the mouth of the dragon, and out of the mouth of the beast, and out of the mouth of the false prophet. For they are spirits of devils, working miracles, which go forth unto the kings of the earth and of the whole world, to gather them to the battle of that great day of God Almighty. Behold, I come as a thief. Blessed is he that watcheth, and keepeth his garments, lest he walk naked, they see his shame. And he gathered them together into a place called in the Hebrew tongue Armageddon."*

The sixth plague describes Satan's last grand deception that he will put on the world. Satan working with two other members of the trinity of evil the beast (Papacy), and the false prophet (United States), will deceive the world to believe in the invasion of aliens, which the Bible describes as "unclean spirits like frogs." This is an accurate description of the small green aliens that for years have been presented in the mainstream media. These "aliens" are actually demons in disguise to fool the people of earth into believing accepting them as friends. They will warn and prepare the remaining people on the planet for the battle of Armageddon, which will be the battle between the armies of the world versus Jesus Christ and His heavenly angels. The great river Euphrates, like the symbol of Babylon, was the river that went through Babylon, signifying the remainder of people on the planet at that time. If waters refer to Peoples and nations, then the drying up of the Euphrates River symbolizes the dwindling of nations, peoples, and tongues that will occur during the 6th plague.

Remember, the sixth seal, the first part of the sixth seal began in 1755, and now the final parts of the sixth seal will occur during the sixth plague. Revelation 6:14-17,

> *"And the heaven departed as a scroll when it is rolled together; and every mountain and island were moved out of their places. And the kings of the earth, and the great men, and the rich men, and the chief captains, and the mighty men, and every bondsman, and every free man, hid themselves in the dens and in the rocks of the mountains; And said to the mountains and to the rocks, Fall on us, and hide us from the face of him that sitteth on the throne, and from the wrath of the Lamb: For the great day of his wrath is come; and who shall be able to stand?"*

The Bible is so precise that it even tells you what the enemies of God will be doing during Christ's 2nd Coming. Those who are

Good Father, Bad Father

drenched with the innocent blood of many on their hands, they will be hiding in elaborate underground facilities located at Area 51, The Ozarks, and Mount Weather and other facilities located throughout the United States and the world. But these underground facilities will be of no avail and no use because they have dug their own graves. Old Testament prophet Obadiah in Ch. 1:3,4 says concerning these End Times,

> *"The pride of thine heart hath deceived thee, thou that dwellest in the clefts of the rock, whose habitation is high; that saith in his heart, Who shall bring me down to the ground? Though thou exalt thyself as the eagle, and though thou set thy nest among the stars, thence I will bring thee down, saith the Lord."*

Some people will think that by going off into space they will be able to escape the wrath of God, but from God's words they won't be able to escape, in the same way they afforded no escape to the many innocent people they killed.

The seventh seal is unsealed in between the sixth and seventh plague. The seventh seal marks the 2nd Coming of Christ to Earth, because there is silence in heaven, which is a rare occasion given the multitude angels that continuously sing in glorious harmonic praises to the Almighty God.

The silence in heaven of the seventh seal is due to Christ and all the angels of heaven have come to earth to fight in the Battle of Armageddon and also to resurrect and gather all of God's redeemed people from the four corners of earth. John describes a scene of Jesus preparing to do battle with the armies of the earth and the fallen angels. In Revelation 19:11-16, John writes the following, "

Eliseo Santos

> *And I saw heaven opened, and behold a white horse; and he that sat upon him was called Faithful and True, and in righteousness he doth judge and make war. His eyes were a flame of fire, and on his head were many crowns; and he had a name written, that no man knew, but he himself. And he was clothed with a vesture dipped in blood: and his name is called The Word of God. And the armies which were in heaven followed him upon white horses, clothed in fine linen, white and clean. And out of his mouth goeth a sharp sword, that with it he should smite the nations: and he shall rule them with a rod of Iron: and he treadeth the winepress of the fierceness, and wrath of Almighty God. And he hath on his vesture and on his thigh a name written, KINGS OF KINGS, AND LORD OF LORDS.*

The first time Christ came to earth he sought peace when he humbly rode on a donkey into Jerusalem. However, His 2nd Return will be everything and more in which the Jewish people of Christ's era were expecting in the Messiah. Christ will come to put an end to evil and all those who took pleasure in evil. Many did not understand the significance of Christ until after His death and resurrection. But He will return to earth wielding unlimited power and glory to save and rescue His people from their human and spiritual oppressors. It will be during the Battle of Armageddon in which the armies of the world will be told to fight against an invading threat, but they won't be told that the invading threat is Jesus Christ and His heavenly fleet of angels. Many will have great disappointment not because of Jesus Christ's arrival but because they were lied to by their superiors about the arrival of Christ. Instead of welcoming His 2nd Coming many will be misled to oppose to the KINGS OF KINGS, AND LORD OF LORDS. John describes the Battle of Armageddon in Revelation 19:17-21,

Good Father, Bad Father

> *I saw an angel standing in the sun; and he cried with a loud voice, saying to all the fowls that fly in the midst of heaven, Come and gather yourselves together unto supper of the great God; That ye may eat the flesh of kings, and the flesh of captains, and the flesh of mighty men, and the flesh of horses, and of them that sit on them, and the flesh of all men, both free and bond, both small and great. And I saw the beast, and the kings of the earth, and their armies, gathered together to make war against him that sat on the horse, and against his army. And the beast was taken, and with him the false prophet that wrought miracles before him, with which he deceived them that had received the mark of the beast, and them that worshipped his image. These both were cast alive both into a lake of fire burning with brimstone. And the remnant were slain with the sword of him that sat upon the horse, which sword proceedeth out of his mouth: and all the fowls were filled with flesh.*

John here describes that Battle of Armageddon, which will be a one-sided battle. God and His Forces infinitely outmatch the opposing armies in such a way that only one angel is really necessary to take care of all of the armies of the world. The angel of this passage calls upon the ravenous and carnivorous birds such as vultures, and others to come eat the overwhelming amounts of dead flesh of those evil people of the world. The Beast, (the papacy), and the false prophet (those who compose Apostate Protestantism and leadership of the United States,) will be caught and thrown alive into the lake fire once and for all until they will be consumed.

Finally, John describes the final plague and the ending scenes of earth's history in Revelation 16:17-21,

> *"And the seventh angel poured out his vial into the air; and there came a great voice out of the temple of heaven, from the throne, saying, It is done. And there were voices, and thunders, and lightening there was great earthquake, such as was not since men were upon the earth, so mighty an earthquake, and so great. And the great city was divided into three parts, and the cities of the nations fell: and great Babylon came in remembrance before God, to give unto her the cup of the wine of the fierceness of his wrath. And every major island fled away, and the mountains were not found. And there fell upon men a great hail out of heaven, every stone about the weight of a talent: and men blasphemed God because of the plague of the hail; for the plague thereof was exceeding great."*

At the last and final plague Christ will finish and complete His Day of Justice and righteousness on evil and humanity. Humanity had been led to God's final justice against evil and those who took pleasure in evil. The Creator of the Universe and His Holy Army of Angels now turn to gathering those who died with Jesus Christ and worthy of entering the heavenly Kingdom, and also those who lived and witnessed the 2nd Coming of God and His display of His infinite greatness. Another important event to take note is the theme of the Resurrection.

Chapter 31: Resurrection to Eternal Life or To Receive God's Judgment

Much like the resurrection of Christ, those who died believing in Christ and after the investigative judgment were found worthy to enter heaven will be resurrected to eternal life. At the 2nd Coming of Jesus Christ there will be a group, who will be living in the world while the plagues are falling. This special group won't be harmed by the seven last plagues and they will be a part of special group of God's chosen who will go to heaven without dying like Enoch and Elijah. Both groups will be united together at the 2nd Coming of Christ.

It is important to first explain the state of the dead. The dead are unconscious of their surroundings and as if they are in a deep sleep. In Ecclesiastes 9:5-6 it states, "For the living know that they shall die: but the dead know not anything, neither have they any more a reward; for the memory of them is forgotten. For their love, and their hatred, and their envy, is now perished; neither have they any more a portion forever in anything that is under the sun." Therefore, when someone dies then they will no longer have any type of interaction with the living world. The apparitions of ghosts and "hauntings" of dead people and other paranormal phenomena are actually part of the deceptive works of Satan. He does these deceptive works to maintain the lie of the immortality of the soul. The reason why the immortality of the soul is Satan's lie is because it does away with a judgment of

God, who is the only one who can say whether a soul remains conscious forever or will remain dead forever. In reality, individuals are either resurrected to eternal life or resurrected for final judgment and punishment. The consequences of God's judgment and punishment are eternal, which means eternal death awaits those sinners who won't make it to heaven. As Paul states in Hebrew 9:27,28 "And as it is appointed unto men once to die, but after this the judgment. So Christ was once offered to bear the sins of many, and unto them that look for him shall he appear the second time without sin unto salvation." Paul summarizes the essence of the reality of God's judgment, and salvation in Christ when he states in Romans 6:23, "For the wages of sin is death, but the gift of God is eternal life through Jesus Christ our Lord."

There are several different types of people who will be grouped into different categories in heaven. This is the scene described by Paul, In 1 Thessalonians 4:16-17, "For the Lord himself shall descend from heaven with a shout, with the voice of the archangel, and with the trump of god: and the dead in Christ shall rise first: Then we which are alive and remain shall be caught up together with them in the clouds, to meet the Lord in the air; and so shall we ever be with the Lord. Wherefore comfort one another with these words." As Paul describes at the second Coming of Christ there will be many are already alive, either they are part of a special resurrection or they are part of the 144,000. In Revelation 14, John gives an important description of the 144,000 thousand. Revelation 14:1-5, states

> *And I looked, and, lo, a Lamb stood on the Mount Sion, and with him, an hundred forty and four thousand, having, his Father's name written in their foreheads. And I heard a voice of heaven, as the voice of many waters, and as the voice of a*

great thunder; and I heard the voice of harpers harping with their harps: And they sung as it were a new song before the throne, and before the four beasts, and the elders: and no man could learn that song but the hundred and forty and four thousand, which were redeemed from the earth. These are they which were not defiled with women; for they are virgins. These are they which follow the Lamb whithersoever he goeth. These were redeemed from among men, being the first fruits unto God and to the Lamb. And in their mouth was found no guile: for they are without fault before the throne of God.

Here John presents the 144,000, which is the symbolic number of individuals who will be redeemed of their sins and will not experience death, because they devoted themselves to Christ when they lived on earth. Another unique characteristic of the 144,000 is that they will go through most intense period of tribulation and trouble on the planet. In Revelation 7:14-17, it states

And I said unto him, Sir, thou, knowest. And he said to me, These are they which came out of great tribulation, and have washed their robes, and made them white in the blood of the Lamb. Therefore are they before the throne of God, and serve him day and night in the temple: and he that sitteth on the throne shall dwell among them. They shall hunger no more, neither thirst any more; neither shall the sun light on them, nor any heat. For the Lamb which is in the midst of the throne shall feed them, and shall lead them unto living fountains of waters: and God shall wipe away all tears from their eyes.

Many of those who will be part of the 144,000, will have to toil with hunger and thirst until the 2nd Coming of Jesus Christ. They will be made clean through Christ's intervention in their lives and through Christ's bloodshed on the Cross.

There will be some who will be resurrected at the 2nd Coming of Christ for the sole purpose to be ashamed of seeing God and to be confused, and to have contempt. Throughout history there have been many men who did not believe in God, and their unbelief went to such an extreme that they committed horrible actions, and even set themselves up in their minds and the minds of their followers to being a god. All of these people, the people who killed Christ and made fun of Him, and those Jewish religious leaders who led the people astray and did not believe in Christ as God, and atheists throughout history who have proposed false ideas of reality, will be resurrected so that they can see with their own eyes their errors of their perceived reality. Daniel 12:2 says, "And many of them, that sleep in the dust of the earth shall awake, some to everlasting life and some to shame and everlasting contempt. And they that be wise shall shine as the brightness of the firmament; and they that turn many to righteousness as the stars forever and ever."

All people in human history fall into four categories either they live forever never dying (Enoch, Elijah, and the special 144,000 living today), everyone else who go to heaven die once and then will be resurrected to eternal life following the example of their God, savior, Jesus Christ. The last two groups, the majority of people on the earth who lived throughout history will by default die two times, once in this life and then resurrected temporarily to receive judgment and punishment , which is eternal death via the consuming fire of God. The final group will be the most evil people who have lived on the face of the earth will be resurrected twice and thus will die three times. Their first resurrection will be during the second coming of Christ, and then the second resurrection will be to receive judgment and punishment along with everyone one else who did not make it to heaven.

Concerning those who take part in the first resurrection, John writes in Revelation 20:4-6,

> *And I saw thrones, and they sat upon them, and judgment was given unto them: and I saw the souls of them that were beheaded for the witness of Jesus, and for the word of God, and which had not worshipped the beast, neither his image, neither had received his mark upon their hands; and they lived and reigned with Christ a thousand years. But the rest of the dead lived not again until the thousand years were finished. This is the first resurrection. Blessed and holy is he that hath part in the first resurrection: on such the second death hath no power, but they shall be priests of God and of Christ and shall reign with him a thousand years.*

Therefore, those that are redeemed by Christ will be either part of the first resurrection and or they will be part of the 144,000. Those who are part of the second resurrection will all resurrect 1,000 years after the 2nd Coming of Christ. During the 2nd resurrection Satan will be released temporally from his prison on the planet earth and as he starts to see people resurrected he again thinks of more evil to do. This time he will unite all the unsaved generals from throughout time, and the unsaved men of science to unite and join forces to attempt to takeover God's Holy City brought from heaven. However, as they attempt the impossible, it will start to rain down fire on all the unsaved sinners from Cain to the very last in our era. John writes in Revelation 20:7-15,

> *And when the thousand years are expired, Satan shall be loosed out of his prison, And he shall go out to deceive the nations which are in the four quarters of the earth, Gog and Magog, to gather them together to battle; the number of whom is as the sand of the sea. And they went up on the breadth of the earth, and compassed the camp of the saints about, and the beloved city: and fire came down from God out of heaven, and devoured them. And the devil that deceived them was cast into the lake of fire and brimstone, where the beast and the false prophet are, and shall Be tormented day and night forever and ever. And I saw a great white throne, and him that sat on it, from whose face the earth and the heaven fled away; and there was found no place for them. And I saw the dead, small and great, stand before God; and the books were opened: and another book was opened, which is the book of life: and the dead were judged out those things which were written in the books, according to their works. And the sea gave up the dead which were in it; and death and hell delivered up the dead which were in them: and they were judged every man according to their works. And death and hell were cast into the lake of fire. This is the second death. And whosoever was not found written in the book of life was cast into the lake of fire.*

Therefore, unlike the conception of hell that many people have of it being an everlasting inferno, for every man that has ever lived, they will be judged on their actions, and thus their punishment will fit with all the wrong doing that was done during their lives. The more evil and unrighteousness that an individual did in the sight of God, then the more time the person will face punishment. As for Satan, the beast, and the false prophet, they will last a very long time burning for being the primary people responsible for the ruin of many of God's creation. They will continue burning until they will become devoured and consumed by God's fire. A sign that one day evil, Satan, and all the fallen angels will not exist is that in Revelation 21:4 states, "And God shall wipe away all tears from their eyes; and there shall be no more death, neither sorrow, nor crying, neither shall there be any more pain: for the former things are passed away." When John mentions "the former things are passed away" that means evil, hell, Satan and all who did evil will no longer exist and will be forgotten, forever.

Chapter 32: New Heaven and New Earth

By far the greatest of all the prophecies of the Bible is the prophecy which lasts forever. It is the prophecy of the New heaven and New Earth, in which God and His redeemed live together in harmony for eternity. Many new lessons wait to be learned by those redeemed, who will live under the sight and protection of the God of the universe. Never again will evil in any of its forms exist. Never again will there be opposition to the Word of God.

In Revelation 21, John speaks of the opposite of the fallen Babylon, and this is the New Jerusalem. The saved inhabitants had sought on earth the purification that only Christ can give, through His Blood and His atonement. The clean and pure woman of Revelation 12 or God's pure church throughout the ages, is now represented by John as a bride prepared to meet its bridegroom. In other words, that the Redeemed people have made themselves clean through the help of Jesus Christ and His grace. John states in Revelation 21:1-3,

> *"And I saw a new heaven and a new earth: for the first heaven and the first earth were passed away; and there was no more sea. And I John saw the holy city, New Jerusalem, coming down from God out of heaven, prepared as a bride adorned for her husband. And I heard a great voice out of heaven saying,*

Eliseo Santos

'Behold the tabernacle of God, is with men, and he will dwell with them, and they shall be his people, and God himself shall be with them, and be their God."

In order to be able to practice the promise of eternal life, you should strive to live daily within this life and in the next life with the All-Mighty God. As the Good Father, wants the best for His Children, so does God want to you live forever, for this is something no man can give, but only Jesus Christ of Heaven.

John describes the river of life and the tree of life, in Revelation 22:1-7

And he showed me a pure river of water of life, clear as crystal, proceeding out of the throne of God and of the Lamb. In the midst of the street of it, and on either side of the river, was there the tree of life, which have bare twelve manner of fruits, and yielded her fruit every month: and the leaves of the tree were for the healing of the nations. And there shall be no more curse: but the throne of God and of the Lamb shall be in it; and His servants shall serve Him: And they shall see his face; and his name shall be in their foreheads. And there shall be no night there; and they need no candle, neither light of the sun; for the Lord God giveth them light: and they shall reign forever and ever. And he said unto me, These sayings are faithful and true and the Lord God and of the holy prophets sent His angel to shew unto his servants the things which must shortly be done. "Behold, I come quickly: blessed is he that keepeth the sayings of the prophecy of this book."

Therefore, after John explains the river and the tree of life, he mentions that the people of God through Christ's redemption will be able to see God. There will be no sun there for all of the infinite light of truth and the warmth of the infinite love of God will be with the redeemed forever and always. As John said in his first letter, "God is light, and in Him is no darkness at all," (1 John 1:6) and "God is love," (1 John 4:16). Thus, based on the history presented by the Book of Revelation, it establishes the truth and fulfillment of the things, which are soon to take place on the world.

Every individual will have the opportunity to seek eternal life and to take part in the Work of God. If you are ready to live a life of commitment to Christ and His Words, then pray now and ask for God and the Holy Spirit in your life. Confess your sins and unbelief; you will be forgiven through the blood of Christ. Let us do all we can now to read and study His Holy Words and promises for they are the basis of reality. Let us hear and do what God asks of each of us in keeping His Law and His Commandments. Let us pray to God, and ask Him to help us to keep His law, and abide in His love. Remember and don't forget the words of Christ in John 15:10, "If ye keep my commandments, ye shall abide in my love; even as I have kept my Father's commandments, and abide in his love." Pray and ask daily for forgiveness of sins and do all we can to repent and stop sinning. Confess any and all sins done in secret, that only God and the enemy will know. For it is by removing sin from our lives through the grace of Jesus Christ, that we prepare ourselves to live with the infinite Good Father God forever and always, Amen.

Letter To The Reader

Dear Friend in Christ,

Thank you for taking the time to read my book.

I would appreciate if you would spread the word about the biblical truths contained in this book and share it with your friends and family members.

Please leave an honest review at either
http://www.Amazon.com/author/EliseoSantos   or
http://www.goodreads.com/

Also, You can follow us on Facebook at
https://www.facebook.com/emergingtruth

You can follow the author at https://www.facebook.com/ems1005

If you have any questions pertaining to the subject matter of the book, bulk sales, or any other media requests you can contact us :

Via Email: Emergingtruth@yahoo.com
Via Mail:
Eliseo Santos – Emerging Truth Productions
P.O. Box 785
Phillipsport, New York 12769

Thank You and God Bless.

Notes

1. Date of Birth of Christ - Keep in mind Jesus was born in the fall of 4 B.C. and died and resurrected in the Spring in the spring of 31 A.D. The reason why it's 4 B.C. and not the year 1 A.D. is due to a sixth century error discrepancy in calculating the new system of years of Anno Domino from the old Roman year.

Just so you are not confused, the calendar change in the sixth century changed the year, not the actual calendar months. The present-day calendar months are still the same months that were changed by Augustus Caesar, who changed the sixth month of the year to Augustus (now known as August), and his parent Julius Caesar changed the fifth month of the year to Julius(now known as July),("Calendar." Microsoft® Student 2009 [DVD]. Redmond, WA: Microsoft Corporation, 2008.)

The calendar year was changed in the 6th century (525 A.D.) by the Roman Catholic monk Dionysius Exiguus (also known as Dennis the Little), who incorrectly dated the year of Christ's Birth to the year of Rome 753 and as year 1 A.D. Keep in mind, that when the change occurred in 525 A.D. , the people at that time believed the year to be either 1285 from the founding of Rome or the year 248, based on the first year of the reign of Diocletian, ("When does the Millenium End and Does it really matter?, By David Ewing Duncan, Encarta Yearbook, November 1999). This incorrect chronology was later introduced into historical writings by Bede the Venerable in the 8th century. ("Chronology." Microsoft® Student 2009 [DVD]. Redmond,

WA: Microsoft Corporation, 2008.) Another important point, that must be known in order to alleviate the confusion, is that all numbers at that time were written using roman numerals. There was no concept of a zero and thus, there is no 0 A.D. For example 10, 100, and 1000 were written using roman numerals X, C, and M. The concept of zero reached Europe in the 14th century, (Duncan, ibid).

2. The Ten Persecutions of Christianity by the Roman Empire.

1. Nero (66 A.D.).

2. Domitian (93 A.D.).

3. Trajan (102 A.D.)

4. Marcus Aurelius, and Lucius Verus (166 A.D.).

5. L.Septimus Severus which commenced about (201 AD -ended 213 AD) under Sons Antonius Caracalla and Septimus Geta- continued under Alexander Severus, son of Antonius (223 AD).

6. Maximin, the Giant – Persecution went on and off from (237 AD),.

7. Decius (251 AD).

8. Valerian and son Gallien (259 AD).

9. Aurelian (273 AD)

10. Diocletian (302-312AD),

(Pg.49-120, The Bloody Theatre, Martyr's Mirror By Thielem J. Von Bracht, translated by L.Daniel Rupp, Published by David Miller, Near Lampeter Square, Lancaster County, PA., 1837).

3. Examples of gruesome cruelty of the Romans toward Christians (Pg. 50-51, The Bloody Theatre, Von Bracht, Thielem, Translated by L. Daniel Rupp, 1837, Published By David Miller, Near Lampeter Square, Lancaster County, PA)

Good Father, Bad Father

1. Christians were nailed to a pillars.

2. Christians had a boiling hot mixture of tar pitch, tallow, and wax poured on their bodies.

3. Christians were set on fire to become a burning corpse light at night-time,

4. Animal skins were sewed onto the Christians

5. Christians had hunting dogs chase them to death

4. Doctrine of discovery – was doctrine in which Roman Catholic Church gave authority to the many Catholic monarchs of Europe to discover land and claim it for their own country or kingdom. By claiming foreign land as theirs, they would subjugate, and enslave native indigenous peoples and use their lands and natural resources for their benefit. Papal bulls Dum Diversas June 18, 1452, and the Bull Romanus Pontifex (Nicholas VI) January 8, 1454 are examples of such the Papacy's role in Era of exploration and slavery. More information can be found at www.doctrineofdiscovery.org

5. In the 1300's, John Wycliffe was the first to translate the Bible from Latin to English. It was however done by hand and very tedious. Thus, Wycliffe organized the Lollards to help produce and distribute copies of the Bible.

Appendix 1 - Old Testament Prophecies of Jesus Christ and Their New Testament Fulfillment

Old Testament Prophecies about Christ	New Testament fulfillment
Numbers 24:17	Matthew 1:1-2, 2:2
Isaiah 40:3	Matthew 3:1-3
Isaiah 7:14 (Emmanuel means 'God is with us')	Luke 1:28-31
Micah 5:2 (Ancient of Days means God)	Matthew 2:1-2
Isaiah 61:1,2	Luke 1:28-31
Isaiah 35:5,6	Matthew 9:35
Zechariah -9:9	Luke 19:35
Psalm 41:9	Matthew 26:20-22
Zechariah 11:12, 13	Matthew 27:3,7
Psalm 69:4	John 15:25
Isaiah 64:1-2	1 Peter 3:10
Psalm 22:16	Luke 23:33
Isaiah 53:12	Luke 23:24-25
Psalm 22:18	John19:24
Psalm 22:1	Matthew 27:26
Psalm 31:5	Luke 23:46
Isaiah 53:9	Matthew 27:57-60
Zechariah 12:10	John 19:36-37
Isaiah 53:7	Acts 8:32-35
Psalm 22:27-28	Matthew 28:19,20

Appendix 2 - Differences Between Teachings Found in the Bible and Teachings taught By The Little Horn

Doctrines Taught by Christ and Apostles (1 Tim. 3:15)	Doctrines Changed by the Little Horn (Daniel 8:12)
The dead sleep and know nothing – (John 11:11, Ecclesiastes 9:5)	Prayers to dead – introduced in 310 AD
Worship God in Spirit – John 4:23,24	Religious candles lit during religious ceremonies – 320 AD
Adoration of only God – Rev. 19:10	Veneration of Angels and Saints – 375 AD
Saturday, the Holy Day - Exodus 20:8-11	First Sunday law – 321 AD
No graven images – Exodus 20: 4-6	Veneration of images – 375 AD
Only One Sacrifice of Christ - Hebrews 9:26	The daily sacrifice of the daily mass – 394 AD
Jesus Christ our only Mediator – 1 Timothy 2:5	Mary venerated as Mediatrix - 432 AD
Priesthood of all Believers – 1 Peter 2:9	Priesthood introduced to the People - 500 AD
Prayer for sick for healing – James 5:14	Extreme Unction before death - 526 AD
Death then Judgment Hebrews - 9:27	Doctrine of Purgatory – 593 AD
Don't teach in strange languages – 1 Cor. 14:9	Pope Gregory I makes Latin into official language - 600 AD
Prayers only directed to God – John 14:13	Prayers to Mary and Saints – 600 AD
Christ only Foundation – 1 Cor. 3:11	The Pope made fundamental – 610 AD

"Call no man 'Father'" – Matthew 23:9	The Pope is called "Holy Father" – 610 AD
Never Prostrate before another man – Acts 10:26	People Start Kissing the Pope's feet – 709 AD
Christ rejects Temporal Kingdom – John 18:38	Pope receives temporal Kingdom – 750 AD
Only the blood of can cleanse sins – 1 John 1:7-9	Adoration of the cross and relics - 786 AD
Blessing only through Christ – Ephesians 5:26	The Holy Water with a Little salt – 850 AD
Christ enthroned at heavenly Kingdom – Hebrews 8:1	Pope enthroned before cardinals – 927 AD
Worship the Lord Your God – Matthew 4:10	The Worship of Joseph is introduced – 890 AD
All believers are saints – 1 Corinthians 1:2	Canonization of dead – Saints 995 AD
Bishops should Marry – 1 Tim 3:2-5	Celibacy enforced by boniface – 1079 AD
Don't use vain repetition while praying – Matthew 6:7	Introduction of the Rosary – 1090 AD
Jesus never used force – Rev. 22:17	Pope starts Inquisition – 1184 AD
Salvation through faith – Rom 5:1	Sale of indulgences – 1190 AD
The Last Supper Symbolic – Luke 22:19	The transubstantiation introduced – 1215 AD
The Confession of Sin to God – Psalm 32:5	Confession of a priest – 1215AD

Only God Pardons or forgives sins – Mark 2:7	The Priest forgives and pardons sins - 1215 AD
God condemns idolatry – Exodus 20:4	The Worship of the host – 1220 AD
Jesus orders to search and study the Bible – John 5:39	The Bible is banned from the common people - 1229 AD
The Bible Bans Fetishism - Revelation 21:8	The scapular used to protect from evil forces – 1287 AD
"Drink everyone from the cup" – Matthew 26:27	The cup is prohibited from the laity – 1414 AD
Only Two sacraments – Matthew 26:26, 28:19	Doctrine of 7 sacraments – 1439 AD
Christ condemns traditions – Mark 7:7-13	The tradition has same authority as the Bible – 1545 AD
You should not add to the content of the Bible – Rev. 22:18	Apocryphal books added -1546 AD
We are all sinners – Rom. – 3:23	Dogma of Immaculate conception -1854 AD
God is only infallible – Matthew 19:17	Dogma of Papal Infallibility – 1870 AD

Other unbiblical doctrines without exact dates are infant baptism, aspersion, original sin, etc. .

Index

1260 days prophecy, 225

144,000, 306, 307, 308, 309

1st head fell

Gregory in 1846, 264

2300-Day prophecy, 273

2300-Day Prophecy, 6, 271

2nd beast, 37, 239, 241, 278, 279, 282

2nd Coming of Christ, 1, 3, 4, 39, 88, 119, 124, 128, 181, 182, 185, 194, 243, 263, 269, 275, 276, 291, 296, 298, 301, 305, 308, 309

2nd Coming of Jesus Christ,, 187

2nd head fell

Leo in 1903, 264

2nd Seal, 5, 79

3rd head fell

Benedict in 1922, 264

3rd Seal, 5, 93

4th head fell

Pius in 1958, 264

4th Seal, 5, 115

5th seal, 173

666, 6, 259, 260, 262, 265, 266, 269

7th Day Sabbath, 58, 90, 91, 100, 112, 159, 242, 285

a mixture of different pagan traditions, 47

a prophetic day equals an actual year, 200

Africa, 70, 91, 112, 151, 163, 184, 214, 231

Akiba Ben Joseph, 88

Alamanni, 101

Albi, 130

Alumbrados, 247

Ancient Babylon, 259

Ancient Greece, 42, 44

Ancient Rome, 100

Anglo-Saxons, 101

anti-Christian things the Roman Church, 149

Apostate Protestantism, 240, 278, 279, 282, 288, 295, 303

Apostle John, 3, 4, 9

Apostle Paul, 2, 4, 198

Apostle Peter, 24, 51, 137

Apostle Philip, 12

Area 51, 301

Armageddon, 299, 300, 301, 302, 303

Armenia, 102

Asia, 65, 70, 91, 163, 182, 214

Asia Minor, 65, 70, 91

At least nine of Paul's letters had been in distribution after 90 AD, 77

Babylon, 5, 33, 34, 35, 36, 37, 43, 44, 48, 52, 69, 89, 94, 98, 118, 136, 157, 176, 260, 261, 277, 287, 288, 293, 300, 304, 313

Balak, 93, 95

Beast, 6, 136, 183, 231, 240, 241, 259, 279, 282, 303

Because Christ died for us on the Cross and resurrected, thus Christ has no equals, 266

Belisarius, 101, 201, 202

Belshazzar, 43, 45, 261, 277, 278, 288

Berthier, 201, 203, 238, 263

Bible, 5, 6, 1, 2, 4, 6, 7, 9, 17, 23, 24, 25, 28, 30,

31, 33, 34, 41, 44, 45, 52, 53, 61, 62, 70, 75, 76, 77, 85, 88, 90, 93, 95, 103, 105, 107, 108, 110, 114, 116, 119, 120, 121, 124, 126, 127, 128, 131, 133, 134, 136, 138, 143, 144, 146, 147, 148, 151, 153, 154, 156, 160, 161, 163, 171, 173, 174, 176, 178, 180, 184, 185, 187, 194, 195, 196, 199, 202, 203, 215, 217, 218, 222, 224, 225, 226, 227, 228, 229, 234, 235, 237, 239, 241, 246, 251, 252, 255, 259, 260, 262, 263, 265, 267, 269, 271, 273, 274, 279, 280, 286, 288, 292, 293, 299, 300, 313, 321, 323, 349

Bible Prophecy,, 34, 156, 194, 269, 274

Blood of Christ, 82

Bloodshed on the Cross, 307

Book of 2 Thessalonians, 268

Book of Daniel, 12, 13, 23, 24, 26, 31, 33, 67, 81, 202, 218, 260

Book of Genesis, 62

Book of Revelation, 25, 52, 62, 63, 65, 136, 191, 195, 245, 297, 315

brothers and sisters., 52, 287

Burgundians, 101

Calendar., 319

Cardinal Ratzinger, 171, 264, 269

Cassander, 42

Ceremony of the Eucharist, 109

China, 91, 92, 112

Christ is everything to Christianity, 53

Christ will come to put an end to evil and all those who took pleasure in evil, 302

Christianity, 29, 46, 49, 50, 53, 60, 71, 75, 78, 80, 91, 93, 94, 95, 96, 100, 102, 112, 115, 117, 121, 122, 123, 127, 130, 131, 135, 140, 149, 155, 156, 178, 200, 217, 229, 234, 236, 320

Christmas, 47, 48, 49

Church of Ephesus, 5, 69, 70, 71, 130, 144, 179, 196, 217, 222, 291

Church of Laodecia, 6, 264, 291, 292

Church of Pergamos, 5, 93, 94, 98, 102, 104, 106, 108, 110, 111, 127, 278

Church of Philadelphia, 5, 180, 181, 182, 183, 185, 195, 204, 221, 229, 230, 231, 271

Church of Sardis, 5, 143, 145, 152, 173, 178, 204, 205, 231

Church of Smyrna, 5, 79, 81, 102, 111

Church of Thyatira, 5, 115, 116, 117, 122, 124, 143, 223

Claimed to be the literal body of Christ, 109

Colonial expansion became very lucrative for the monarchies that were involved in acquiring new land and natural resources overseas in the New World, 207

Conquered Medo-Persians in 331 BC, 42, 44

Consistent with the Bad Father of lies and the Roman Empire, 117

Constantine, 49, 81, 89, 95, 96, 97, 98, 99, 100, 105, 107, 113, 127, 128, 129, 278

Constantine and Pope sought to gain power and control to build a kingdom on earth, 97

Constantinople, 97, 103

Council of Tarragona, 120, 121, 132

Council of Toulouse, 120, 121, 131

Creation, 12, 20, 90, 99, 114, 139, 156, 226, 243

Creator, 1, 6, 7, 12, 63, 66, 67, 68, 100, 118, 119, 159, 187, 191, 226, 243, 286, 289, 304

Creator God, 68, 187

Crusade, 131, 134

Crusades, 103, 130, 134, 149, 178, 215

Daniel, 5, 12, 13, 14, 23, 24, 26, 31, 33, 34, 35, 36, 37, 40, 41, 42, 43, 44, 45, 46, 56, 67, 69, 72, 81, 82, 87, 97, 100, 101, 118, 127, 128, 129, 133, 135, 136, 141, 152, 153, 157, 160, 184, 195, 200, 201, 212, 215, 218, 225, 228, 241, 260, 261, 266, 272, 274, 277, 308, 320

Dark Day of New England, 184, 185, 188

Day, 6, 46, 57, 58, 89, 91, 98, 99, 100, 112, 129, 145, 159, 160, 184, 185,

186, 187, 188, 189, 192, 195, 201, 227, 229, 230, 242, 243, 271, 273, 275, 283, 285, 289, 304

Days of the week have continued to be uninterrupted, 286

Death, 28, 116, 133

Death,, 116

Describes the alienation of mankind from the tree of life, 62

Developed a comprehensive plan for the activities of the order, 165

Did so much for the living beings on this planet, 285

Died for our sins, 125

Diocletian, 81, 319, 320

Drew the ire of the Vatican, 178

Earth, 6, 3, 159, 175, 301, 313

Easter, 26, 27

Edict of Nantes, 179

Egypt, 27, 29, 44, 52, 55, 58, 60, 86, 91, 94, 98, 106, 118, 198, 223

End times, 298

End Times, 6, 2, 4, 14, 119, 128, 183, 184, 185, 187, 189, 192, 194, 195, 226, 259, 268, 273, 274, 276, 288, 289, 293, 301

Enforced the fasting rule on the Sabbath, 114

Eternal kingdom of God on earth, 39

Eternal life, 80, 269

Eternal Life, 1, 2, 6, 305

Eucharist, 98, 106, 109, 117, 254, 255, 287

Fall of Babylon,

89, 157, 287, 288

Feast of Tabernacles, 58, 59, 60

Feast of unleavened bread,, 28

First Pope to claim to hold the two keys of Peter, 106

Foreign Bible society, 228

France, 101, 120, 130, 178, 179, 180, 209, 211, 215, 221, 226, 227, 249, 252

France would remain a republic without a monarchy, 226

Francis I, 178

Francis is a Jesuit, 268

Franks, 101

Frederik of Prussia, 248

Freemasonry, 257

French government in banning all forms of religion they actually killed the Word of God, 227

French revolution, 226, 227

French Revolution, 6, 180, 183, 185, 219, 221, 227, 228, 230, 237, 239, 249

Garden of Eden, 18, 40, 61, 62

Germanic Kingdoms, 101

Gnosticism, 71, 94

God, 2, 3, 5, 6, 1, 2, 3, 4, 5, 6, 7, 9, 10, 11, 12, 13, 15, 16, 17, 18, 19, 20, 23, 25, 27, 28, 30, 33, 35, 36, 37, 38, 39, 40, 41, 43, 45, 46, 48, 49, 50, 51, 52, 53, 58, 59, 60, 61, 62, 63, 65, 66, 67, 68, 70, 71, 73, 76, 81, 83, 84, 85, 87, 88, 90, 94, 95, 98, 100, 102, 106, 107, 108, 109, 110, 111, 112,

Good Father, Bad Father

114, 115, 117, 118, 119, 120, 121, 124, 125, 126, 127, 128, 129, 130, 131, 133, 134, 135, 137, 138, 139, 140, 141, 143, 144, 145, 147, 148, 149, 152, 153, 154, 155, 156, 157, 158, 159, 160, 161, 163, 165, 168, 170, 173, 174, 175, 176, 178, 180, 181, 182, 183, 184, 186, 187, 194, 195, 196, 197, 198, 200, 202, 204, 206, 211, 217, 218, 221, 222, 223, 224, 225, 226, 227, 228, 229, 230, 231, 232, 234, 235, 236, 237, 240, 241, 242, 243, 246, 249, 254, 255, 259, 260, 261, 262, 264, 266, 268, 269, 273, 274, 275, 277, 278, 280, 281, 282, 283, 285, 287, 288, 289, 291, 292, 293, 295, 296, 297, 298, 299, 300, 301, 302, 303, 304, 305, 307, 308, 309, 310, 313, 314, 315, 317, 349

God is light, 315

God is love, 10, 315

God of the universe, 140, 278, 313

Good Father, 1, 2, 5, 2, 3, 7, 9, 11, 19, 20, 23, 30, 31, 52, 58, 61, 63, 76, 82, 84, 85, 87, 92, 93, 97, 98, 103, 106, 111, 117, 119, 122, 124, 126, 129, 131, 139, 140, 152, 156, 161, 163, 168, 196, 234, 238, 274, 275, 280, 289, 293, 296, 314, 315

Good Father God, 2, 3, 9, 30, 76, 82, 85, 111, 122, 124,

129, 161, 234, 238, 275, 123,

Gratian, 104

He does these deceptive works to maintain the lie of the immortality of the soul, 305

He is really the Son of God, 139

He will return to earth wielding unlimited power and glory to save and rescue His people from their human and spiritual oppressors, 302

Heaven, 6, 3, 21, 66, 68, 86, 110, 183, 193, 274, 292, 313, 314

Heavenly Sanctuary, 195

Hell, 169

Help you recover and overcome all the effects of sin in your life, 198

Henry II, 178

Henry IV, 179

Heruli, 46, 101, 201

His death can cover all the death penalties and sins of every human being that believes in Him, 139

History, 5, 23, 57, 112, 113, 114, 129, 167, 201, 206, 207, 208, 209, 210, 217, 236, 248, 256

Holy Spirit, 1, 7, 9, 11, 19, 23, 51, 55, 70, 82, 86, 89, 94, 96, 103, 106, 119, 132, 135, 156, 159, 160, 175, 202, 217, 239, 273, 283, 287, 288, 292, 293, 315

Host, 109

Huguenots, 178, 179, 180, 215

Human principles, 186, 187, 246

Ignatius Loyola, 165

Illuminati, 247, 248, 249, 257

Immediate feelings of happiness, security, 123

India, 91, 112, 184, 208

Infinite God, 28

Inquisition, 5, 131, 134, 135, 149, 151, 170, 171, 173, 174, 175, 177, 210

Inquisitions, 171

Investigative Judgment, 6, 271

Is now in heaven hearing our prayers, 118

Isaiah, 13, 99, 286, 298

Isaiah 45 18, 286

Israel, 10, 27, 28, 48, 49, 50, 54, 55, 58, 59, 60, 85, 88, 91, 93, 95, 123, 196, 253, 283

Its many biblical truths, 146

Jerusalem, 15, 33, 58, 63, 70, 84, 86, 87, 88, 182, 193, 272, 273, 278, 302, 313

Jesuits, 5, 145, 162, 165, 166, 167, 168, 169, 170, 180, 183, 205, 206, 207, 208, 209, 210, 211, 212, 213, 214, 215, 216, 217, 218, 221, 246, 248, 249, 250, 251, 256, 265

Jesuits going against Biblical principles and morals, 213

Jesuits use the name of God in vain, 170

Jesus Christ, 6, 1, 2, 3, 5, 9, 10, 11, 12, 13, 14, 15, 19, 20, 26, 28, 30, 33, 46, 47, 49, 50, 51, 52, 53, 55, 56, 57, 58, 60, 61, 65, 66, 67, 69, 70, 75, 77,

Eliseo Santos

81, 82, 83, 84, 85, 87, 88, 94, 98, 103, 105, 110, 113, 114, 115, 116, 117, 118, 120, 122, 124, 125, 127, 129, 130, 132, 136, 138, 140, 141, 146, 148, 151, 153, 154, 156, 157, 158, 159, 161, 162, 167, 173, 174, 176, 177, 178, 179, 182, 183, 184, 187, 194, 196, 197, 198, 203, 204, 208, 228, 229, 250, 254, 255, 256, 261, 262, 264, 266, 269, 274, 275, 277, 280, 286, 289, 291, 292, 293, 296, 299, 300, 302, 304, 305, 306, 307, 308, 313, 314, 315, 322, 349

Jesus Christ and His words and not take the, 183

Jewish religious leaders, 1, 12, 15, 83, 84, 85, 86, 88, 211, 308

Jezebel, 115, 118, 120, 124

John, 3, 4, 5, 9, 10, 11, 12, 13, 15, 20, 25, 38, 51, 54, 56, 61, 62, 65, 66, 67, 68, 70, 77, 81, 90, 98, 119, 133, 149, 150, 153, 156, 173, 175, 176, 178, 191, 192, 195, 196, 197, 199, 200, 203, 204, 211, 221, 222, 224, 225, 227, 237, 239, 240, 241, 245, 246,랜252, 255, 257, 263, 264, 267, 277, 280, 282, 283, 287, 289, 293, 295, 298, 299, 301, 302, 303, 307, 309, 311, 313, 314, 315, 321

John Calvin, 178

John describes the importance

of the two witnesses and their significance to the Church of Philadelphia, 221

John the Baptist, 51, 54, 56

John the son of Zebedee, 51

Joseph I, 205, 210

Justinian, 101, 121, 200, 201

Killed Christians to continue the existence of the false good, 134

King Ahab, 124

King Artaxerxes, 273

King Herod, 54, 85

King of Moab, 95

King Shapur II, 112

Kingdom of God, 38, 40, 168

Language, 11, 34, 37, 76, 77, 105, 116, 120, 151, 173, 212, 224, 228, 242, 245, 269, 281, 282, 283

Law of God prepares you to live forever with God, 98

Leaders both in the political and religious world, have sought to use the sacred

vessels of God, as if they were God, 278

Limits access to the Bible, 127

Lisbon Earthquake, 185, 205

Little Horn, 6, 37, 40, 41, 42, 81, 89, 97, 100, 127, 128, 133, 135, 136, 152, 153, 160, 200, 212, 218, 268, 323

Little Horn,, 81, 100, 128, 200, 268

Lombards, 101

Louis XIV, 180, 209

Love of God, 10, 90, 154,

Eliseo Santos

180, 225, 229, 277

Loyola, 165, 215, 247

Lysimachus, 42

M.Martin, 208

Many Protestants were now able to read and study their Bibles, 271

Many readers of the Bible were keenly awakened by the widespread devastation, 185

Mark of the beast, 242, 278, 281, 283, 289, 295, 297

Marquis de Pombal, 205

Martin Luther, 5, 76, 143, 147, 148, 149, 150, 152, 153, 154, 161, 163, 217

Mass, 28, 110, 117, 138, 254

Medes and Persians, 44, 261, 277

Middle East, 55, 58, 70, 91, 102, 112, 115, 157

Monarchs, 205

Monstrance, 28

Moses, 10, 27, 59, 114, 198

Mount Weather, 301

Mount Zion, 39, 262

Musacus, 112

Napoleon, 197, 201, 203, 205, 219, 238, 249, 250, 251, 252, 263

Nebuchadnezzar, 33, 34, 35, 36, 43, 97, 157, 241, 261, 278

Nero, 72, 82, 320

Never again will there be opposition to the Word of God, 313

New Testament, 6, 1, 3, 24, 50, 53, 75, 77, 78, 89, 120, 121, 129, 131, 149, 194,

198, 224, 261, 322

Nicolatians, 71, 97, 107

Noah, 193, 194, 276, 277

Of the inquisition, 178

Old Testament, 6, 10, 11, 28, 50, 75, 76, 77, 83, 84, 85, 87, 91, 95, 112, 118, 152, 198, 224, 242, 280, 282, 301, 322

Oppose any Protestants that openly opposed papal authority, 168

Ostrogoths, 46, 101, 201

Ozarks, 301

Pagan, 80, 96, 106, 126, 134

Papacy, 46, 100, 101, 117, 121, 122, 128, 129, 133, 141, 147, 150, 153, 154, 155, 160, 161, 163, 175, 176, 195, 203, 204, 212, 216, 217, 218, 236, 237, 239, 246, 251, 252, 256, 263, 265, 281, 300, 321

Passover, 27, 28, 54, 58, 60

People were killing priests, and other ministers of religion, 226

Persecution, 81, 93, 320

Plagues, 6, 295

Pontifex Maximus, 104, 105, 109

Pontius Pilate, 50, 56

Pope Benedict XVI, 264, 267, 268, 269

Pope Clement XIV, 211, 218, 247, 251

Pope Damasus, 105

Pope Francis, 263, 267

Pope Gregory

IX, 120, 131

Pope Gregory XI, 160

Pope Gregory XIII, 160

Pope Innocent I, 114, 130

Pope Innocent III, 130

Pope Paul III, 166

Pope Pius VI, 197, 202, 203, 204, 219, 238, 249, 251, 252, 256, 262, 263, 265

Pope Pius VII, 203, 249, 251, 256, 265

Pope Silverius, 201

Pope Sylvester, 107, 113

Pope Syricius, 107, 108

Pope Vigilius, 200, 201

Portugal, 101, 186, 205, 206, 210, 211, 215, 221

Prayer, 140, 166

Promises, 3, 111, 124, 156, 176, 197, 199, 237, 271, 294, 315

Protestant reformation, 143, 152, 163

Protestant Reformation, 5, 76, 142, 143, 144, 147, 154, 163, 217, 223

Protestant reforms were a step in the right direction, 145

Protestantism, 6, 72, 145, 154, 155, 166, 170, 173, 174, 180, 204, 218, 231, 235, 236, 240, 246, 278, 280, 282, 288, 295, 303

Protestants were during this time unfettered from the Roman Church and other authoritative Protestant religions, 271

Prussia, 180, 248, 265

Ptolemy, 42

Resulted in many more martyrs, 146

Resurrected, 188

Resurrection, 6, 87, 304, 305

Revelation, 5, 6, 4, 15, 16, 23, 25, 28, 39, 52, 61, 62, 63, 65, 66, 67, 68, 72, 77, 97, 103, 106, 111, 116, 119, 132, 136, 144, 153, 156, 157, 173, 176, 182, 183, 191, 195, 196, 197, 199, 203, 204, 221, 223, 224, 225, 226, 231, 237, 239, 240, 241, 245, 246, 251, 252, 259, 260, 262, 263, 265, 267, 269, 279, 280, 282, 285, 287, 288, 292, 295, 296, 297, 298, 299, 300, 301, 302, 303, 306, 307, 309, 310, 313, 314, 315

Revelation 14, John gives an important description of the 144,000, 306

Revelation 17 9-11, 259

Roman Catholic church, 109, 145, 213

Roman Catholic Church, 26, 27, 76, 81, 89, 95, 96, 97, 103, 105, 107, 109, 111, 116, 117, 122, 126, 127, 128, 130, 131, 133, 136, 142, 145, 147, 148, 149, 150, 151, 153, 154, 156, 157, 159, 160, 161, 165, 170, 175, 180, 183, 195, 204, 205, 207, 214, 215, 216, 217, 223, 231, 232, 234, 238, 239, 245, 246, 253, 256, 260, 262, 268,

Eliseo Santos

280, 282, 287, 321

Roman Catholic Mass, 28, 109, 254

Rome, 29, 45, 49, 52, 55, 56, 70, 72, 77, 80, 94, 95, 96, 97, 98, 100, 101, 103, 104, 107, 109, 121, 126, 147, 157, 169, 201, 202, 252, 259, 287, 299, 319

Russia, 248, 265

Sabbath, 54, 58, 89, 90, 91, 98, 99, 100, 112, 114, 129, 159, 184, 215, 226, 242, 281, 283, 285, 289

Sabbath was also kept in Scotland and Ireland, 113

Satan, 3, 4, 5, 6, 16, 17, 18, 19, 20, 31, 48, 52, 58, 61, 62, 71, 73, 79, 82, 83, 84, 92, 93, 95, 98, 111, 116, 122, 126, 127, 132, 134, 136, 139, 154, 156, 175, 182, 187, 196, 197, 199, 217, 225, 231, 238, 239, 246, 251, 256, 268, 282, 289, 299, 305, 309, 310

Sebastiao Jose De Carvalho y Mello, 205

Seleucus, 42

Seven Churches, 5, 65, 67, 69

Seven Trumpets, 67

Sign of God, 281

Simon Bar Kokhba, 88, 89

Something this world will never give you, 194

Sought another Christ, 87

Souls under the altar, 146

Source of the genuine and true Christianity that Jesus and his disciples, practiced and endorsed,, 121

Spain, 101, 113, 176, 186, 206, 211, 215, 221

Spanish Inquisition, 173, 177

Spiritual exercises were a set of controlled movement and experiences in which an individual, 165, 167,

Study your Bibles, 194

Sunday, 27, 49, 84, 90, 97, 98, 99, 100, 112, 120, 145, 159, 183, 234, 242, 278, 280, 281, 282, 287, 288, 289, 295

Sunday law, 49, 100, 242, 278, 281, 288, 295

Symbolic of all of God's people throughout time, 175

Ten Commandments, 5, 10, 31, 37, 38, 59, 65, 88, 90, 98, 103, 108, 110, 111, 119, 123, 124, 126, 129, 135, 138, 149, 156, 159, 170, 187, 194, 197, 225, 226, 234, 236, 240, 242, 243, 249, 261, 277, 280, 282, 283, 286, 295

Teutonic goddess, 26

The 1st beast of Revelation 13, 203

The 7th seal, 181

The Bible is the great equalizer for the common man, 132

The Book of Hebrew, 12, 139

The Eighth, 267

The general public of the Middle Ages had no stable foundation for their

Christian faith, 152

The Jesuits, 5, 146, 165, 166, 167, 168, 169, 205, 206, 207, 208, 209, 211, 217, 247, 249, 250, 251

The more evil and unrighteousness that an individual did in the sight of God, then the more time the person will face punishment, 310

The techniques the Jesuits used to spark rebellions against Protestant monarchs was now being employed against the Pope who expelled them from the Roman Church, 218

The Word, 10, 15, 117, 155, 193, 302

This will culminate when the mark of the beast is proclaimed as the mark of allegiance to those who set themselves as a god instead of allegiance to the God of the universe, 278

Three angels messages, 288

Three Hebrew youths, 158

Tiberias Caesar, 56

Transubstantiation, 28, 110, 131, 137, 138

Tsar Alexander I, 248

Undermines the infinite power and grace of the priesthood of Jesus Christ, 118

United States, 232, 236, 237, 238, 239, 240, 246, 256, 279, 282, 300, 301, 303

Vandals, 46, 101, 201

Visigoths, 101

Waldenses, 121, 215

Wants for Christians to repent of their sins and to seek God in the Holy Scriptures, 119

Wants you to see the truth and the truth originates and ends with Him and His words in the Bible, 124

Waters, 25

Where many Protestants found a home in America, 204

Whore of Revelation 17, 153

Will remain in power until the 2nd Coming of Christ, 89

William Miller, 271, 273

Year, 55, 160

Yuletide, 48

Zachariah, 53

ABOUT THE AUTHOR

Eliseo Santos was born and raised in New York City. His life journey and quest for the truth that began as a youth from The Bronx to the Ivy League has led him to the origin of all truth, which is the Word of God and Jesus Christ in the Bible. Eliseo is a life-long Christian and has decided to devote his life to uphold the 10 Commandments and Principles of God found in the Bible that has been proven true through his personal research and experiences. Eliseo is a blogger for the Emerging Truth Blog where he shares his insights with the world. To learn more you can visit http://www.emergingtruth.net .

Made in the USA
Middletown, DE
16 November 2015